JAMES
HERRIOT

James Herriot, Photograph by Derry Brabbs. Used with the permission of the photographer.

JAMES HERRIOT

A Critical Companion

Michael J. Rossi

CRITICAL COMPANIONS TO POPULAR CONTEMPORARY WRITERS
Kathleen Gregory Klein, Series Editor

Greenwood Press
Westport, Connecticut • London

Library of Congress Cataloging-in-Publication Data

Rossi, Michael John.
    James Herriot : a critical companion / Michael J. Rossi.
       p.   cm. — (Critical companions to popular contemporary
    writers, ISSN 1082–4979)
    Includes bibliographical references and index.
    ISBN 0–313–29449–6 (alk. paper)
    1. Herriot, James.   I. Title.   II. Series.
    SF613.H44R67   1997
    636.089'092—dc20   96–25014

British Library Cataloguing in Publication Data is available.

Library of Congress Catalog Card Number: 96–25014
ISBN: 0–313–29449–6
ISSN: 1082–4979

First published in 1997

Greenwood Press, 88 Post Road West, Westport, CT 06881
An imprint of Greenwood Publishing Group, Inc.

Printed in the United States of America

The paper used in this book complies with the
Permanent Paper Standard issued by the National
Information Standards Organization (Z39.48–1984).

10 9 8 7 6 5 4 3 2 1

For Joan, Martha, Rebecca,
and our own creatures great and small

Contents

Contents

Series Foreword

The authors who appear in the series Critical Companions to Popular Contemporary Writers are all best-selling writers. They do not have only one successful novel, but a string of them. Fans, critics, and specialist readers eagerly anticipate their next book. For some, high cash advances and breakthrough sales figures are automatic; movie deals often follow. Some writers become household names, recognized by almost everyone.

But novels are read one by one. Each reader chooses to start and, more importantly, to finish a book because of what she or he finds there. The real test of a novel is in the satisfaction its readers experience. This series acknowledges the extraordinary involvement of readers and writers in creating a best-seller.

The authors included in this series were chosen by an Advisory Board composed of high school English teachers and high school and public librarians. They ranked a list of best-selling writers according to their popularity among different groups of readers. Writers in the top-ranked group who had not received book-length, academic literary analysis (or none in at least the past ten years) were chosen for the series. Because of this selection method, Critical Companions to Popular Contemporary Writers meets a need that is not addressed elsewhere.

The volumes in the series are written by scholars with particular expertise in analyzing popular fiction. These specialists add an academic focus to the popular success that the best-selling writers already enjoy.

The series is designed to appeal to a wide range of readers. The general reading public will find explanations for the appeal of these well-known writers. Fans will find biographical and fictional questions answered. Students will find literary analysis, discussions of fictional genres, carefully organized introductions to new ways of reading the novels, and bibliographies for additional research. Students will also be able to apply what they have learned from this book to their readings of future novels by these best-selling writers.

Each volume begins with a biographical chapter drawing on published information, autobiographies or memoirs, prior interviews, and, in some cases, interviews given especially for this series. A chapter on literary history and genres describes how the author's work fits into a larger literary context. The following chapters analyze the writer's most important, most popular, and most recent novels in detail. Each chapter focuses on a single novel. This approach, suggested by the Advisory Board as the most useful to student research, allows for an in-depth analysis of the writer's fiction. Close and careful readings with numerous examples show readers exactly how the novels work. These chapters are organized around three central elements: plot development (how the story line moves forward), character development (what the reader knows about the important figures), and theme (the significant ideas of the novel). Chapters may also include sections on generic conventions (how the novel is similar to or different from others in its same category of science fiction, fantasy, thriller, etc.), narrative point of view (who tells the story and how), symbols and literary language, and historical or social context. Each chapter ends with an "alternative reading" of the novel. The volume concludes with a primary and secondary bibliography, including reviews.

The Alternative Readings are a unique feature of this series. By demonstrating a particular way of reading each novel, they provide a clear example of how a specific perspective can reveal important aspects of the book. In each alternative reading section, one contemporary literary theory—such as feminist criticism, Marxism, new historicism, deconstruction, or Jungian psychological critique—is defined in brief, easily comprehensible language. That definition is then applied to the novel to highlight specific features that might go unnoticed or be understood differently in a more general reading of the novel. Each volume defines two or three specific theories, making them part of the reader's understanding of how diverse meanings may be constructed from a single novel.

Taken collectively, the volumes in the Critical Companions to Popular

Contemporary Writers series provide a wide-ranging investigation of the complexities of current best-selling fiction. By treating these novels seriously as both literary works and publishing successes, the series demonstrates the potential of popular literature in contemporary culture.

Kathleen Gregory Klein
Southern Connecticut State University

Acknowledgments

Many people helped to make this book possible. I wish to thank Kathleen Gregory Klein and Barbara Rader for their editorial advice and for their encouragement and patience. I am grateful to MaryKay Mahoney, Albert DeCiccio, Kathleen Shine Cain, and Martha Rossi for their helpful comments on several chapters. Merrimack College assisted with a faculty development grant. Special thanks also go to my family—Joan, Martha, Rebecca—for their encouragement.

JAMES HERRIOT

1

The Life of James Herriot (James Alfred Wight)

James Herriot was "born" during a soccer match in the late 1960s, when an obscure Yorkshire veterinarian, James Alfred Wight, chose to use a Birmingham player's name as his pseudonym in writing about his experiences as a vet. As Wight later explained, he was concerned that publication using his own name might be seen as violating the veterinary profession's prohibition against advertising. Using the Birmingham goalkeeper's name brought together two of Wight's greatest enthusiasms: practicing his profession and following soccer.

EARLY LIFE

James Alfred Wight, known throughout his life as "Alf," was born on October 3, 1916, in Sunderland, England. When he was three weeks old, his family moved to Scotland, where he grew up and attended school in Hillhead, on the western edge of Glasgow. At the time, the area was partly city and partly country, with views of the Clyde to the west and the unspoiled Scottish landscape to the north and south. His Scottish childhood left him with a slight Glasgow accent, which is occasionally mentioned in his books and which can be heard in his reading of his work on audiotape.

His mother, Hannah Bell Wight, was a professional singer whose repertoire included opera (Brower 97). His father, James Henry Wight, was a musician, playing the piano and the organ. He was also leader of an orchestra providing background music for silent films (Woods 14). Growing up in this musical household, Alf Wight developed a love for music. He took piano lessons as a child, and his parents hoped that he might pursue a career in music (*Maclean's* 4). Although he did not show promise as a pianist, he enjoyed playing the piano and listening to music—interests that continued throughout his life. One outgrowth of this musical background was his fanciful choice of the pseudonyms Siegfried and Tristan for the Sinclair brothers in his books. In *All Creatures Great and Small,* he probably writes with his own family in mind when he attributes these names to their father's love of Wagnerian opera.

As an only child, Wight was often on his own. He found amusement in reading and in hiking the Scottish countryside. In the 1920s, when he was growing up, organized activities for children were rare. Outdoor play involved informal games with neighborhood children and exploring. Evening entertainment outside the home, still uncommon for all ages, was limited mainly to musical and theatrical performances— whether amateur or professional—and to the increasingly popular silent movies. Except for radio, which had begun to bring outside entertainment into the home, people continued to make their own entertainment in the evening. Visits with neighbors or family remained the most common form of socializing, while reading and handicrafts were popular individual pursuits. From an early age, Wight's reading was extensive. Starting with comic books, he moved on to the books in his family's library; later he recalled in particular works by Rider Haggard, Conan Doyle, and H. G. Wells. By the time he was in high school, his strongest subjects were English and languages.

He also developed a love for the Scottish countryside and for animals. He roamed the Scottish hills for nearly fourteen years with his Irish Setter, Don, and school friends. He spoke later of walking as much as thirty miles a day in the hills to the southwest of Glasgow (*JHDS* xi) and of camping at Rosneath with his friends on weekends throughout the summer in his college days (*JHY* 24). There were always cats waiting to greet him when he returned home from school or from hiking with his dog.

As Wight grew up, he realized that he preferred an outdoor life to working in an office and began to look for a suitable career. At the age of thirteen, he found the answer when he read the article "Veterinary Surgery as a Career" in *Meccano Magazine,* a popular magazine for boys. He mentions this episode in his first book, in several interviews, and in the introduction to the collection *James Herriot's Dog Stories*—his most extensive discussion of his schooldays. As he describes it, he suddenly recognized that a veterinary career offered him the opportunity to combine earning a livelihood with his love for dogs and cats and his preference for the outdoors. He decided on the spot that a veterinary career was for him. Then he began to think about whether it was an achievable goal. The odds seemed to be against it, because he disliked sciences and was not taking science courses at Hillhead High School. He was also a poor math student.

Shortly after reading the article in *Meccano,* he had an opportunity to hear the Principal of Glasgow Veterinary College, Dr. Whitehouse, speak at his high school. It was 1930. The combined effects of the economic depression and the passing of the workhorse had begun to make veterinary medicine look like a dying profession. The veterinary colleges, including the one in Glasgow, were having difficulty staying afloat, because few new students were being attracted to the profession. Wight found encouragement in Dr. Whitehouse's appeal for students to become veterinarians. As a result, he went to see Dr. Whitehouse personally at the college about his chances of becoming a vet with no high-school physics or chemistry, no time to begin a science sequence before graduation, and no aptitude for math. Dr. Whitehouse's answer was reassuring. The necessary science background could be handled in the first year of veterinary college, and the college entrance requirements throughout Britain could be met at the time by outstanding performance on tests in his strong areas: English, Latin, and French. Even in math, he was told, little more than an ability to figure receipts would be necessary.

In retrospect, Wight viewed this information as a mark of the unscientific character and desperate condition of veterinary education in the 1930s. At the time, he understood it to mean that a veterinary career was possible for him, and became determined to achieve that goal. He studied harder to gain high scores on the tests in his better subjects, especially Latin. He also worked at his math and passed the qualifying exam in it. Even in his early teens, Wight was capable of making a decision, acting boldly on it, and working with single-minded determination to carry it out. It is a pattern he would repeat almost forty years later, when he accepted the challenge to act on his talk of writing a book about his veterinary experiences.

When Wight entered Glasgow Veterinary College, he found it a dramatic change from the strict discipline and high academic standards he had known earlier. Students in Scottish schools were still punished physically with a leather belt in those days, and he had felt its strokes regularly for laughing in class. Hillhead High School also demanded that students approach their education with seriousness and diligence. In contrast, self-discipline or no discipline at all was the norm at the veterinary college. If students chose not to care about their education, no one else seemed to care. No one would insist that they pay attention in class or even go to classes, and many students did not complete their degrees. The college's financial condition, however, was so strained that students who continued to pay to attend would not be thrown out for failing classes; one notable student had completed less than two years of coursework after fourteen years at the college. It seemed to Wight that many students passed their time playing poker and many aged professors had lost interest in teaching, although he also recognized that the college had a number of serious students and dedicated professors.

Wight found this new freedom tempting. He was drawn to playing poker with the idle, long-term students and quickly found himself saddled with gambling debts at the age of sixteen. He was still young enough to remember reading novels intended to warn children about bad habits bringing young men to ruin, and he was shocked to think of himself that way. The thought of becoming a disappointment to his parents also overwhelmed him with guilt. He decided to reform and to clear his gambling debts. Gradually, he saved enough money. He economized by eating cheap, filling food and by walking part of the way each day between the college and home, where he was still living. He managed to focus his attention on serious study again and developed the self-discipline necessary to succeed in the less structured environment of the college.

In Chapter 18 of *All Creatures Great and Small,* he tells of a similarly chastening experience early in his time at the veterinary college. On that occasion, a horse taught him a lesson in humility by helping him to see how little he knew in comparison to what he thought he knew. Both that experience and his experience with gambling served to temper the overconfidence fostered by his success in meeting the admission standard and by his newfound freedom.

Since he was most interested in working with dogs and cats, he was disappointed by the almost exclusive emphasis in veterinary education—and in the majority of veterinary practices—on commercially valuable farm animals: horses, cows, sheep, and pigs. Glasgow Veterinary College, in Wight's recollection, was weak on classroom instruction but very strong on practical experience. As a student, he saw general practice with

Donald Campbell of Rutherglen. He was also fortunate enough to work with William Weipers of Glasgow in a practice specializing in small animals and set up on standards far ahead of the times. He even found himself, at nineteen, filling in for a vet for two weeks entirely on his own—a frightening but immensely valuable educational experience (*JHDS* xx). As an approach to education, however, learning by being thrown into situations with minimal preparation does have drawbacks. Wight's equine education included a program of weekly horseback riding in which students who had not been given riding lessons were placed on horses and, as a result, were frequently thrown. Instead of gaining expertise in horsemanship, Wight suffered a concussion and several days of amnesia after being thrown (*JHDS* xvii). He refers frequently in his books to a continuing unease with horses, to just not being a "horsey" person.

VETERINARY CAREER AND MARRIAGE

In 1938, Wight graduated from Glasgow Veterinary College as a qualified veterinarian, a Member of the Royal College of Veterinary Surgeons (M.R.C.V.S.), and entered Donald Sinclair's veterinary practice in Thirsk, in Yorkshire, England. Jobs were still extremely scarce as a result of the economic depression, and Wight's prospects were discouraging until he was offered an interview in Sinclair's large animal practice in Yorkshire. His mixed feelings of relief over the possibility of a job, disappointment over working with large rather than small animals, and surprise that the Yorkshire landscape had so much to offer are described in *All Creatures Great and Small,* along with the details of his first meeting with his future employer, his subsequent interview, and the offer of a job. Later, in interviews and in *James Herriot's Yorkshire,* Wight insisted that this account in his first book was entirely true, down to the smallest detail—including his falling asleep in the garden while awaiting the return of Donald Sinclair, the Siegfried Farnon of his books. He also continued to describe Donald and himself as very compatible opposites (Gonzalez 59).

Within the first few weeks, Wight's heart was won by the landscape and people of Yorkshire. Although he continued to regret giving up his dream of working with small animals, he knew that he wanted to stay in Yorkshire. And his certainty increased over the years. As he gained experience and the farmers' acceptance, he also grew increasingly comfortable about remaining in a large animal practice. He recognized that one advantage it held over a small animal practice was the necessity of making rounds to the farms rather than staying indoors and waiting for patients to come. He had succeeded in finding a career in which he could earn a living while enjoying an outdoor life in beautiful country—one of his two original goals. Doing rounds as a country vet was, for him, "like a paid holiday" (Green 97).

During his first two years in Thirsk, Wight found that his other goal of working with dogs and cats could also be satisfied in the Sinclair practice. As he made his rounds, he discovered a large population of dogs and cats. In addition, since many vets still avoided small animal work as not rough enough to be taken seriously, he found demand for his services among dog and cat owners. Donald Sinclair, eager to take the horse cases himself, was happy to leave the small animal work to Wight and agreeable to his expanding that part of the practice. As a result, although he would remain primarily a large animal vet, Wight succeeded in building "what amounted to my own small animal practice, with clients coming from far around to our little town to seek the services of a vet who actually wanted to treat their pets" (*JHDS* xxiv). When veterinary schools began to increase instruction in the care of dogs and introduced instruction in the care of cats, Wight took the opportunity to learn as much as he could from students and assistants (*JHCS* x).

On November 5, 1941, Wight married Joan Catherine Danbury and became a partner in the Sinclair practice. As described in the final chapter of *All Creatures Great and Small,* the couple spent their honeymoon doing tuberculin testing while staying at the old Wheatsheaf Inn in Carperby (*JHY* 155–56). In his books, Wight presents their courtship as a comedy of errors by focusing on the mishaps that befell them and on his anxiety over wanting Joan (Helen in the books) to like him. Wight's concern for maintaining a degree of privacy even while seeming to reveal all is evident in this handling of the courtship. Their quiet moments together, long walks, and visits at the farm, although mentioned briefly, remain safely in the background, while Wight focuses attention on their most public, and often his most humorously embarrassing, moments. For the next two years, until Wight's service in the RAF, the couple lived on the top floor in the practice headquarters. For another eight years after the war (*JHY* 170), they had the Georgian house to themselves and their growing family. Donald and Brian Sinclair had moved out, one to marriage and the other to a job with the Ministry of Agriculture.

In the early years of World War II, when veterinarians were excluded from the draft, Wight and Donald Sinclair volunteered for service in the

RAF, prompted by patriotism, duty, and a romantic spirit of adventure. Wight was attracted by the idea of flying and the prospect of becoming a dashing pilot. On October 3, 1943, his twenty-seventh birthday, he was called up for service, and shortly after left his pregnant wife for military induction in London. Brian Sinclair waited and was drafted with other veterinarians into the Army Veterinary Corps.

While in training at Scarborough, only about three hours away from Thirsk by bus, Wight hazarded the consequences of being caught AWOL to make two brief, unauthorized visits to his wife, which he later minimized as "playing hookey" (*JHY* 163). Although carefully planned, the visits were a bold and impulsive action at odds with Wight's image of himself in the books as a basically steady and unimaginative type. On the second of these visits, on February 13, 1944, he arrived in Thirsk to find himself a father. His son James had just been born at Sunnyside Nursing Home, and he took the opportunity to see his wife and son sooner after the birth than was customary at the time. In *All Things Wise and Wonderful,* he describes his shock at the infant's bruised appearance, which he found so different from that of newborn farm animals, and the indignant reaction of Nurse Brown (in reality Nurse Bell). His daughter Rosemary was born in the same room at Sunnyside Nursing Home on May 9, 1949.

Following training, Wight entered the pilot training school at Windsor. Although he was somewhat older than the other pilot trainees, he succeeded in qualifying as a pilot. He never saw combat, however. Shortly after qualifying, he underwent an operation for an old injury and, as a result, his fitness rating was downgraded and he became ineligible to fly. In 1945 he received a medical discharge and returned to his wife and son in Thirsk.

In the years after the war, Wight continued to work in partnership with Donald Sinclair. The new drugs available and the new medical procedures made those years an exciting time to be a vet. In the 1940s Wight became the first vet in his part of Yorkshire to do large animal surgery (Green 97). In the unusually heavy snows of 1947, he demonstrated an adventurous spirit once again by attempting to use skis to make calls to isolated farms. He abandoned the effort only after getting caught in a snow squall made him recognize it as too dangerous (*JHY* 124–27). Later, in 1961 and 1963, the spirit of adventure moved him again when he served as vet accompanying a shipment of sheep by sea to the Soviet Union and a shipment of cows by air to Istanbul.

When he returned to practice after the war, he also found special enjoyment in his children. First Jimmy and then Rosemary accompanied him—until reaching school age—while he made his daily round of calls to the farms. As a result of this early experience, both children developed a strong interest in becoming vets. Herriot later expressed regret in interviews and in both *The Lord God Made Them All* and *Every Living Thing* about having encouraged his son but discouraged his daughter, in the belief that large animal practice was still very rough in the 1950s and would be too dangerous a career for a young woman. Jimmy eventually became a vet and Rosemary, with her father's encouragement, a medical doctor. Wight knew well the dangerous nature of being a vet, having suffered a succession of injuries over the years. One of his most serious injuries was caused by a kick he received from a horse in his first year as a vet, which left him bruised and with a permanent cavity in his thigh muscle. In 1992, in *Every Living Thing,* he revealed a far more serious consequence of being a vet in the 1950s, telling of vets who suffered serious medical problems as a result of picking up a brucellosis infection from treating cows for the disease. He describes there how he himself suffered recurring bouts of delirium (not unlike residual malaria attacks) from brucellosis throughout the 1950s, until his attacks gradually disappeared.

THE VET BECOMES A WRITER

In Wight's bachelor days in Thirsk, he and the Sinclairs had been in the habit of telling each other about the interesting people and situations they had encountered on their rounds. Socializing at pubs also involved sharing reminiscences or stories of local people and events. Whether carefully told or informal and artless, stories were a regular part of life and a source of entertainment in the days before television.

After his marriage, Wight would tell his wife each day about the funny things that had happened. He began to feel that a book should be written about the experiences of a country vet, and he began to fancy himself writing it. Over the years, he would regularly say of the more striking incidents that he was keeping them to put in his book. Finally, after twenty-five years, his wife grew tired of humoring him and pointed out one day in 1966 that "someone who's 50 years old and has never written a line isn't going to start writing books at that age" (*Maclean's* 5). Wight took her comment as a challenge and became determined to do it.

He had little idea of the work involved in writing. In school he had been good at essay writing, and he had read widely. But he had written very little for thirty years. He brought an old typewriter into the sitting room in the evening and began learning to use it and trying to put his experiences on paper. Writing at first in the ornate style of Macaulay's essays, Wight found that his first efforts disappointingly resembled "a very amateurish school essay" (Moorehead 12).

He soon realized that his material required a more natural, informal style—that it should sound the way he "would tell the tale in a country pub" (Green 92). But he still found it difficult to make his prose sound that way. He bought books on the craft of writing, like *Teach Yourself to Write* and *How to be a Writer*. He looked more closely at the writing style of other writers, especially Salinger, Hemingway, Conan Doyle, and Dickens. Wight may have learned from Dickens techniques for quickly sketching and individualizing a large cast of characters. He attributes his learning how to handle flashbacks to his reading of Budd Schulberg's novel based on F. Scott Fitzgerald's declining years, *The Disenchanted*, which flows smoothly and frequently between time periods as well as between reality and alcoholic fantasy. As he learned his craft, he submitted short stories to several magazines and had all of them rejected (Moorehead 12).

Working in front of the television, often for only half an hour at a time, between calls to care for animals, Wight developed his craft and completed his first short book over about eighteen months. He intended to send the manuscript to a London publisher, Michael Joseph, who had recently published a successful series of books about the experiences of a medical doctor. But he sent it to another publisher on the advice of a friend. It stayed there for eighteen months before it was returned rejected. Discouraged, Wight threw the manuscript in a drawer with the intention of leaving it there. His wife Joan, however, insisted that he try to do something with it. This time he sent it to a literary agent, who read it, liked it, and promised to place it with a publisher. Shortly after, the agent succeeded in placing the book with the publisher that Wight had originally intended to try.

If Only They Could Talk, his first British book, was published in 1970 under the pseudonym James Herriot, with other individuals and its Yorkshire localities also given pseudonyms and thinly disguised. Darrowby in the book is Thirsk with a mix of Richmond, Leyburn, and Middleham (*JHY* 15). Descriptions of individuals and physical details in the stories are likewise often composites or imaginatively altered, although Wight maintained that all of his stories are "90 per cent true"

(Moorehead 12). As he explained later, "I didn't want to write anything that I thought might hurt anyone's feelings. That's why I keep my writing about thirty or forty years behind the actual events. Nearly everyone I've been writing about is now dead" (Gonzalez 58). His first book sold only twelve hundred copies. Meanwhile, he completed the manuscript of a second book, *It Shouldn't Happen to a Vet*, which was published in Britain in 1972.

Wight's fortunes changed dramatically when the president of St. Martin's Press, Thomas McCormack, returned to the United States with a copy of *If Only They Could Talk*, which he had been given while in London in search of promising books for American publication. Wight's book, among others, remained unopened on McCormack's bedside table until his wife happened to read it. She was charmed and insisted that he publish it (Del Balso 181). Impressed by her enthusiasm, he read the book and enjoyed it. He was interested in publishing it but concerned about its marketability as a short book, so he acquired a copy of Wight's second book in order to consider a combined edition (Dudar 2). To further enhance its marketability, he asked Wight to bring the love story to a more definite conclusion. Wight was agreeable and added the final three chapters containing the proposal, marriage, and working honeymoon (Del Balso 181). McCormack found the result better than he had hoped—"the perfect wrapup" (Dudar 2). With a title from a popular Anglican hymn and $25,000 worth of publicity (Moorehead 12), *All Creatures Great and Small* was an immediate best-seller when it was published in the United States in 1972. It rapidly became an international best-seller.

All Creatures Great and Small was followed by the British publication of *Let Sleeping Vets Lie* in 1973 and *Vet in Harness* in 1974. These two books were combined, with some reorganization and deletions, and published in the United States as *All Things Bright and Beautiful* in 1974. Two more British books followed, *Vets Might Fly* in 1976 and *Vet in a Spin* in 1977. These were the last of the separate British editions of Wight's work. They were combined and published in the United States in 1977 as *All Things Wise and Wonderful*. From this point on, Wight's books were published in the same form in Britain and in the United States.

Wight continued to write between calls while watching television in the evenings. As he observed later, his earliest books were written from memory. He found that he had a strong memory for dialogue and that by looking through old veterinary textbooks and records of cases he would recall long-past situations and dialogue. Early in his career, he had begun keeping a daybook listing details of cases and treatments, and this proved especially helpful for reminding him of the interesting people and situations he had encountered. After his books became popular, he began to make notes of interesting situations as they occurred. He also found that he could write in his head as he drove to and from calls, working through stories in preparation for writing them down. He began carrying a pad with him in his car to jot down ideas, and he eventually began carrying a recorder so he could dictate ideas as he drove. In addition, he began to type notes of ideas for future stories, recording their key features in what he termed vignettes, which could be developed into complete stories later. By 1978, he had accumulated nearly six-hundred vignettes (*Maclean's* 5), enough for at least ten more books.

As the popularity of Wight's books spread, his identity became more widely known and admirers sought him out in Yorkshire. He was not very difficult to find, in spite of his changing the names of people and places in his books. Although always courteous to visitors, he continued to guard his privacy as much as possible. He also continued to work full-time as a vet and to identify himself primarily as a vet rather than a writer. Throughout his life, he autographed his books with his pen name, James Herriot. As he observed in a rare, early interview and in a story in his fourth American book, a farmer with a sick animal "couldn't care less if I were George Bernard Shaw" (Moorehead 12).

Although he enjoyed his success, he clearly did not enjoy the consequences of becoming famous. Fame was simply irrelevant both to his work as a vet and—it would appear—to the personal satisfaction he found in writing books. The income that his books provided also seemed to matter little to him beyond an improvement in financial security. Although the British government took 83 percent of his earnings in taxes, he refused to take up residence abroad, as so many other writers had done. He continued to live quietly, adding only a few simple conveniences to his home, updating his old stereo system, and later building a new, modest home with a view of the Yorkshire landscape. Wight avoided interviews and public appearances, insisting that he simply did not have time as a working vet to play the celebrity. As he put it, "It's nice to meet [the glamorous people in the literary world], to be friendly with them, but not to go into their world. It's not my world" (*Maclean's* 6).

LATER YEARS

The continuing popularity of Wight's books led to film and television versions of his work, which, in turn, increased his popularity and led to honors, awards, and more demands for personal appearances. In 1974, the movie *All Creatures Great and Small,* starring Simon Ward, was filmed on location in Yorkshire. In 1978, the BBC began a serial based on his books. Entitled *All Creatures Great and Small* and starring Christopher Timothy, the series began its initial several-year run on PBS television in the United States the following year and greatly boosted Wight's already considerable popularity. A second film, *All Things Bright and Beautiful,* starring John Alderton, was produced in 1979.

At the urging of his American publisher, Wight made two brief promotional tours of the United States in 1973 and 1974, in conjunction with publication of his first two American books. Although he found the trips enjoyable—the second more so, because his wife Joan accompanied him—he also found them tiring and felt that they were taking him away from the profession and setting he loved. The longer of these tours, at three weeks, was the longest time he had been away from Yorkshire since his arrival in 1938.

Wight became President of the Yorkshire Veterinarian Society in 1973–74, and other honors followed. In addition to book awards, honorary degrees, and the establishment of the James Herriot Award by the Humane Society of America, he was honored by the American Veterinary Medical Association for his contribution to enhancing public appreciation of the profession. His books produced an upsurge of interest in veterinary medicine as a profession, which resulted in increased enrollments in veterinary colleges, as well as a successful public outcry against the proposed closing of Glasgow Veterinary College as part of a cutback in the funding of higher education. The paramount mark of his success was his being made an Officer of the Order of the British Empire in 1979. Yet another honor that undoubtedly meant much to him was being made a Fellow of the Royal College of Veterinary Surgeons in 1982.

Wight continued to write. In 1979, with the publication of the beautifully photographed *James Herriot's Yorkshire,* he permitted readers to have a peek beneath the cloaking pseudonyms in his books. In descriptive comments rather than story form, he identifies the locations featured in the books, comments on the authentic characteristics of individuals in them (still withholding names), and offers additional details about his life. His fourth American book, *The Lord God Made Them All,* dealing with his postwar experiences, appeared in 1981.

Over the next fourteen years, Wight mined his previously published stories. A series of collections appeared, including *The Best of James Herriot* (1982), *James Herriot's Dog Stories* (1986), and *James Herriot's Cat Stories* (1994). A series of illustrated books for children also appeared. Each contains an adaptation of a previously published story and attractive watercolor illustrations—the earliest ones by Peter Barrett and the later ones by Ruth Brown. The eight books in the series are *Moses the Kitten* (1984), *Only One Woof* (1985), *The Christmas Day Kitten* (1986), *Bonny's Big Day* (1987), *Blossom Comes Home* (1988), *The Market Square Dog* (1989), *Oscar, Cat-About-Town* (1990), and *Smudge, the Little Lost Lamb* (1991). A collected edition, *James Herriot's Treasury for Children,* followed in 1992. *James Herriot's Yorkshire Calendar* also appeared.

With advancing age, Wight gradually retired as a practicing vet, cutting back to two days a week and turning over the practice to his son. Although continuing to appear remarkably fit and youthful, he began to feel the effects of arthritis in his hands. No longer able to sign books easily and not wishing to disappoint visitors seeking his autograph, he began to provide bookplates that he had signed at home (Dowling 68). Wight also appeared to have retired from writing, having limited himself to writing introductions to collections of previously printed stories. His days, he said in 1988, were sufficiently filled with enjoying his four grandchildren, hiking mornings and afternoons, and reading histories and biographies (Dowling 68).

He surprised everyone—including his family, it seems—when he produced the manuscript of a new book, *Every Living Thing,* which was published in 1992. Bringing the account of his life to the present, the book also served as his swan song. After being ill for three years with prostate cancer and carrying on despite difficulties and pain, James Alfred Wight died on February 23, 1995.

During his lifetime, Wight was occasionally asked to speculate on the popularity of his books, particularly in the United States, where he met his greatest success. His views changed slightly over the years, especially as his initial surprise over the magnitude of his success passed. Moving from an astonished protest that he had no idea why they had gained such popularity (Moorehead 12), he then speculated that his American readership's love of animals might be responsible or that his books were benefiting from a "backlash" against the generally pornographic nature of modern novels (*Maclean's* 5). Later, he thought that their hardy Yorkshire farmers might have appealed to the pioneering spirit of Americans (Gonzalez 58). He routinely rejected the tendency of some readers to find "weighty, humanitarian, sociological meanings" in his books (*Maclean's* 6). He saw a more straightforward meaning in them: "My books are a restatement of old values: hard work and integrity. You can see them on the farms here in Yorkshire all the time and it's quite a contrast to what one finds in city life today" (Gonzalez 89). Regardless of the views readers take of their meaning, Wight's books have delighted readers and perhaps left their mark on them much as Wight believed his Jack Russell terrier Hector left his mark on Yorkshire. Hector, he suggested, changed the bad-tempered character of his breed "in great widening ripples" as he sired good-natured puppies who, in turn, passed on their good nature to their puppies (*JHDS* xxvii).

Ultimately, Wight's books tell the story of his life and experiences as a vet. At his death, his editor of many years at St. Martin's Press in New York observed, "More than any other author I've met, he was in his books" (Tabor A19).

Genre: Autobiography and Short Story

James Herriot is often viewed as a masterful storyteller rather than as an autobiographer. He is, of course, both. Autobiographies can take a wide variety of prose forms, including poetic, dramatic, or cinematic. As a result, they straddle more than one tradition. Herriot makes the short story form the basic building block of his larger, more complex volumes of autobiography. He gives autobiography—the story of a life—a twist by making his autobiography the sum of the stories that he tells from his life.

AUTOBIOGRAPHY

Autobiography and autobiographical writing have become increasingly popular and varied in nature in the twentieth century. This trend has also been accompanied by an increasing willingness to recognize a wider range of materials as autobiography. At the same time, modern critical theories have caused scholars to question tidy, compartmentalized, traditional definitions of genres as too narrow and often misleading. Together, these trends have raised uncertainty about how to define autobiography as a genre. As one critic remarks, "Everyone knows what autobiography is, but no two observers, no matter how assured they may be, are in agreement" (Olney, "Autobiography and the Cultural Moment" 7).

What Is Autobiography?

Autobiographers tell the story of their lives. In this common description lie the two most distinctive features of autobiography.

First, autobiographers present their own lives. They do not present the lives of characters who exist only in their imagination, as fiction writers do, nor the lives of real people who have led lives separate from their own, as biographers do. Like all nonfiction writers, they are limited to working with actual facts; but they also have the mixed blessings of having more material available to them and of knowing their material intimately, in ways no other nonfiction writer can. In a sense, they are limited to the truth, but they have access to truths that only they are in a position to know. (See below for more on the special nature of "truth" in autobiography.)

Second, autobiographers present their own lives within the framework of conventional narrative forms, essentially turning their lives into story, and so must shape the written version of their lives to meet conventional expectations of their chosen form. At the very least, these expectations call for a greater degree of organization, focus, logical connection, and coherence than is immediately visible in life's chaotic mixture of activities and events. Thus, autobiographers must edit their lives, selecting only those pieces that seem to them to be most relevant and to fit together in some reasonable way. As a result, autobiography has been viewed as an exercise in self-definition—an effort to define one's own identity and the meaning of one's own life, for either personal or public purposes.

Autobiographical writing, by contrast, is writing based on, but not mainly about, a writer's own life and experiences. To the extent that all writing grows out of personal experience—writers are commonly advised to write about what they know—all writing might be said to be autobiographical in a very general sense. More specifically, however, the term applies to writing governed largely by public rather than personal aims. While autobiographical writing obviously draws on and frequently parallels aspects of the writer's life, it also departs from the writer's life either by fictionalizing it or by focusing attention elsewhere. It may use personal experience as inspiration and raw material for literary fiction (the autobiographical novel) or as evidence in support of a proposition (the autobiographical essay). In autobiographical novels, a character having much in common with the writer will also be a distinctly different individual, serving different thematic ends. Many of Dickens's novels, for example, are autobiographical, but David Copperfield and Pip, despite being partly Dickens's alter egos, differ from him and from each other and serve different thematic purposes. Similarly, an autobiographical essay may use personal experience in a variety of ways to call attention to an essentially public issue. Herriot's travelogue, *James Herriot's Yorkshire,* presents details of his personal history in the manner of an autobiographical essay, in order to facilitate a descriptive survey of notable features of the Yorkshire countryside. The focus of attention is quite different from that of his other works.

Autobiographical writing does not engage in introspection in order to clarify or define the writer's life, as autobiography commonly does. On the other hand, autobiographers often engage not only in self-definition, but also in presenting a broader vision of life, society, and the world. Thus, the greater the autobiographical writer's fidelity to the facts of his or her life, the less distinct may be the difference between autobiographical writing and autobiography.

The nature of autobiography can be understood more clearly through comparison with biography. Both autobiography and biography deal with an individual's life, but an autobiography is a self-told biography. While both may include interpretation, biography focuses primarily on the historical, factual record of a life. It is an outsider's view. It must draw its authoritative content from the public record and from statements by the individual and other first-hand observers. As a result, it necessarily emphasizes the *what* of a life. While most modern biography does seek to understand and explain an individual's actions as a function of personality, it can deal with the *why* only to a limited degree and with much speculative uncertainty. Autobiography, in contrast, is the insider's view. It focuses more strongly on the interior life and personal development of the individual. It emphasizes, even if not explicitly, the *why* of a life.

Thus, the most distinctive feature of autobiography is that it is extended writing about one's own life as such, with an effort to achieve some understanding of its significance. Until recently, forms of writing about the self that focus primarily on recording events, opinions, or reflections—like diaries, slave narratives, letters, and journals—were not considered to be autobiography. These narrower and generally less extended forms of writing about the self are now gaining greater acceptance as forms of autobiography, partly as a result of recognition that they too represent their writers' conscious selection of material and implicit definition of themselves and their world.

Similarly, the memoir has also been seen as distinct from autobiography, because it typically focuses on exploring the writer's world and acquaintances rather than on exploring the self. Defined in those terms, the memoir is still commonly seen as distinct from autobiography. Recently, however, the distinction between memoir and autobiography has become blurred, as writers have used the term "memoir" to designate an autobiography with a narrow time frame. By this definition, the memoir is a writer's treatment of a portion of his or her life, while the autobiography deals either with the writer's entire life to date or with the writer's life from birth to fame or to some notable turning point (Zinsser 11). Except for the difference in scope, the terms memoir and autobiography are now commonly used almost interchangeably.

The History of Autobiography

Autobiography is an almost exclusively Western literary form, with its roots in the more universal and longstanding tradition of biography, which dates back to biographical records of the accomplishments of kings, legends of heroes, and mythological accounts of gods. While appealing to human curiosity, these early biographies were produced to serve a wide variety of public purposes, from supporting dynastic stability to strengthening a people's identity, to providing ethical and moral instruction. The Bible's various biographical portraits of kings and prophets remain among the most widely read and best known of these early accounts.

Some Greek and Roman biographical portraits convey a convincing impression of a real person, rather than a two-dimensional combination of details. As a result, a suggestion of personality began to emerge, although its historical accuracy was not a concern. The Greek historian Thucydides, for example, brings the major figures of the Peloponnesian War to life by inventing the persuasive rhetoric of their speeches, essentially treating them as dramatic characters. The philosopher Plato similarly makes a number of the speakers in his dialogues, especially Socrates, seem at times convincingly real people rather then mere spokesmen for philosophical positions. The classical rhetoricians' attention to the praise of public figures as a standard rhetorical situation also spurred biographical description.

Plutarch, the best-known early biographer, has been called the father of biography, both because the declared aim of his *Parallel Lives* was to reveal the character of his subjects and because his method was basically to follow their progress from birth to death. Plutarch gives attention to minor events that reveal the person and shows weaknesses as well as strengths. In common with other early biographies, however, the primary purpose of these lives was instructional: they were to serve as examples to be emulated or avoided. Medieval portraits of saints and sinners followed in the same vein. This didactic tradition continued into the English Renaissance with the enormously popular sixteenth-century *Mirror for Magistrates,* where a specific individual's biography serves merely as a pretext for presenting readers with the cause-effect relationship between a particular choice in life and its outcome. No reason, no plausible basis in the individual's life, for the fateful choice is expected or given. A parallel instructional purpose is also present in propagandistic works such as Thomas More's early sixteenth-century biography of Richard III and Foxe's seventeenth-century *Book of Martyrs,* where concern for historical accuracy and character take second place to the writer's political objectives. On the other hand, a number of Renaissance biographies do focus on the personality of the subject—among them Boccaccio's *Life of Dante,* Roper's *Life of Thomas More,* and Vasari's *Lives of the Painters.* Although many types of biography continued to be produced, what is generally considered the modern biography emerged in the eighteenth century. Marked by interest in historical accuracy, character, and the relationship between personality and actions, it is best exemplified by Boswell's eighteenth-century *Life of Johnson.*

The emergence of autobiography as a genre in the nineteenth century can be seen as related to the emergence of modern biography in the eighteenth century, since these two genres represent different ways of exploring the individual personalities of real persons in relation to their environment, actions, and accomplishments. From ancient times through the eighteenth century only a small number of works resembling modern autobiography can be found. The few famous figures of the classical period who wrote about themselves wrote primarily accounts of notable public actions—usually military campaigns—with the aim of explaining or justifying the strategies and decisions behind those actions. These accounts—the most famous being Julius Caesar's *Commentaries*—indirectly reveal something of their authors, but they are far from being exercises in self-analysis and reflection.

The *Confessions* of St. Augustine, often considered the first autobiography, is unusual in being an explanation of an internal battle and, thus, almost inevitably self-analytic and reflective. It recounts Augustine's lengthy spiritual search and struggle leading to his conversion to Christianity, which he marked publicly by abandoning his successful secular career. More than a personal history, the *Confessions* is also a devotional and theological piece, praising God and examining such issues as the nature of sin and free will. These features also contribute to an impression of the account's having the introspective qualities of modern autobiography. Other early autobiographies, such as Peter Abelard's twelfth-century *History of Calamities* or the fifteenth-century *Booke of Margery Kempe,* are similarly aimed at something other than an exploration of the self. Abelard presents himself as a victim of persecution, while the illiterate Kempe defends herself against charges of heresy in her dictated account of her life.

More firsthand accounts by individuals of their actions and life histories appeared in the Renaissance, when biographers became increasingly interested in factual accuracy. Personal accounts of exploration in this age of discovery also became popular, and may have spurred autobiography by making the self-told account of experiences a familiar narrative form. Perhaps even more influential, fictional autobiographies became numerous in the sixteenth and seventeenth centuries. In England, in particular, distrust and condemnation of fictional literature as frivolous, even harmful to readers, prompted the production of fictional autobiographies as a way to disguise fiction as nonfiction. These fictional autobiographies—such as Daniel Defoe's *Robinson Crusoe*—also generally focus on events (plot) rather than character. But, to the extent that their claim of truth was accepted (and evidence suggests it often was), they helped to make the telling of one's own story an established possibility.

Jean-Jacques Rousseau's *Confessions,* written in the 1760s and published posthumously in 1782, is often recognized as marking the beginning of modern autobiography, because it is centered on exploring the individual human consciousness, on looking for the meaning of experience in terms of its effect on character. Rousseau marks a shift to the Romantic and modern conception of human beings as autonomous individuals—each one developing and reacting to the world as essentially an independent, self-contained, often isolated center of consciousness.

Rousseau influenced later autobiography by turning his attention to the childhood years, usually ignored by other writers of lives, and examining the influence of childhood experience on the formation of adult personality. Rousseau's *Confessions* herald modern autobiography's characteristic concern with being an account of inner life.

Forms and Conventions of Autobiography

In writing about their own lives, autobiographers encounter a number of problems, including the need to select and organize incidents from an overabundance of possibilities, the need to choose a rhetorical perspective toward their subject, and the need to determine their purpose in recounting the facts of their lives. Some of the ways that writers can envision their purpose in writing about themselves are evident in the attempts of critics to categorize autobiographies. Common types of autobiography are the egocentric, the confessional, the justificatory, the exemplary, and the developmental. Herriot's memoirs are more closely related to the latter types of autobiography.

The egocentric autobiography assumes that anything and everything concerning the writer's life will automatically be of interest to readers. As might be expected, some egocentric autobiographies, such as the *Autobiography of Benvenuto Cellini,* are driven by boastfulness and an inflated self-image. The confessional autobiography represents a writer's efforts to work out and resolve feelings of guilt over past offenses. Examples include Rousseau's *Confessions* and many twentieth-century autobiographies focused on antagonistic childhood relationships with parents and other figures of authority. While in confessional autobiography writers cope with a wish to blame themselves for something, in justificatory autobiography they resist the efforts of others to find them blameworthy. Justificatory autobiographies defend the writer's choices in life by explaining what led to the choices and by showing them to be reasonable and appropriate choices on either objective or subjective grounds. Also known as apologies (that is, explanations), autobiographies of justification include Cardinal Newman's *Apologia Pro Vita Sua* (concerning his conversion) and Oscar Wilde's *De Profundis.*

The autobiography of example envisions the writer's life as representative of the human condition or human potential, whether in a generalized sense or within a specific group of peers. The *Autobiography of Benjamin Franklin* presents the example of the self-made man and invites emulation of Franklin's rise through study, initiative, and hard work. Nineteenth-century American slave narratives are representative in another sense, with the individual writer's experiences to some extent depersonalized and presented as the situation not simply of an individual but of the writer's people. Other autobiographies seek to be representative of basic human experience. Ann Dilliard's *An American Childhood* focuses on the development of consciousness in childhood. Frank Conroy's *Stop-Time* presents a portrait of twentieth-century isolation and alienation of the individual.

The developmental autobiography (also called intellectual or analytic autobiography) traces the shaping of the mature individual, often trying to disclose the roots of economic, intellectual, or artistic achievement. Essentially, these autobiographers explain how they are a product of early experience and training, how they came to be who or what they are. Eudora Welty's *One Writer's Beginnings* is typical in tracing qualities that play a major role in her fiction back to her earliest awareness of them. Other examples include *The Education of Henry Adams* and the philosopher John Stuart Mill's *Autobiography,* concerning his struggles over his oppressively rationalist education. The *Autobiography of Benjamin Franklin* can also be seen as tracing the development of Franklin's economic and political success. Writers who are uncertain about how they came to be who or what they are often write exploratory autobiographies when they seek to trace their development. Autobiographies that search for and try to make sense of the writer's past include Susanna Kaysen's *Girl, Interrupted*—which explores whether her stay in a mental hospital as a teenager was justified—and Ian Frazier's *Family*—which looks at the social history behind the author.

Herriot's memoirs are primarily forms of the developmental autobiography although they also possess elements of the justificatory and the exemplary. Each of his books centers on a stage in his life, with its particular challenges, choices, and opportunities for self discovery and growth. Each book evokes the essence of his experience; it sets the Yorkshire scene, populates it, and invites readers to enter his world. Each book follows his progress toward a moment of decision or recognition that marks the boundary between two stages of life, capping one stage and launching the next. Thus, *All Creatures Great and Small* deals with his gradually being won over by Yorkshire, ultimately committing himself professionally to being a farm vet and personally to marriage. These choices resolve pressing issues while also raising new uncertainties. *All Things Bright and Beautiful* finds Herriot grappling with the challenges of adjustment to his new life. His adaptation to extraordinary change—to rapid medical progress and to what it means to be married—then finds him again facing new uncertainties as world events intrude and call into question his most basic values. *All Things Wise and Wonderful* chronicles his successful passage through this crisis of doubt. *The Lord God Made Them All* then follows the development of his sense of family and fatherhood, and with the coming of a new generation of vets to Darrowby *Every Living Thing* finds him rediscovering and reaffirming his core values. While Herriot's memoirs are justificatory to the extent that they repeatedly address the rightness of his choices, and exemplary to the extent that they model making choices from the heart, they are primarily developmental in exploring the intersection of personality and environment in the shaping of his life.

As narratives, autobiographies present a series of events in detail. These events may be organized either chronologically or out of sequence, according to a thematic or topical principle. Recollections of earlier events (flashbacks) or descriptions of later events (flash-forwards) may interrupt a chronological sequence, especially when they reveal contributing factors or consequences. When organization is based on thematic or topical principles, events usually appear in the order of their relevance or their immediate usefulness. These are standard narrative features. Autobiographies, however, typically move freely in time while also maintaining a sense of rough chronological order, whether they are organized chronologically or by another principle. Unlike events in a plot, personal experiences that are complete in themselves may not be readily identifiable in terms of their chronology or even their relative order in the writer's life, unless the writer provides that information. At the same time, autobiography's focus on accounting for what the writer has become always suggests an overall movement forward in time to a decisive, defining moment or to the time of writing.

To some extent, these peculiarities in the handling of time are related to narrative point of view in autobiography. Since autobiography is the writer's representation of his or her own life, the narrative point of view is always that of the writer, who is the same person as the main character. Nearly all autobiographies are first-person narratives, in which either the main character or the writer tells the story, speaking as "I." Thus, the teller of the story, the main character, and the writer are openly identified as the same person when an autobiography is a first-person narrative. A very small number of autobiographies are third-person narratives, in which the teller of the story speaks of the main character as "he" or "she," suggesting that they are two distinct persons. The narrator nevertheless speaks for the writer in presenting the writer's vision of his or her own life, and readers of autobiography will always identify the narrator with the writer. Thus, when an autobiography is a third-person narration, the teller of the story is transparently the writer in disguise, or the writer/main character standing outside himself or herself in detached self-assessment. Ron Kovic's *Born on the Fourth of July*, for example, alternates between first-person and third-person narration, partly to illustrate the division between the writer's fully functioning mind and the paralyzed body in which it is trapped and partly to show that it is dehumanizing for people to treat others as objects.

Because the narrative point of view in autobiography is always the writer's view, whether presented as a first-person or third-person narrative, it is always a mix of how the writer saw things at the time and how he or she has come to understand them in looking back at them, often with more information and with the wisdom of greater maturity.

Autobiography as Story: Truth and Fiction

To write autobiography is to shape one's own life and experience into story, to impose order and meaning on the chaotic profusion of events that are part of daily living. To simplify and shorten the telling, some selection must take place. Events may be compressed, leaving out interrupting activities and other concerns that occupied the writer's attention. Events may even be reordered somewhat to make their relationship or their impact more obvious. The cast of characters may be limited by omitting people originally present but not directly involved in the action. Some reshaping is the conscious reshaping of the storyteller. Some of it is the unconscious reshaping that memory produces. The autobiographer has the obligation to tell the truth as he or she knows it—as he or she believes and feels it to be true. Tobias Wolff speaks for all autobiographers in a prefatory note to *This Boy's Life*, where he mentions choosing not to correct some points, including errors in chronology, because his autobiography "is a book of memory, and memory has its own story to tell. But I have done my best to make it a truthful story."

But autobiography is also fiction, because it is a consciously crafted version of the writer's life. What a writer chooses to include as important, or to leave out, is an editing process that makes the autobiography an interpretation of a life.

THE SHORT STORY

The short story is a compact, usually prose form of narrative fiction that is carefully and swiftly handled to achieve a single, unified effect. The modern short story is marked by a strongly realistic representation of life, often in combination with an imaginative treatment of such elements as setting, symbolism, or the psychological state of the narrator.

The History of the Short Story

The short story became established as a literary genre in the nineteenth century, although storytelling predates the invention of writing. In preliterate societies, oral storytelling served both as entertainment and as a means of transmitting cultural values. By necessity, oral stories were structured for the teller's easy recall and designed for the intense engagement of the audience's attention. In literate societies, oral storytelling has survived mainly in the anecdotes that support informal social interaction.

Until the nineteenth century, written stories were essentially written versions of the popular oral forms of storytelling, which include fables, fairy tales, parables, and medieval exempla. These early forms of storytelling are usually fanciful or exaggerated, and they are typically aimed at instructing their audiences concerning appropriate moral behavior. Some of these didactic stories present their message indirectly, by illustrating where different behaviors lead. Many, especially the fable, provide an explicit moral at their conclusion. Both oral and written stories were usually a combination of escapism and instruction up through the eighteenth century.

The written short story moved from the realm of popular culture and gained recognition as a literary genre in the nineteenth century, when writers in the United States, Germany, France, and Russia began to experiment with writing short, realistic fiction. This shift to realism was prompted, in part, by the reading public's loss of interest in fanciful tales. In the seventeenth and eighteenth centuries, middle-class audiences began to prefer to read short prose narratives that were factually descriptive and informative rather than fictional and didactic. Nonfiction sketches of new lands and cultures, as well as short journalistic pieces on a wide variety of subjects, replaced fanciful tales in popularity. Short fiction was also overshadowed by the development of the novel in the eighteenth century. The enormous popularity of the novel, an extended work of realistic fiction, demonstrated that fiction could still win readers and encouraged attention to realism in fiction. Thus, the popularity of both the nonfiction sketch and the novel pointed writers toward experimentation with short realistic fiction in the early nineteenth century.

The modern short story emerged when writers such as Edgar Allan Poe, E. T. A. Hoffmann, Prosper Mérimée, and Nikolay Gogol combined realism with the imaginative quality of earlier stories to go beyond a mere description of the world and explore such matters as a narrator's perception of reality and the feelings a setting prompts. Literary themes replaced the morals found in early stories, and the challenges of working in a form so highly compressed invited constant innovation. By the end of the century, a great number of outstanding short stories had been written. Extensive experimentation continued in the twentieth century and established the modern short story as a popular and versatile literary form.

Conventions of the Short Story

The short story has two key characteristics: it is complete in itself and it proceeds to a striking, even if uncertain, conclusion. These characteristics combine to establish a single, unified effect. A short story must succeed on its own, even when placed in company with other stories concerning the same character, place, or time. A short story proceeds to a conclusion that directs the reader to an understanding of its significance. Unlike early stories, the modern short story rarely states a moral, but its striking conclusion directs readers to ponder the story's effect for an equivalent truth.

The short story's compactness and its aim of achieving a single, unified effect are also responsible for the genre's other notable characteristics. Commonly, the short story deals with a single major character and/or a single major incident. The incident may be a notable event, a chain of actions leading to such an event, or even a series of consequences traceable to such an event. In terms of both character and incident, the short story's scope is narrow, to permit a consistent focus on matters of direct relevance and the exclusion of all that is unnecessary to its aims. The compactness of the short story makes it necessary for every word to contribute something of value to the story. Every character, action, description, detail should be significant. Consequently, the short story must have a plan for the coordination of its parts in support of a single, unified effect. Short stories are marked by a high degree of organization, even if the principle of organization is unusual or not readily apparent. Finally, short stories cannot be static, that is, cannot simply describe a moment frozen in time. Something must happen, progress, change. In other words, short stories must have a plot, although the plot need not be dominant. The plot of a short story may involve the physical activity of successive actions or the mental activity of psychological processes, emotional experience, and motivation. Whether focused on external or internal activity, the plot of a short story is more likely to be concerned with the nature of the relationship between successive actions than with their sequence or the magnitude of their outcome. The emphasis, especially in twentieth-century short stories, is less likely to be on what happens than on understanding how and why it happens.

Short Stories as Parts of Larger Works

Short stories are usually anthologized, or gathered in collections, for publication. Generally, works in an anthology do not build on each other; each one stands primarily on its own without reference to the others. Anthologized works may occasionally share a subject matter, geographic setting, perspective, or set of issues, but the anthology as a whole usually is not designed to have any special coherence or unity.

Some anthologies, however, are arranged according to an organizational plan that connects all its parts and gives a special identity or additional meaning to the collection as a whole. The most common organizational plan is the framework device popular in the Middle Ages, in which a context is created for the presentation of the individual works in the anthology. In short story collections, the frame usually establishes an occasion for the telling of stories, which remain self-contained and often interchangeable. In *The Arabian Nights,* for example, the narrator tells stories to stay alive, buying time with them. In Boccaccio's *Decameron,* ten young Florentines in isolation outside the city tell stories to pass the time and to take their minds off the plague that they are hoping to escape. In Chaucer's *Canterbury Tales,* travelers on a pilgrimage to Canterbury tell stories to make the journey pass more pleasantly and to win a free meal in a contest to tell the best story. In framed collections of stories, especially later Renaissance collections, any interplay between stories and frame or between individual stories is rare. The *Decameron* and *The Canterbury Tales* are the outstanding exceptions. The stories within each day's set in the *Decameron* often play on features of preceding stories, in a combination of one-upsmanship and imaginative exploitation of the day's theme. Boccaccio's stories, however, bear little relation to the personalities of their tellers, which is an outstanding feature of *The Canterbury Tales.* Chaucer's stories reveal the personalities of their tellers, and the juxtaposition of stories dramatizes the relationships between tellers who represent a cross section of society. Later framed collections of stories emulated Boccaccio and Chaucer, but did not succeed in developing a greater degree of unity for the collection.

A related development is the picaresque novel, which appeared in Spain in the sixteenth century and later spread to England and France. A form of fictional autobiography, the picaresque novel is an episodic story of a lower-class rogue, whose comical exploits often provide a satirical commentary on society. Typically, the episodes in a picaresque novel are a series of unrelated adventures that support no real, overall plot. They provide no character development and may even present inconsistent character traits. Essentially, the picaresque novel resembles a collection of stories that have in common only the name of their main character and a focus on vivid, possibly satirical, incidents. Among the better known picaresque novels are the Spanish *Life of Lazarillo de Tormes,* the English *Moll Flanders* and *The Unfortunate Traveler,* and the French *Gil Blas.*

HERRIOT'S WORK AS AUTOBIOGRAPHY AND SHORT STORY

Herriot's books are both autobiographies and collections of short stories. As an autobiographer, Herriot combines the modern view of autobiography as an exploration of interior life with the traditional idea of memoir as an account of the writer's world and acquaintances. He brings these usually divergent approaches together by presenting his interior development as a response to experience. Essentially, he places himself in the position of reading and interpreting his experiences as his readers read and interpret his stories—to understand his world, to discover its values, and to define himself and his values in relation to his world. Much modern autobiography shares a like concern with finding meaning in life, struggling with disconnectedness, and seeking a sense of self and place in a world that offers few ready-made answers or seems to deny the possibility of finding answers. Herriot's autobiography responds to such a world with hope rather than cynicism. What he has termed his "rosy" view is largely an effort to look for the good without entirely denying the existence of the bad. As the first-person narrator of many stories in which he often plays just a modest part, Herriot presents himself not so much as the teller of the story of his life, but as an observer of life, including his own.

As a storyteller, Herriot combines elements of the oral tradition with the formal craftsmanship of the literary short story. At the heart of his stories lie the anecdotes that typically support informal social interaction—the accounts of notable occurrences that he exchanges with Helen at the end of the day, with Siegfried during long evenings of reminiscence, and with friends at pubs. Animals and their personalities figure strongly in his stories, giving them a touch of the fantastic. But the stories remain firmly rooted in realism: they never become beast fables in the manner of Aesop, with the animals simply acting as if they were human beings in animal form. Herriot always presents an animal's personality as partly its temperament and partly an imaginative projection of human qualities introduced by people associated with the animal. Herriot's animals are not humanlike in their own right, but in the eyes of characters who share a common human tendency to anthropomorphize or to sentimentalize animal behavior. The stories themselves are handled with the emphasis on economy, completeness, and achievement of the single, unified effect that is typical of the modern short story.

Part of the popularity of Herriot's books undoubtedly lies in the relatively self-contained nature of their individual chapters. Many autobiographies are episodic, but Herriot's chapters generally work as separate short stories, which makes it possible for busy readers to enjoy a sense of completeness in reading as little as one chapter at a sitting. As collections of short stories, his books resemble picaresque novels, because they present a series of separate adventures, genuinely autobiographical in this case, linked by the main character's presence in each of them. The adventures are often humorous, and focus attention on experiencing the world and on social values. Unlike the picaresque novel, however, his books are not satirical. Nor is the main character a rogue, although Herriot takes pains to paint himself as less than heroic, just an ordinary, fallible, average person. Herriot is the link between stories, both as their narrator and as an involved character. His life provides the frame for the stories, but only one of his books, *All Things Wise and Wonderful*, closely

resembles typical framed collections of stories. There he offers his recollections of his earlier civilian experiences while undergoing training
for the military in World War II. In his other books, the frame is a context
rather than a frame as such. The context for the stories is another stage
in his life, with the issues, challenges, and new experiences appropriate
to that stage. Through the stories, through their topical and thematic
relationships to each other and to his current concerns, Herriot represents
his ongoing process of learning about his world, himself, and what he
values in life.

3

All Creatures Great and Small
(1972)

All Creatures Great and Small achieved a success far beyond anything Herriot had envisioned when it was published in the United States in 1972. Sales of earlier versions in England had been only modest. His New York publisher, nevertheless, thought it would appeal to Americans and backed it with a strong advertising campaign. Americans noticed the book, and a much wider range of people than expected found it appealing. It went beyond mere success to achieve best-seller status, the praise of reviewers, and continuing international popularity.

Reviewers and Herriot himself have speculated on the source of its popularity. Some reviewers said that Americans were ready for a positive alternative to books about alienation and isolation in modern life. They liked its positive outlook on life, especially on work. Others credited the attractive mix of modesty, principles, warmth, and self-deprecating humor that marks Herriot as a character in the book. Still others saw the variety in its content as winning readers and holding their interest. Herriot himself suggested that Americans might simply be more extravagantly fond of animals than anyone thought.

Each view may have an element of truth in it. Stronger reasons for its popularity probably lie, however, in the quality of its writing and in its invitation to share in Herriot's gradual discovery of what is worth valuing in life.

THEMATIC ISSUES

All Creatures Great and Small is a coming-of-age story. Coming-of-age stories focus on a turning point between immaturity and maturity in a character's life, frequently a time in adolescence when a person begins to see the world as an adult instead of as a child. But they can also focus on a time when a person completes the process of growth into adulthood. The turning point could come at any age and takes a different form for each person, but it always marks the passage from one phase of life to another.

All Creatures Great and Small presents James Herriot's first two years of practice in the 1930s as a time of personal as well as professional passage from innocence to maturity. Leaving the sheltered life of a student behind, he has to find his place in the world, make his own choices, and live with the results. Can he make it? It is more than a question of finding happiness or personal fulfillment. In the economic depression of the 1930s, anyone could slip into poverty. Jobs disappeared as businesses failed, and governmental public welfare programs barely kept people from starvation. Herriot's job interview was a lucky break, since, as he says, even experienced veterinarians were desperately offering to work for their keep alone.

As a novice vet fresh from school, he is full of illusions and uncertainties that he needs to recognize and resolve. Herriot's journey to the snow-swept barn where we meet him in Chapter 1, arm deep in a cow and face down in nameless muck on the stone floor, is a journey of adjustment and change. It involves adjusting his tidy, book knowledge gained in veterinary college to the messy, complicated reality of practice. It involves exchanging his heroic vision of being a triumphant healer for a humble awareness of his own and his profession's limitations and strengths. It involves developing a measured confidence, both in himself and in his professional judgment. It involves abandoning the imagined attractions of a clean, comfortable, state-of-the-art small animal practice in favor of the unexpected satisfactions of a messy, physically demanding large animal practice. It involves an urban-bred young man making the adjustments necessary to fit comfortably into rural life, especially the harsh rural life of the Yorkshire Dales. It involves his gradual transformation into a seasoned vet and his coming to know himself. The successful conclusion of his journey is marked at the end of the book by his marriage and his partnership in the veterinary practice. These two events set firmly in place the future course of his adult life and confirm his integration into the Yorkshire community.

Coming-of-age stories often concentrate on what is happening inside the main character during a period of adjustment, showing the character's struggle with complex thoughts and feelings. The focus of attention in *All Creatures Great and Small,* however, is on the external circumstances that stimulate Herriot's thinking and growth. The book describes the people, places, and situations that he encounters. Herriot speaks of being affected by them and shares first impressions and conclusions about them. But he does not analyze his reactions to them or detail the evolution of his thoughts and feelings. He could do so easily, since he serves as narrator and since autobiographical writing is often self-analytic. (See the section on narrative point of view later in this chapter.) Herriot, however, prefers to put readers in the position of assessing the effect that his experiences have on his outlook and life choices. This seems to be his point when, in interviews, he has insisted that *All Creatures Great and Small* is really about the people of the Yorkshire Dales. He directs his readers' attention to those things that have had an impact on him and creates the opportunity for his readers to experience them as well.

The Dales and veterinary practice itself are of particular interest here because the 1930s mark a period of transition. The old ways are passing with the arrival of twentieth-century science and technology. The coming of mechanized agriculture has already begun to make the workhorse disappear from the landscape. The Dales are also feeling the effect of rural electrification, new cures and preventative measures for disease in livestock, modern agricultural methods that favor large-scale operations over small farms, improved communication through radio, film, and telephone, the economic changes of the 1920s and 1930s, and the arrival of outsiders such as middle-class retirees moving to the country. All of these innovations are prompting—even necessitating—social change. And change brings both loss and gain. Part of Herriot's purpose is to recollect a vanished way of life and its distinctive qualities. Neither the old ways nor the new represent an ideal, however. Herriot is careful to observe that they are each as impoverished in some respects as they are enriched in others.

Looking back at this transitional period from the late 1960s, when he begins writing, Herriot calls attention to what is being lost and gained in terms of human qualities and values. He focuses on the positive qualities found in the vanishing breed of small subsistence farmers: principally ruggedness, independence, stoicism, and generosity. These qualities mirror what he sees in the Yorkshire landscape; they are shaped by direct human engagement with that environment in the daily struggle to survive. And they are changing, if not fading, as scientific and technological advances give the farmers more independence from the whims of nature. Herriot develops secondary themes centered on these qualities and on related issues, such as the bond between humans and animals, the essence of positive human relationships, and the definition of success in life. These qualities and issues are at the heart of his passage to maturity. In those first two years of practice, he grows into maturity as he clarifies his values and moves to conform his life to them.

The people, places, and situations that Herriot experienced as a young vet in Yorkshire served to bring about his passage from youth to maturity. He now invites readers to experience them in *All Creatures Great and Small.* Can they touch the readers' lives, in some manner, as they touched his?

PLOT DEVELOPMENT

Herriot's life provides the book's overall structural coherence. *All Creatures Great and Small* covers the period from Herriot's traveling to be interviewed for his first job upon graduation from veterinary college through his first two years of practice. Chapters 1 through 31 are the contents of Herriot's first British book, *If Only They Could Talk,* and cover his first year in practice. Chapters 32 through 64 are the contents of his second British book, *It Shouldn't Happen to a Vet,* and cover his second year in practice. The two British books fit together as a unified work because they establish the foundation of his ongoing thirty-year career as a Yorkshire vet. Chapter 64 ends with his working relationship with Siegfried Farnon firmly established. The three final chapters added for American publication (two of them later appeared in his third British book) reinforce his being settled in Darrowby by presenting his proposal to the daughter of a Yorkshire farmer, their marriage and working honeymoon, and his formally becoming a partner in the veterinary practice.

The first half of *All Creatures Great and Small* emphasizes Herriot's professional growth. He replaces his book knowledge with practical experience and discovers the satisfactions of large animal practice. He also falls so much in love with the scenery and people of the Yorkshire Dales that he decides to stay there. The second half of the book emphasizes personal and social growth. He gains confidence in himself and develops his ability to handle a wide range of social relationships, from getting along with his unpredictable boss to dealing with the stresses of dating and falling in love. He acquires a realistic sense of responsibility and discovers that he can act boldly when necessary—as he does in asking Helen to marry him and in insisting on combining the testing job with their honeymoon. Since each half of the book mixes professional and personal growth despite emphasizing one or the other, the two halves blend completely. At the end of the book, Herriot's professional growth and personal growth are marked symbolically by his nearly simultaneous marriage and partnership.

Within the overall framework of Herriot's first two years of practice, *All Creatures Great and Small* has an episodic structure, which is typical of all his books. Each chapter commonly deals with one or more complete incidents and could stand on its own as a short story. In fact, some chapters have been reprinted as short stories. The typical chapter shares some features with short stories: it has a single aim, and it limits the number of characters, their development, details of setting, plot complications, background information, and analysis to only what supports its aim. The typical chapter also ends in short story fashion, with a striking concluding line that provokes thought about the chapter's aim or point.

Chapters that can stand as independent stories carry the threat of making a book seem fragmented. The overall framework of Herriot's first two years in practice is only partly helpful here. Many chapters are so loosely connected to the two-year timeline that they could be moved to other positions in the book without seeming to be out of place. Some are tied only by a reference to the season of the year. Herriot, however, avoids the problem of fragmentation by setting up connections between chapters in several ways. Similar connections also appear in his later books.

First, he encourages readers to see a plan instead of a problem here. At intervals, he repeats two characteristics of veterinary practice: its variety and its unpredictability—which can have a vet looking good or foolish at any moment. Both of these ideas serve as a rationale for the wide variety of incidents and individuals that are presented in the book. They encourage readers to see difference as a connection between chapters. In other words, variety and unpredictability turn into intentional features that link chapters as part of a unified whole.

Second, Herriot also links chapters in more conventional ways. Although the action started in a chapter is usually completed within it, sometimes the action continues into a second or third chapter—which provides a strong impression of continuity. The pair of chapters about Tristan's experience with the pig-raising scheme and the pair of chapters about trouble with Isaac Cranford are examples. A variation on this pattern is a broken series of chapters presenting independent incidents that develop a plot line or reveal a specific character's qualities. This type of series is usually interrupted by chapters dealing with other incidents. Examples of this pattern include the series of chapters presenting incidents in Herriot's courtship of Helen and the series dealing with the "war" between Siegfried Farnon and Miss Harbottle. Here the sense of continuity provided by the related chapters carries over to the interrupting chapters.

Herriot strengthens the book's unity in other ways as well. Some chapters establish links to much earlier chapters by bringing back characters for new adventures. The returns of Mrs. Pumphrey and Angus Grier are notable examples. Many chapters also set up connections to earlier chapters by presenting similar situations and issues, which invite readers to notice points of comparison and contrast. Individual chapters frequently mirror this pattern by presenting several incidents that show a range of possibilities within one type of situation. Finally, the chapters are strongly linked through their thematic relationship. The incidents and individuals in them add to a picture of the values and issues that Herriot is pondering. They offer different examples of dedication, regard for animals and other human beings, choices of lifestyle, and so on. Sometimes they present small degrees of difference, and sometimes they offer sharp contrasts.

Since more than one of these linking techniques often applies to a chapter, they overlap and reinforce each other to provide unity and structure within the overall framework of Herriot's first two years of practice.

NARRATIVE POINT OF VIEW

All of Herriot's books are first-person narratives. In a first-person narrative, the narrator is a character living within the world of the story and can be the main character, a minor character, or a witness who is not a participant in the action. First-person point of view limits the narrator to telling only what he or she knows personally, knows secondhand from other characters, can find out or figure out, and thinks or feels in a situation. Essentially, it limits the narrative to what a real person involved in a real situation might be able to know and tell about it. In contrast, a third-person narrative is told by someone outside the story. Third-person point of view allows the narrator to know and tell everything about anything, including the future and what each character is thinking. A third-person narrator can shift between telling what he or she knows and telling how various characters see things from their limited points of view.

One form of third-person narration may seem similar to first-person narration. In *limited* third-person narration, the narrator concentrates on how only one character experiences things. The limited third-person narrator, however, is still a separate individual who knows—and can tell readers—a great deal more than the character could. In this respect, limited third-person narration differs greatly from first-person narration: the first-person narrator is not a separate individual and cannot have additional outside knowledge to tell. In general, a first-person narration is also more likely to show the effects of such things as the personality, abilities, and mental state of the character serving as narrator. This increases the likelihood of an *unreliable narrator,* one whose narrative commentary is at odds with what readers can see on their own in the story.

Since James Herriot is both the narrator and the main character in *All Creatures Great and Small,* this is a first-person narrative. James gives only information that anyone in his situation could know or could easily learn. He also shares his analysis of all he experiences. He observes people and situations, thinks about them and about his own attitudes and performance, and shares his conclusions. Analysis and speculation are his only way into the minds of other characters. He is usually a reliable narrator; readers are never given cause to doubt his reliability, except, perhaps, in his tendency to undervalue himself and his standing with others.

Double Narrative Perspective

The narrative perspective of *All Creatures Great and Small* is more complex than it appears at first. A double narrative perspective emerges here, and versions of it will return in Herriot's other books.

The usual narrative point of view throughout is that of the young James Herriot, sharing his experience and thoughts at roughly the time that the events occurred in the 1930s. In addition, a second, slightly different narrative point of view occasionally enters the narrative; James is still the narrator on these occasions, but he is a different James. For example, as he and Siegfried admire rows of bottles in the dispensary in Chapter 3, the narrator observes somewhat ironically that these medicines were "nearly all useless" (23) and soon to be banished by new discoveries. With such a comment, the narrator is transformed briefly into an older James Herriot, who is looking back on his early experience from some thirty years in the future. It is a comment that the young James could never make, because a first-person narrator cannot know the future the way a third-person narrator can. But a first-person narrator can know about the past, and for the older James what will come in the young James's future is already in the past. The older James can know it as a first-person narrator, and this additional knowledge separates him from the young James. Their viewpoints differ simply in the older James's ability to set events of the 1930s in their historical perspective. His comments usually concern later discoveries in veterinary medicine and changes in the Dales landscape and lifestyle. They concern what anyone from the vantage point of thirty years in the future might be able to identify as correct, incorrect, mistaken, or different—especially about veterinary medicine's procedures, diagnoses, and medications. Thus, his infrequent comments complement what the young James as narrator can tell readers. As a result, the double narrative perspective encourages readers to appreciate Herriot's experience in the 1930s on its own terms without forgetting to keep a broader perspective as well.

Unifying the Double Perspective

Even if brief and infrequent, the presence of a second narrative voice can easily become a problem if it seems to be just a lapse in narrative consistency. Herriot, therefore, encourages readers in several ways to accept the double narration as essentially unified.

First, the difference between the two narrative perspectives is minimal. The narrator remains James Herriot. The older James differs from the young James only in having a knowledge of later events and possibly more experience and understanding. Both narrators show detachment, the ability to stand back and view things objectively. The detachment that marks the older James's comments is typical of characters looking back on earlier events in their lives. Detachment is also one of the defining characteristics of the younger James as he is depicted in the book (see the section on characters and character development, in this chapter)—which is uncommon in characters looking at very recent events in their lives.

Second, readers are encouraged to accept occasional shifts from the book's usual 1930s perspective to a 1960s perspective by the way time sequences shift in young James's narrative. Events are frequently told out of chronological order. As a result, although the narrative present stays the 1930s in general, what is treated as present time at any moment in the narrative may become past or future in relation to the events surrounding it. Distinctions between narrative past, present, and future begin to blur. The first chapter, for example, shifts the narrative present in a conventional way by beginning in medias res, literally in the middle of things. Opening in the middle of a struggle with a cow, Chapter 1 then backs up to fill in the start of the episode before concluding the action.

The opening chapter also starts the entire book in medias res, by presenting an episode seven months into James's first job. Chapter 2 then backs up to give an account of his bus trip to Darrowby to be interviewed for the job. Despite the seven-month time difference, both chapters present themselves as present-time accounts. Both chapters also digress: Chapter 1 weaves memories of James's schooling into the unfolding action, while Chapter 2 weaves in memories of first-job horror stories he had heard from schoolmates and side trips into fantasy visions of his future employer. The present time of Chapter 1 is the future of Chapter 2. Thus, the opening chapters prepare readers to be tolerant of time shifts. As the narrator continues to juggle past, present, and future, the mix begins to seem as natural as straightforward chronology.

Finally, the double narrative perspective plays off the autobiographical nature of the book. The natural tendency of readers is always to think of narrator and author as the same person. This is seldom true in fiction, where the narrator is likely to be a product of the author's imagination. But narrator and author are nearly always the same in autobiography, which by definition is the author's telling of his or her own story. Readers are, of course, aware that the author and the main character/narrator have the same name in *All Creatures Great and Small.* Whenever the voice of the older James enters, it reminds readers that the young James will continue his career to become that older James, the experienced vet. It also reminds readers that the young James and the older James are versions of the author, who is a veterinarian of thirty years' experience according to the brief biographical note included in the book. As a result, the older James serves as a bridge between the world in the book and the real world, inhabited by the author and the readers. At the same time, however, readers learn so little about the author from the biographical note that he seems less real than the characters in the book. He remains, like the shadowy older James, little more than a promise of the young James's future success. Those readers who are also aware that James Herriot is a pen name will find the line between the real world and the world of the book blurred even further.

The result of the double narrative point of view in *All Creatures Great and Small* is a blending of the limited viewpoint of the young James Herriot with the more fully informed viewpoint of the older James Herriot. More important, it brings together involvement and detachment as complementary instead of opposing attitudes. Consequently, it encourages readers to respond to the text with both involvement and detachment, to resist being uncritical in their appreciation of the attractions of both the past and progress.

CHARACTERS AND CHARACTER DEVELOPMENT

Since *All Creatures Great and Small* presents Herriot's first encounters with the people of Yorkshire, readers are introduced to a very large number of characters. A few appear regularly throughout the book and command continuing attention. Others star more briefly and command attention—usually primary attention—for the moment. Thus, a distinction between characters who are central in the book (major characters) and those who are central in any of its smaller parts (minor characters) may be helpful. In general, major characters figure directly in James's unfolding story of his life, while notable minor characters dominate the stories that are part of his experience as a vet. These notable minor characters are distinct from the many additional minor characters who appear in supporting roles and remain little more than names.

Character development does not take place in Herriot's books in the usual sense of a character's being led to change by circumstances. Instead, it takes place as the gradual revelation of a more complete and complex personality. All of Herriot's characters begin as types. A type is an easily recognized category of people who share common qualities—for example, artists, hunters, optimists, or hotheads. Many of Herriot's characters are introduced as representative Yorkshire types, as examples of categories found in the Dales. They may also be recognizable as literary types, that is, as belonging to categories frequently shown in literature. Although few of Herriot's characters develop in the sense of changing over time, many of them become more individualized. In addition to having qualities in common with others in their category, they begin to stand out as having unique personal qualities. This individualizing occurs as characteristics and idiosyncrasies are revealed in subsequent situations, dialogue, and details. Development in this sense is obviously more common to the book's central characters, since they have the advantage of being seen over a longer period of time.

Herriot usually begins depicting characters with a physical description and a brief personality description or label that identifies them by type. He then follows up by showing the characters speaking and acting. This pattern—a "tell, then show" pattern—is sometimes altered and even reversed for variety. In addition, Herriot plays off the widespread tendency to associate physical features with personality traits. The physical descriptions and key personality traits of his characters are usually linked according to popular conceptions—the open face is associated with innocence, the firm jaw with determination, and so on. Here too he occasionally works against the pattern, by twisting the expected connection so that the personality trait suggested by a character's physical features actually turns out to be the complete opposite of the character's real personality.

The mix of these patterns and their variations is well represented in the first three chapters of the book. The eight characters (other than James and Siegfried) introduced there follow the "tell, then show" pattern. Brief, linked physical and personality descriptions are followed by a demonstration in speech, action, or both. Typical are the Dimsdales, father and son, who are described as "long, sad, silent" (3) men of gloomy disposition and are shown speaking only a total of ten words by the end of Chapter 1's two-hour action. Uncle Dimsdale, Mrs. Hall, Bert Sharpe, Mulligan, Diana Brompton, and the unnamed farmer with the Clydesdale follow the same pattern. So do the three versions of Siegfried introduced in the first two chapters, although the three versions together build a picture of Siegfried by contrasting each other. James himself follows the opposite, "show first" pattern: he is introduced through his actions and through his words both as a participant in the action and as the narrator. Only much later in the book are personality labels applied to him by other characters.

A more typical example of the "show first" pattern is the introduction of Mr. Soames in Chapter 5. His somewhat rude and belligerent speech on the telephone brings James's immediate assessment of him as an "aggressive know-all" (35). This view is confirmed later by James's first sight of him as thick-set and dapper from a distance, and then unpleasant close-up with his "thick, red neck, a ruddy face and small, fiery eyes" (36). One of the rare examples of contrasting physical features and personality traits is the depiction of Jeff Mallock in Chapter 28. He is the opposite of what would be expected from his gloomy trade as knacker and from the smelly, nightmare world of his slaughter yard: a pink, cherubic man with an unusually attractive and healthy family.

Whether in one meeting or over a series of meetings, Herriot's characters slowly reveal more of their personalities. Readers get to know the people of the Dales as James does, little by little, thus sharing in his process of discovery.

Major Characters

James Herriot. James approaches even the most difficult of people and animals with empathy. He imagines what makes them as they are and even how they see him. In doing so, he reveals much about himself. Readers see a man capable of detached objectivity, able to step back and look at himself clearly and honestly. They also see a man who displays warmth and sympathy toward others, whether human or animal. As he reveals his understanding of the thoughts and feelings of others based on observation and reflection, he never gives cause to doubt his reliability. He tends, however, to underestimate his standing with others. This tendency actually works to reinforce his credibility as a naturally modest and fair observer. It also demonstrates his youthful anxiety over gaining acceptance.

As a narrator, James can reveal his own thoughts and feelings directly, but the thoughts and feelings of others only indirectly, as he sees them. Much of what he reveals of himself, however, seems as indirect as what he reveals of others—it seems distanced from the immediate action being presented. He only occasionally shares what he is thinking and feeling while involved in the action; more commonly, he supplements the action and dialogue with a commentary that appears to be based on thoughtful reflection regarding the situation and everyone in it, including himself. Thus, what readers are permitted to see directly of James is as limited and controlled as what they are allowed to see of other characters. Much remains private for him as well as for them.

James occasionally identifies himself explicitly as an observer. At a professional meeting of veterinarians in Chapter 21, for example, he speaks of how it "amused me to look round the crowded room and try to guess what the little knots of men were talking about. That man over there . . . And the one with his arm out . . ." (140). In Chapter 23 he mentions how, when Siegfried and Miss Harbottle join battle, "it gave life an added interest to observe the tactics of the two sides" (155). And in Chapter 36 he speaks of "times I often seemed to stand outside myself, calmly assessing my progress. It was easy to flick back over the years" (246).

When he looks at himself, he takes a balanced view. He presents, without extended apology, his mistakes, his failures, and the limitations under which veterinary medicine labors. Similarly he presents, without claiming undue credit, his successes, flashes of insight, and solid professional competence. He displays his ability to laugh at himself and to appreciate the absurdity of situations that were clearly painful for him to experience. He regularly sees himself as lacking qualities he admires in others: the decisiveness and charm of Siegfried, the mental agility and worldly social ease of Tristan, the polished sophistication of the well-bred Richard Edmundson. On the other hand, his warmth and professionalism shine in the courtesy he extends even to the most annoying, undeserving people he encounters—from Uncle Dimsdale to Mr. Sidlow to Mr. Cranshaw—and in his effort to see reasons for their actions.

He does not judge. For him, people and animals seem to come in a full range of personalities, including the vicious—and they remain true to type. Thus, to recognize an antisocial person or animal is partly to understand its actions. This is evident in his treatment of the greedy Mr. Dumbleby, the butcher. When he playfully tests whether Mr. Dumbleby can escape a basically greedy nature to commit a generous act, Dumbleby remains true to type. James treats Dumbleby's choice as confirming the wisdom of accepting people as they are instead of condemning them for failing to be something else. Similarly, James accepts Siegfried's personality and does not try to change it. He begins to find ways to live with Siegfried's inconsistencies in word and deed after realizing that Siegfried will never acknowledge inconsistency.

As the book progresses, James is the character who comes closest to conventional character development, that is, to changing as a result of his experiences. Change is at the heart of a coming-of-age story, for it is a fundamental before-and-after difference in a character that shows a turning point between one phase of life and another has been passed. For James, the change is essentially his discovery and acceptance of who he really is. He proceeds from the insecurity of youth, with its professional and social anxiety, to the security of a satisfying job, experience, and acceptance. He adjusts to the hardships of his job and to the eccentricities of his employer and clients. As he does so, he discovers a love for the Yorkshire countryside, the people of Yorkshire, and the life of a country practice, which clarifies and firmly establishes what he wishes his future to be. James slowly comes to terms with that future. After recognizing early in the book that such a choice involves abandoning a desire for worldly success in favor of personal fulfillment, he begins to accept that future and finally comes to the certainty that he has no regrets. As the book progresses, he also learns, to trust his professional judgment, even as he becomes increasingly aware of the limits of medical knowledge. He continues doing as well as he did when he acted decisively on his first solo visit, but he also develops greater and better-founded confidence.

Having progressed in his professional life, he begins a parallel development in his private life. When he meets Helen in Chapter 40, he realizes how long it has been since he thought of anything but work. He functions very well in the bachelor household of the Farnons and in social situations arising directly from his role as a veterinarian—chatting with clients, sharing meals, and drinking together in pubs—but in other social contexts he is troubled by feelings of anxiety and inexperience. As he becomes interested in dating, he shows his need to develop in his social life some of the same mature qualities that he has developed in his professional life: trust in his judgment, confidence to be himself, and an ability to act decisively when what he values is at stake. The example of the socially adept Farnon brothers adds to his feelings of inadequacy. James's contrasting levels of confidence in his professional and social life are highlighted for readers on the occasion of Mrs. Pumphrey's party, in his early encounters with Helen, and in his dealings with her father. Initially, he follows Tristan's advice, but his dating disasters push him to become more self-reliant. He reasons that he cannot do worse on his own. When he acts independently and results improve, his progress is clear. Eventually, he finds himself capable of acting as decisively in his personal life, by asking Helen to marry him, as he has in his professional life, by diagnosing and administering emergency treatments without hesitation. He finds that his empathy can guide him to do the right thing in social as well as professional situations, as his interview with Mr. Alderson in Chapter 66 shows. In the end, James achieves a high level of maturity in both sides of his life, which come together and mesh in his working honeymoon.

Siegfried Farnon. The one character, other than James, who receives constant attention throughout *All Creatures Great and Small* is Siegfried Farnon. His presence is so strong that Siegfried's preference for calling Herriot "James" rather than "Jim" (as Helen and others do) makes it irresistibly "James" in this book for readers as well. In addition to bringing James to Yorkshire, he helps to define some of the special qualities that win James to life as a country vet in the Dales. Siegfried emerges more as a colleague and friend than as an employer. James finds with him a satisfying sense of common enterprise and camaraderie. He experiences that feeling again later with the Yorkshire farmers, when he sees himself as "a tiny wheel in the great machine of British agriculture" (247). Above all, Siegfried fascinates James in much the same way that Yorkshire fascinates him. Readers see so much of Siegfried primarily because James finds it challenging to try to understand him and to discover how best to adjust to living with his peculiarities.

Herriot introduces Siegfried in Chapters 2 and 3 by presenting James's conflicting conceptions of him. Before they meet, James tries to imagine what he will be like. Thinking that Farnon may once have been a German name, he draws on popular English stereotypes of Germans to imagine two, opposite possibilities. James's brief, initial vision of him as Herr Farrenen is that of an ideal boss, imagined as the stereotypically roly-poly, jovial German commonly associated with festival and beer-hall scenes. Then he quickly turns to the opposite conception of Siegfried as the embodiment of the worst features of bosses from undergraduate horror stories, building a nightmarish image of Herr Farrenen as a "hulking, cold-eyed, bristle-skulled Teuton" (11). This Siegfried is cast in the mold of the negative stereotype of German military officers popular in English World War I propaganda. In addition, the bombastic speech patterns and actions James imagines link Siegfried to a long tradition of stage parodies of soldiers as excitable, strutting blowhards. Even as James continues to build on his negative vision of Herr Farrenen, he finds hints of a different Siegfried in Skeldale House and its visitors. When James awakens, in more ways than one, to the real Siegfried at the end of Chapter 2, Herr Farrenen is replaced with a stereotypical Englishman. He is "just about the most English-looking man" with his humorous face, sandy hair, trim mustache, and casually tweedy clothing. His voice too is "the most English voice" (20).

This ordinary Englishman displays appropriately attractive English qualities from the moment he gives the just-awakened James a friendly, slightly amused greeting and apologizes for his faulty memory. As he shows James around, Siegfried displays his enthusiasm for his profession, his delight in showmanship, his pride in modernizing the practice, and his optimism. To some extent, this ordinary Englishman is cast in the mold of the rural English upper class: he is a born horseman; he is casually elegant, whether in his rumpled tweeds or in evening dress; he is charming and carelessly attractive to a succession of beautiful, well-bred young women; he is even slightly eccentric, as shown by his burst of song at James's praising his equipment, his unorthodox driving style, and his car's loose passenger seat on runners. Siegfried, however, is clearly a working vet, not a hobbyist. Having bought a run-down practice, he has rebuilt it in a year to the point where it is turning a profit and promising to improve with a few more years of work. He has the aura of the upper class but the practical concerns and dirty hands of a working country vet. The real Siegfried ultimately emerges as more than the stereotypical Englishman he initially seems to be. Oddly enough, the real Siegfried also reveals himself to be not entirely unlike the two imaginary Herr Farrenens. The good humor of one reappears in him as a more sedate English benevolence and the excitable nature of the other reappears as part of his attractive English eccentricity.

Siegfried's basic decency becomes evident early, when he genuinely thanks James for opening every gate—usually a routine, thankless chore for students. His decency becomes evident again later that first day, when he invites James for a drink in a pub and offers to hire him on generous terms at a time when unemployment is so high that new veterinarians are desperate for work and might easily be exploited. In James's first weeks, Siegfried displays additional admirable qualities. He answers Soames with unhesitating support for James's professional judgment and competence. He displays genuine pleasure rather than a bruised ego when the farmers begin to accept James and to ask for him specifically. From the start, he relates to James primarily as a friend and colleague, a rough equal in all but experience, who does not emphasize his superior status (an approach exemplified later, for contrast, by Angus Grier).

Siegfried's excitable nature becomes evident when his younger brother Tristan appears in Chapter 6. His reaction to Tristan's failed pathology exam is surprising—dark flush, glaring eyes, wildly bellowed accusations, and the abrupt firing of the offender. His reaction recalls James's vision of Herr Farrenen looking shocked, "quivering with rage" (19), spluttering wild accusations, and rejecting him for his offenses. But the antagonistic rage that defines Herr Farrenen is just a rare expression of Siegfried's flare for the dramatic. More common is the pattern in the tactics that precede it in this meeting with Tristan. Siegfried adopts an attitude of unconcern so clearly at odds with his objective that it greatly magnifies the tension of the situation and focuses attention on him. His pose invites an unsuspecting James to rush to his fate and dares a cautious Tristan to escape certain doom. In the scene with Tristan, Siegfried's tactical pattern resembles that of a predator stalking its prey, a cat toying with a captive mouse. Used later with the redoubtable Miss Harbottle, his tactics belong in a chess championship or tactical warfare for high stakes. A similar pattern is also evident whenever Siegfried finds it necessary to reason with James. He adopts an obviously patient attitude at odds with his usual manner, draws James toward a trap with a chain of seemingly innocent questions, and finally pounces to make his point, but with a crow of triumph rather than a bellow of rage.

Such scenes with Tristan and James, however, are followed inevitably by a reversal of Siegfried's position. As Tristan observes to James after being fired, "He's always sacking me and he always forgets" (48). As James himself repeatedly discovers after losing a reasoning match, Siegfried is ready to adopt an entirely different position, without ever admitting error, when circumstances make his earlier position unsuitable. This mercurial nature is for James one of the most fascinating and frustrating aspects of Siegfried's personality.

Ultimately, Siegfried emerges as more complex than any of James's three initial stereotypical visions of him. He defies categorizing. Even James's frequent label for him, "mercurial," is too narrow and superficial, because it suggests that he is merely a bundle of contradictions or even that his defining characteristic is an unpredictable changeability. James does emphasize the inconsistent nature of Siegfried's behavior by observing and puzzling over it throughout the book, but he also recognizes that it follows a predictably recurring pattern. Moreover, such a pattern is entirely consistent with what James describes of Siegfried's personality: his mercurial behavior is recognizably an outgrowth of his personality.

The situations James cites to illustrate Siegfried's mercurial nature are examples of rapid decisions gone bad. As James observes, Siegfried is a man of action. He hates inactivity, rushes about energetically, and embraces innovations. His desire for action also leads him to make quick judgments. James sees good and bad in this. Siegfried's decisiveness is one of the qualities James most admires in him, seeing its advantage to veterinary practice. But he also realizes that Siegfried's rush to act sometimes leads him to focus his attention so narrowly that he misses the larger picture. What is appropriate for part of the picture may not fit the picture as a whole. This character trait is behind his unorthodox driving style, with its cliff-hanger switching between complete attention to the scenery and attention to the road. It is also behind frequent instances of apparent inattention or faulty memory, such as his maddening cross-purpose conversation with Jim in Chapter 52. And it sets the conditions for his rapid reversals of position: since Siegfried, unlike James, doesn't second-guess himself or worry over the wisdom of his decisions, he presses energetically onward until circumstances force him to change his mind. For example, his decision to hire James can be seen as one of his typical rapid decisions, and his support of James in front of Soames can be seen as a typical refusal to reconsider a decision. Hiring James proved wise and fortunate, and James's admiration of his decisiveness suggests that most of his decisions proved similarly advantageous. But the disadvantage of this approach lies in the risk of making an obviously foolish choice and looking more foolish for sticking with it.

So it is with Siegfried. His reversal of position generally occurs when he discovers firsthand that the situation requires different handling. Sometimes it comes from having refused to listen to others, as it does when he recognizes that the brakes on James's car are gone only after driving the car himself and narrowly escaping a crash. Sometimes it comes from having attended to only one of several competing values, as it does in his ill-fated economy drives and his firings of Tristan. Frequently it comes from the fact that Siegfried is simply too generous to do in a real situation what he decided should be done on the basis of cold logic or good business sense alone. His heart wins over his head in the "you must attend" episode, in the suture economy episode, and ultimately in the outcome of every confrontation with Tristan. In most of these instances, Siegfried's change of position is really a new quick decision based on his new perception of the situation. He never really recognizes his mistakes. Or, if he does, he never admits it. His habit of shifting blame elsewhere is a maddening but effective way to shut off discussion of the past and to hasten to move forward.

As the book progresses, Siegfried does not change as much as readers' perceptions of him, like James's, change upon further acquaintance and observation. Although practical, talented, and hard-working in building his practice, he is far from being the hotheaded Herr Farrenen, an Angus Grier, or even a Miss Harbottle. Generous and easygoing, he is also far from being a Stewie Brannon. His attitude toward money is an instance of this realistically human complexity. On the one hand, he is casual about handling money—stuffing it haphazardly into a pewter pot on the mantel—and careless about keeping records of visits for billing and records of expenditures. On the other, he worries a great deal about money whenever financial stability seems to be threatened. Thinking about the high cost of medical supplies and equipment, he launches economy drives until his concerns shift to quality of care. Thinking about the financial drain of Tristan's schooling weighed against his failed exams, his carousing, and his loafing about the practice, Siegfried rages until other concerns demand his attention. Thinking about the overall amount owed the practice by deadbeat clients and the hard work he has done for nothing, he launches collection drives until his normal perspective returns. In the end, Siegfried emerges as a more complex character than he first appears and displays a more consistent core of attractive human qualities than his surface contradictions at first suggest.

Tristan Farnon. Siegfried's brother Tristan is a veterinary student who assists in the practice when not at school. A practical joker keen on battles of wits, Tristan introduces a strain of comic relief and playfulness into the demanding routine of veterinary practice. He also adds a touch of ironic humor to the book when his ingenious schemes misfire so that the joke is on him.

Tristan has Siegfried's voice, but is different in physical appearance and temperament. He is small, dark-haired, boyish-faced, and charming in a puckish rather than elegant way. In contrast to Siegfried's energy and activity, he is distinguished by his fully relaxed posture when sitting and his absorbed enjoyment of his cigarette and newspaper. His immediate reference to partying the night before his arrival in Darrowby quickly suggests the stereotypical partying student. The suggestion is reinforced shortly after, when Siegfried accuses him of being a lazy, boozing woman chaser and when Tristan tells James that he has actually flunked not just one, but both of his latest exams.

From the moment he meets Tristan, however, James feels that he is "in the presence of a quicker and livelier mind" (45). It soon becomes clear that Tristan does not lack ability. He can pass his exams easily if he tries—he passes the retake of his two flunked exams at Christmas without appearing to have studied. His progress seems unaffected by extending his school vacations so far beyond official length that James wonders if he has a special arrangement with the school. He even gives ample evidence of mental agility, charm, and social skills equal to Siegfried's. He simply shows it in escaping work, outwitting his brother, devising practical jokes, weighing the merits of pubs for miles around, and charming everyone with his conversation and companionship.

While Siegfried enthusiastically applies himself to his profession, Tristan shows some enthusiasm only about socializing. His participation in Siegfried's hen and pig raising scheme is revealing. Tristan becomes interested in the personalities of the hens and the pigs rather than their ability to produce eggs or pork; therefore, he neglects them completely when they lose their charm. Similarly, when he is assigned to collect money from the practice's clients on market day, he enthusiastically adjusts his conversation in order to charm each individual. But he puts off recording the payments in the ledger and then loses his only record of the payments. Although Tristan calls these and other mishaps bad luck, they seem to result from bored inattention to details, arising from a lack of interest in the real objective of his activity.

Beneath Tristan's carefree attitude and clowning is a well-hidden element of deep unhappiness. His lack of enthusiasm for work and studies is more than just laziness: it is an expression of his genuine aversion to the future that lies before him. This becomes clear in a revealing moment soon after his arrival, while he is assisting James in an especially messy and bloody struggle to stuff a displaced uterus back into a cow. When they are pausing together for breath with their faces almost touching, James is "able to look deep into [Tristan's] eyes and [to] read there a deep distaste for the whole business" (75). It would appear that Tristan is not lazy or lacking ability, but that he is repulsed by the unpleasant realities of veterinary practice. James too finds some aspects of practice unpleasant, but, unlike Tristan, he comes to accept them as the price to pay for pursuing its rewards. Apparently Tristan cannot make that adjustment. As a result, when James later terms Tristan "Siegfried's reluctant student brother" (247), the word "reluctant" points to something much deeper in Tristan than his school record. His unhappiness stays well hidden, however, because Tristan insists throughout on taking his troubles lightly.

Helen Alderson. Meeting Helen at the Alderson farm in Chapter 40 reawakens James to thoughts of love. Helen is an attractive woman with a warm smile. Her unconventional, daring choice of clothing for the 1930s—green linen slacks—shows an independent turn of mind. The slacks combine practicality and style, suggesting a similar combination of qualities in her. Helen seems to embody traditional Yorkshire values and at the same time to be a modern, independent woman. She is making bread in the farm kitchen when James arrives, but she is equally comfortable doing ten minutes of hard walking or handling a calf expertly for him while he sets its broken leg. Helen and James seem well matched as they chat blissfully on the sunny hillside and share an appreciation of the rugged countryside. She has won his heart by the time he leaves. His prospects seem bright when Helen remarks on their shared love of the Yorkshire landscape: "I'm glad it appeals to you too—a lot of people find it too bare and wild. It almost seems to frighten them" (282). Helen's attractiveness and strength find additional confirmation shortly afterward in Tristan's admiring whistle and in Siegfried's admiration of her as a "lovely girl" (282) who has looked after her father, younger brother, and sister since her mother died.

In spite of Helen's importance in the book, however, readers are given little more direct evidence of her personality. She is shown almost entirely through James's eyes, and the picture is clouded by his anxiety over whether she can like him as much as he likes her. Siegfried's comment that "half the young bloods in the district are chasing her" but she is being "choosy" (283) awakens in James doubts about his prospects. Instead of seeing Helen as the woman beside him on the hillside, he begins to imagine her as too sophisticated for a humble country vet. Instead of being himself, he feels that he must try to be dashing and sophisticated to compete with the "young bloods" for her interest. Proceeding on this basis through much of his early courtship, James misinterprets her feelings and actions. As a result, he misdirects readers about her character. As events unfold, the original picture of Helen's character is first distorted and then once again revealed.

Thinking himself unworthy of her, James is slow to pursue Helen. Then he makes the mistake of trying to impress her on their first date instead of just being himself. After the elegant dinner dance that Tristan advised proves a fiasco in Chapter 48, James misreads Helen's strained expression and trembling voice as she thanks him as misery politely masked. He believes that he does not have a chance with her. Later, in Chapter 57, he jumps to the same conclusion when he meets Helen with the polished Richard Edmundson. He reads into her smile and strained eyes his own embarrassment over her finding him on a drunken date with a nurse. Remembering the dinner dance, James decides to ignore Tristan's advice and tries a less impressive, presumably safer movie for his second date with Helen. After this date also proves a fiasco, James is again in the process of misreading Helen's "twitching and frowning" reaction as barely controlled scorn when he is suddenly interrupted by Helen's bursting into helpless laughter, which indicates that she has been struggling all along to avoid laughing. Helen has appreciated the humor in their dating disasters and tried to avoid hurting his feelings by laughing. Anxiety has clouded his vision.

In spite of being misdirected, readers are likely to recognize far sooner than James that Helen likes him. Her reactions throughout the disastrous first date appear good-humored or uncertain at worst. Her interest in James seems quite clear when she provides him the opportunity to ask her for a second date by going to the surgery and asking him to see her dog. Readers may also suspect before her laughter in Chapter 62 that her values and interests really are what they appeared to be in that idyllic first meeting. The truth of this is later confirmed by the success of their working honeymoon, doing tuberculin testing at the top of the Dale, as a time of "laughter, fulfilment [*sic*], and cameraderie [*sic*]" (491).

Minor Characters

Many characters take a turn being the center of attention in only one chapter or a few successive chapters. They include Mr. Soames, Frank and George Copfield, the Bellerbys, Mr. Dean and Bob, Miss Harbottle, the Coopers, Phineas Calvert, Jeff Mallock, Isaac Cranford, Mr. Handshaw, Nugent, Mrs. Mallard, Terry Watson, Mr. Worley, Sam Broadbent, the Hugills, Miss Stubbs and her animals (Prince, a.k.a. "Mr. Heinze," Ben, Sally, Arthur, and Susie), John Skipton, Mr. Sidlow, Harold Denham, the Rudds and Strawberry, Dennis Pratt, Horace Dumbleby, Tip, Mr. Myatt, the Taverners, the Altons, Stewie Brannon, Candy and Mr. Alderson, and the Allens. Some central characters also make brief appearances or reappearances as part of the Yorkshire community, for an advance introduction, or in a postscript on their story. A few have more than one turn in the spotlight: Mrs. Pumphrey and Tricki Woo are a notable example, as is Angus Grier. Interestingly, only a few of the many animals that James is called to help become featured characters in their own right: Bob, Nugent, Mrs. Stubbs's companions, Strawberry, Tip, Candy, and, chief among them, Tricki Woo.

Mrs. Pumphrey, Tricki Woo, and Nugent. James finds relief from the harsh physical conditions of large animal practice in occasional small

animal work, especially in his visits to Mrs. Pumphrey and her Peking-
ese, Tricki Woo.

Mrs. Pumphrey is a wealthy elderly widow with a magnificent house,
numerous servants, and an excessive affection for Tricki Woo. She is also
an unusually likable person who makes James's visits times of luxurious
comfort, entertainment, and ego-soothing appreciation. Her warmth is
immediately apparent when she greets James. She seems to be almost as
happy as Tricki, who leaps from his cushion to welcome him. Her good-
natured eccentricity is also immediately apparent. She names James uncle to Tricki. She calls symptoms of impacted anal glands "flop-bott" (a
term suggesting Victorian delicacy). She pampers the little dog beyond
good health (rich diet and overexcitement inducing hysterical attacks she
calls "crackerdog"). And she creates elaborate stories with Tricki as star.
The Tricki Woo of her fantasy is a descendent of Chinese emperors, a
philanthropist, an unmatched judge of racing form, and a solicitous
nephew.

James doubts, however, that Mrs. Pumphrey is slipping into senility.
He suggests that she may instead be indulging in these fantasies as a
type of game to add interest to her pampered but otherwise dull life. He
points out that Mrs. Pumphrey is intelligent as well as amusing. Her
sharpness of mind is certainly evident behind Tricki's record of very
shrewd, successful betting on horse races. Her stories of Tricki's exploits
also suggest some conscious fictionalizing, as in her choice of "Mr. Ut-
terbunkum" as Tricki's proposed alias in the story of his unsolicited
financial contribution to an animal magazine. But it remains unclear to
what extent she realizes that her stories of Tricki's exploits are fictional.
James is aware that he is playing a game in going along with Mrs. Pumphrey's fantasies, but he is also certain that she takes the game seriously
and is not laughing at him for going along. He repeatedly observes that
she has a "blind spot" regarding Tricki. Later, she reveals a similar blind
spot in her inability to see how it might be inappropriate to keep a pig
as a pet in her house and in her worry that keeping Nugent the pig
outdoors might be unhealthy for him.

Part of the seriousness of the game may lie in its usefulness as an outlet
for her intelligence and her affectionate, generous nature. As an extremely wealthy widow, Mrs. Pumphrey may need a more fulfilling existence than her status and class permit. She bestows her affection on a
willing and responsive animal, as many people do. In addition, she finds
an acceptable outlet for her imagination by creating elaborate fictions in
which Tricki is the main character. Above all, as a woman who "gave

widely to charities and would help anybody in trouble" (97), she works through Tricki to help people who are not exactly in trouble but can use a boost: Tricki's activities often serve as a way to do good more widely without risking a refusal of her help and without making anyone feel obliged to her. Thus, she regularly brightens James's life with little luxuries that are much easier for her to give and for him to accept in Tricki's name. Similarly, she provides unsolicited support for the publication of *Doggy World.* Tricki's whim is to do the good she actually wishes to do, and the wise recipient plays the game. James discovers this when he notices that Mrs. Pumphrey is pleased by his thanking Tricki for gifts, while she is "rather cool" (100) when he thanks her.

The real Tricki makes the game easier to play because he is unusually good-natured, affectionate, and attractive with his wide grin and silky, golden coat. James finds Tricki so "equable" and intelligent that he admits to being "genuinely attached to him" (96–97), suggesting that Tricki is a dog worthy of being doted upon. Tricki's only flaw, as James observes later, is greed. He is unable to refuse any food offered him at any time. In the episode of his hospitalization, Tricki emerges as similar to Harvey Cheyne in Kipling's *Captains Courageous* and to many other spoiled storybook children of basically good character who become unspoiled once they are forced to undergo the hardships of a vigorous, unprivileged life. Tricki's dieting and his living as an ordinary dog with the gang of Skeldale household dogs restore his health. When he returns a new dog to his pampered life, some of the more wholesome life also continues. His romps in the garden with the Skeldale dogs are replaced by romps with Nugent the pig in Mrs. Pumphrey's garden.

Tricki's new companion, Nugent, is similar to Tricki Woo in being so unusually good-natured and equable that he invites being doted upon. He looks for people to visit him and, like a dog, rolls over on his side when his back is scratched. Nugent is also similar to Tricki in being a source of misery to Hodgkin, the dour old gardener who dislikes pets of any type. Hodgkin hates pampering the pig even more than tossing rings for the dog. Although James mentions it only briefly, Nugent also follows Tricki in being generous to his Uncle Herriot with gifts including a signed picture like those from Tricki. By emphasizing their unusual personalities, James tries to rationalize Mrs. Pumphrey's and his own unusual behavior toward these animals. In other words, Nugent is so like a pet dog in personality that it seems unreasonable to treat him as just a farm animal, while Tricki is more like a person than an ordinary dog.

Angus Grier. In Angus Grier, James finds a living example of the nightmarish boss. Siegfried warns him that Grier is a "cantankerous Aberdonian" (145) who is notoriously abusive to students and likely to harass anyone who rubs him the wrong way. At first sight, James finds Grier's appearance unpleasant and showing signs of a drinker. Grier is fiftyish, with a blotchy complexion, blurry eyes, a blue-veined nose, and a "permanently insulted expression" (145). He quickly justifies his negative image by greeting James with a grunt, abusing his current student, and offering "a long recital of wrongs suffered at the hands of wicked clients and predatory colleagues" (146). Grier's attitude is the opposite of Siegfried's upbeat and supportive disposition. He also demonstrates his mean streak when he takes offense at James's reluctance to get dirty unnecessarily and engineers the humiliating practical joke of encasing him in an elaborate rubber suit to provide minor assistance at a cleansing. In him, Tristan's capacity for drink and relish in practical jokes find a mean-spirited equivalent.

Later, when James substitutes for the injured Grier for three weeks, he finds Grier using whiskey liberally for pain relief, which confirms his first impression of Grier as a drinker. He also finds Grier's household a dreary contrast to the comforts of Skeldale House. The thin "tight-lipped" (234) Mrs. Grier serves soggy porridge for as many meals as possible, spies and hovers disapprovingly, and urges penny-pinching in the dispensing of drugs. Miss Harbottle's oppressively rigid organization and efficiency seem praiseworthy in comparison to Mrs. Grier's demeaning surveillance. Siegfried's economy drives are no match for her extreme stinginess. Siegfried's changes of position and his tendency to shift blame in private for his mistakes are far more benign than Grier's public scapegoating of James for the treatment of Adamson's cow and more tolerable than Grier's poisonous silence afterward. James himself shares with Grier a Scottish background and accent, but he is as strikingly different from Grier in personality as in accent—his "glottal Clydeside" versus Grier's "rasping Aberdeen" (234).

Mean as they are, however, Mr. and Mrs. Grier seem understandably human. Angus Grier achieved professional success quickly by marrying his boss's daughter, but at the cost of life with Mrs. Grier. She achieved marriage and kept the family business, but at the price of life with Grier and without children. Neither has a personality likely to help the other develop a positive outlook on life. In fact, it is easy to see how they would only have soured each other's lives more and more with the passing years. James encounters a further hint of the unhappy human beings beneath the mean exterior when he accidentally discovers that Grier is having an affair with the romantic, fortyish Mrs. Mallard.

Miss Harbottle. Siegfried's choice as the perfect secretary for the practice is Miss Harbottle. She is a retired secretary of thirty years' experience in business who was recommended to him as a "model of efficiency" (103– 104). She is a big woman in her fifties, with dark curls, glasses, "a round healthy face," a strong chin, austere clothing, and "an air of effortless command" (104). James and Tristan quickly recognize from her crushing handshake that Miss Harbottle is used to running things her way. It also becomes clear that her organized, efficient way of running things is at odds with Siegfried's haphazard, messy way of running the business side of the practice. When her horrified tour of the office puts Siegfried on the defensive, James becomes worried and Tristan is amused. They can see that a battle is coming. Given Siegfried's retreat throughout the tour, the odds seem to favor Miss Harbottle's determination to "straighten things out" over Siegfried's assurance that he "can handle her" (106).

Miss Harbottle is shocked by what she sees because she is genuinely the efficient office manager that Siegfried set out to hire after Tristan's billing mishap. She sees disaster brewing in the jumble of paperwork on the desk, in the unreadable daybook and ledger, and in the overflowing pot where all of the practice's cash is kept. When she promises to "straighten things out," she clearly believes that she was hired to rescue the practice from chaos by setting everything up the way it is usually done in business.

The rescue mission becomes a battle for power when she discovers that, in order to succeed, she must straighten out Siegfried first. He thwarts her efforts, because he is the source of the worst disorder. In the battle that follows, Miss Harbottle positions her desk to gain a tactical advantage and tries to intimidate Siegfried into better behavior. Many of their meetings resemble confrontations between stern parent and naughty child, or between a judge and a juvenile delinquent. Siegfried adopts the childish tactics of avoiding her and of sticking to his old habits while promising to change. At one point, he reverses roles by scolding her for the inefficiency he has actually been causing. The battle seems to end in a stalemate when she provokes him to explode in Chapter 23, thus taking their psychological battle to the brink of physical violence. She is still there later in the book, with no sign of continuing warfare between them.

A MARXIST READING

Marxist criticism is a form of sociological criticism that is popular today. All sociological criticism views literature in relation to social forces deep within a society. It sees these forces as responsible for the basic structure of the society and for its accepted attitudes and values. Sociological criticism looks at how a literary work, as a product of the society, has been shaped by these forces and how it, in turn, supports them. The author may or may not be conscious of this, since these social forces are so basic a part of society that people are usually unaware of their influence. Thus, sociological criticism considers part of its purpose to reveal these social forces. Chief among them are unequal power relationships between groups of people in society.

At the center of sociological criticism is an ideology, which is a concept of what the powerful forces in society are and how they operate to shape the basic attitudes and values of the society. The sociological critic looks for how a given ideology is reflected in a literary work. In other words, a sociological critic's ideology determines his or her focus of attention in reading a work. Marxist critics focus on economic forces in society.

Marxist criticism has grown out of the nineteenth-century writings of Karl Marx and Friedrich Engels. Observing the wretched social conditions brought by the emerging Industrial Revolution, they theorized that groups of people (social classes) have competed for economic dominance throughout history. They theorized that a minority of economically powerful people in every age succeed in exploiting those who have less economic power. The exploited people do most of the actual labor required to support economic activity in a society, but the powerful people enjoy all the benefits of that hard work. Thus, the exploited workers are oppressed, because they carry the burden without getting any of the benefits of their work. The people who exploit, or live off them are their oppressors. In preindustrial Europe, the oppressors were the nobility, who held the political power and the land, while the oppressed were the serfs, who were basically enslaved farm laborers. In industrial Europe, middle-class factory owners and investors (capitalists) were becoming the oppressors and factory workers the oppressed. In addition to being unjust, exploitation and oppression are dehumanizing. People lose some of their human qualities when they are treated as the equivalent of machinery and, consequently, robbed of any dignity and satisfaction in their work.

Marx and Engels also theorized that the prevailing attitudes and values in a society are those that benefit—and, therefore, are supported by—the dominant class. These societal attitudes and values shape the thinking of people in the exploited class, who are led to believe that how things are is the only way they can be. Moreover, the exploited class is influenced to believe that things should be that way and, therefore, is inspired to help keep them that way. In other words, the workers are trapped in a system of oppression that makes them unknowing accomplices in their own oppression. Marx and Engels believed that the working class would eventually realize this and break free by revolting. They tried to hasten the workers' revolution by revealing this system of oppression in their writings. They encouraged workers to revolt and to set up an economic system in which the people who do the work have the power.

Marxist literary criticism, however, has little interest in promoting revolution, or even in promoting one political system or party over others. It tends to be "political" only in the larger sense of focusing attention on social injustice. It does so by encouraging readers to go beyond looking at a literary work in isolation and to consider, instead, how the literary work embodies the effects of the class conflict, competing economic interests, and power relationships that shape society.

Because *All Creatures Great and Small* takes place during the economic collapse known as the Great Depression, it offers promising ground for a Marxist reading. The effects of the Great Depression were so severe and widespread that concern about the economic structure of society became an unavoidable subject of discussion in everyday life. A book set in this period would inevitably be touched in some way by this heightened economic concern.

All Creatures Great and Small responds to this concern, in part, by rejecting and challenging the capitalist economic structure. The Great Depression is clearly on James's mind in Chapter 2, as he travels to Darrowby for his job interview and thinks about how veterinarians are unable to find work. It becomes, however, a silent frame of reference, a contrasting world left behind, once he arrives in the Dales. After he gets his job, the Great Depression barely touches his life or the lives of the people he meets, since the Dales are very nearly a world apart. They are not, however, a utopian alternative to capitalism, for the day of an economic order based on family farming is passing even in the Dales. Instead, the Dales are a world that demonstrates the possibility of alternative social relationships. In the situations in the book, Herriot sketches alternatives to the exploitation, competitive power relationships between social classes, and dehumanization of workers that were so painfully evident in the capitalist system during the Great Depression. In doing so, he delivers a powerful rejection of the existing economic order and a challenge to develop a new order, characterized by more equitable social relationships.

The Darrowby veterinary practice provides the strongest example of an economic relationship free of exploitation, class competition, and dehumanization. First, Siegfried's goal is clearly not to maximize profit by exploiting James's or his brother Tristan's labor. He hires James on terms generous enough by several measures to suggest that James will be enjoying the benefits of his own labor. The reference to vets desperate to work just for their keep indicates, for example, that Siegfried could easily have hired an assistant without offering four pounds a week beyond keep—and the four pounds probably mean slipping below profitability, since the practice has just begun turning a profit.

Second, the association between Siegfried and James is closer to a partnership throughout than an employer-employee power relationship, despite Siegfried's ownership of the practice and James's references to him as his "boss." Only experience, not unequal power, separates them. Even at the start, Siegfried speaks of the thriving business that "we," not "I" will have in a few years. As James observes repeatedly, they function as friends and coworkers, splitting the same hard work between them. They are also mutually supportive. Siegfried, especially, encourages James to succeed, and rejoices without a trace of jealousy or resentment when he does succeed. James's offer near the end to combine the testing with his honeymoon rather than leave Siegfried overburdened makes clear that their relationship has already become a partnership in all but name. Siegfried, not James, worries that the working honeymoon could be a form of exploitation.

Finally, the relationship between them makes their work an enriching rather than dehumanizing experience. As James and Siegfried say repeatedly, they find a strong sense of pride in their work and a sense of accomplishment in each successful conclusion of a case. Their working lives are entirely free of feelings of oppression. They are doing what they enjoy, and they enjoy doing it. Their only depressing moments come not from being robbed by the economic system of any enthusiasm for their work, but from their recognition of the limits of scientific knowledge, which sometimes bring the disappointment of losing a patient. Unlike exploited, oppressed workers, they have a personal and economic interest in the product of their labor.

The positive example of the Darrowby practice is made clearer by several contrasting situations. Angus Grier's practice displays the exploitation, power relationships, and dehumanization that Marx considers typical of the capitalist system. Grier's location in a more urban part of the Dales allows him to attract a steady supply of veterinary students who need to see practice as part of their education. Like industrial workers in a profit-driven economic system, the students are easily exploited because they can always be replaced if they resist exploitation. This type of situation robs workers and students alike of the power to control their own lives. Grier exploits his students as free labor. Instead of helping them to learn about practice and to gain confidence, as Siegfried does with James as a novice vet, Grier shifts the burden of his hard or uninteresting work onto his students. He enjoys the benefits of his student's labor, while they see none of the financial benefits and few of the educational benefits of their labor. The exploitation probably also extends to providing the minimum in room and board necessary for survival. As James discovers when filling in while Grier recovers from an accident, the food at the Griers is cheap and tasteless. Maximization of profit directs the course of Mrs. Grier's life and her joyless household.

Grier also exploits his power relationship to abuse as well as use his student workers. He intentionally humiliates them and makes their working conditions more demoralizing than necessary. As a result, the dehumanizing effect of economic oppression is vividly illustrated. Readers first meet a Grier who is constantly criticizing his current student assistant and questioning his masculinity. Grier then sets out to humiliate James in the cleansing episode, and succeeds because James does not wish to antagonize him by refusing. Later, he abuses James's professional competence when he orders him to treat Mr. Adamsons's cow inappropriately. James feels compelled to follow Grier's order because his function as Grier's replacement is to do as he is told. But doing so puts James and his work in conflict, just as Grier's student finds his self-concept under attack in his work experience. Lack of power leads to the inability of workers to find meaning in their work and, in turn, leads to a denial of meaning in their lives. Grier's practice is in sharp contrast to Siegfried's, where James can feel fully responsible for his work and, therefore, can see it as a meaningful part of his life that builds and confirms his sense of identity.

The positive example of the Darrowby practice is also emphasized by the disruptive entry of Miss Harbottle and by Siegfried's brief economy campaigns. Miss Harbottle's successful thirty-year business career and glowing references identify her with the profit-centered capitalist system. She immediately creates strain in the practice. Her organization and efficiency focus on the record-keeping necessary to determine profit and threaten to transform labor from a source of satisfaction into a commodity. Her conflict with Siegfried is caused by the incompatibility of their economic goals. Siegfried's brief economy drives produce a similar strain in the practice and emphasize his usual focus on the intrinsic value of work rather than its profitability. Unlike the Griers' profit-centered economy measures, which serve their aims, Siegfried's economy drives are always abandoned when he recognizes and rejects the consequences of their application.

The possibility of a classless, cooperative, alternative economic system is also illustrated in the relationship between the Darrowby vets and the Yorkshire farmers. Herriot minimizes class difference by showing that both vets and farmers spend much of their working life in the same muck and facing the same harsh conditions. Moreover, differences in education and leisure time, which often form the basis of social class distinctions, seem to be offset by the vet's typical working conditions in the book. Frequently the vet is shirtless and in the muck or exposed to the weather while engaged in strenuous physical activity. The farmers typically watch as the vet labors on their behalf. This situation places the vet in the role of the exploited providing labor and the farmer in the role of the exploiter benefiting from another's labor. Once typical superior-subordinate roles are reversed this way, a potential class distinction between vet and farmer is difficult to assert. The Darrowby vets and farmers are shown meeting socially as equals in pubs, at cultural events, and at local dances. James comes to see himself engaged in a common enterprise with the Yorkshire farmers; he thinks of himself, with satisfaction, "as a tiny wheel in the great machine of British agriculture" (247). The value of his work is not defined in terms of money.

The example of Sam Broadbent makes the same point. Imitating the sound of a warble fly is the only thing Sam does well, but its effectiveness in herding cows is unmatched. Given Sam's limitations, the monetary value of his labor in general would be small; even his one skill would have little monetary value. His neighbors, however, recognize and value his skill for its usefulness to them, which, in turn, makes it a source of value and dignity to Sam. By their positive or negative examples, many other individuals and situations in the book also serve to challenge the capitalist economic structure and to emphasize the value and dignity of individuals and their labor.

In *All Creatures Great and Small* James goes through a process of growth by discovering who he is in the most basic sense. He discovers his capabilities, his place in the world, and his values by reflecting on his own experience and on the example of everyone he meets. But what he discovers can have no value unless acted upon: his coming of age does not lie in the process of discovery or in what he discovers, but in his choosing to conform his life to what he has learned is right for him.

James's choice is analogous to the instinctive one Siegfried makes, without regret, in Chapter 64, when he renews his acquaintance with Stewie Brannon in place of pursuing his dream to be a race course vet. Stewie himself and Siegfried's life in Darrowby on the one hand and General Ransom's party and the race circuit on the other hand represent opposite values and lifestyles. Siegfried would have to become someone else to live his dream. As he later recognizes, he would be "miserable" (474) as a result. Other people do not choose as wisely as Siegfried and James. Perhaps another reason for the popularity of *All Creatures Great and Small* is its gentle reminder of the importance of choosing wisely— and its definition of "wisely."

All Things Bright and Beautiful
(1974)

All Things Bright and Beautiful justifies Herriot's reputation as a writer of animal stories to a greater extent than *All Creatures Great and Small*. Despite the popularity of Tricki Woo in Herriot's earlier work, few animals emerge there as distinct individuals with personalities of their own. They seem instead to reflect their owners' personalities and concerns, just as Tricki does, and serve mainly as the reason for James's encounters with their owners and as challenges to his veterinary skill. In *All Things Bright and Beautiful,* animals continue to mirror their owners' personalities and, in the narrator's eyes, various human concerns and relationships, but many of them also emerge as distinct individuals. Stories featuring animals as central characters appear throughout the book.

In many ways, *All Things Bright and Beautiful* delivers more fully on the promise of its predecessor while matching its strengths. Unlike many sequels, it offers more than a follow-up on the earlier story. It presents a new process of growth and brings James, now Jim, to another decisive moment from which there is no turning back. It tightens the episodic structure of the earlier book, by reducing the number of chapters by more than a fourth and the number of pages by more than a tenth. It continues and makes more extensive use of its predecessor's complex narrative point of view. And it builds on, rather than repeats, character portrayals and secondary themes introduced in the earlier book.

THEMATIC ISSUES

All Things Bright and Beautiful deals with the bittersweet nature of change and response to change. Although both gain and loss come with change, attitudes toward change are colored mainly by one or the other. To focus on loss is to invite being consumed by regret. To focus on gain is to invite being buoyed by optimism. Recognizing both is rare, and that still leaves open the question of whether to embrace or to resist change.

This question barely arises in Herriot's earlier book, because, despite its recognition that the world of 1930s Yorkshire is passing, *All Creatures Great and Small* focuses on a gradual process of personal growth rather than on dealing with change. At the end, marriage and veterinary partnership simply mark the completion of the growth process and a turning point between two stages of life. In contrast, the turning point at the end of *All Things Bright and Beautiful* initiates change and breaks the pattern of Jim's life. The break is especially strong because much of the book concerns his continuing growth as a vet and his adjustment to marriage. Instead of confirming his gains from that process, the end threatens to wipe out those gains when it tears him abruptly from his career and marriage.

The turning point at the end of the book is Jim's call-up to military service in World War II. The call-up is anticipated early in the book, with the mention in Chapter 2 that both Siegfried and Jim had volunteered for service and been deferred temporarily on the basis of their occupation. The war then fades from view until it makes a sudden return to the book in Chapter 41, on the eve of Siegfried's leaving for service. Their farewell evening of reminiscence and Jim's concern about soon having to leave his pregnant wife give the chapter a funereal quality, a mix of mourning and warmth. World War II and the departure of Herriot and the Farnons to military service is bringing an end to what they had together in Darrowby. It is also bringing the forced separation of Helen and Jim. The future is full of uncertainty: even if the war should prove only an interruption and they all return safely, the world will be different when they return. They may be different too. These lessons of World War I prompted people to view World War II with foreboding, as the characters do. Herriot also relies on his readers to bring their own sense of foreboding to the story, based on their knowledge of World War II. As in the earlier war, many did not, in fact, return. The world and lives were, in fact, changed by it.

The impact of World War II itself is only part of, what will make the postwar world different. The impact of other changes already under way will also mark the war as a turning point. In the chapters where the war is far from mind, change in general is still at the center of attention, as are hints of revolutionary change to come. This is especially clear near the middle of the book, when Chapter 19 focuses on the disappearance of the draft horse and on the example of Cliff Tyreman, an expert horseman. Almost overnight, in Jim's three years of practice, mechanized agriculture took over the Dales. Draft horses went from numerous to the point of being almost entirely replaced by tractors. Since old-time veterinary practice centered on horses, their disappearance was as serious a blow to vets as to horsemen. Neglected areas such as small animal work suddenly became important to vets, simply as a matter of economic survival. Cliff Tyreman, as Jim explains, represents the typical farm worker in his making the best of change. Although Cliff feels a loss in replacing horses with tractors, he also appreciates how this has made his work easier. Instead of complaining, Cliff takes to tractors and to the idea of learning shepherding at almost seventy with enthusiasm. Will veterinarians facing a future without the draft horse be as willing to adapt? The future in small animal work that, as Herriot says, veterinary education had refused to recognize is exemplified in Granville Bennett's animal hospital and his expertise.

Throughout, Herriot points readers to a future quite different from what veterinary medicine had known up to then. He presents Bennett as a vision of the future and gives him special emphasis by visiting him at three roughly equally spaced intervals in the book. He tells readers that the Darrowby practice and all vets would eventually move in Bennett's direction. He also points to the future in Jim's efforts to develop the small animal side of the Darrowby practice and in Jim's being among the first country practitioners to try surgical procedures on stock. Similarly, his mentions in Chapters 6 and 21 of the Veterinary Surgeons' Act of 1948 point to a new, higher level of professional standards in the future. No longer will unqualified persons, including veterinary students, be allowed legally to treat cases as they did during the time of the book, before the war.

The strongest indication of a radically different future comes near the end of the book, with the introduction of the first new lines of drugs that successfully fight infection and disease. With the new drugs veterinary medicine finally has the means to separate itself completely from black magic. One effect of World War II would be to hasten development of these modern drugs, first to treat human victims of the war. As a result, the end of the war would bring new opportunities to succeed in treating animals in cases where formerly science could do no better than magic. The old, quaint, unscientific veterinary world of the thirties would pass as the draft horse had passed.

At the end of *All Things Bright and Beautiful*, it is clear that Yorkshire is being caught up in both war and change. The war would mark a dividing line between past and future, between one world of veterinary medicine and another. Will it be a loss or a gain, the end or the beginning? That is the question that Herriot poses at the end of the book. Jim's taking Black's Veterinary Dictionary with him is clearly an effort to hold on both to all he values in the past and to some connection with his rapidly advancing profession while he is away from it. As he tells readers in the last line, he felt strongly that it would be "the end of everything" (438), although he knows now that it was the beginning. Both responses are equally possible. Both loss and gain come with change. As most of the incidents in the book show, what matters most is the response to change.

PLOT DEVELOPMENT

All Things Bright and Beautiful covers the period (compressed to months from about two years) between Herriot's marriage and his call-up to military service in World War II. In contrast to *All Creatures Great and Small*, however, its overall structural coherence depends on its thematic concerns rather than on chronology. In *All Creatures Great and Small*, his first two British books were placed one after the other to make the larger American book, focusing attention on the young veterinarian's progress over his first two years of practice to the crowning point of his marriage and partnership (see Chapter 3). In his second American book, Herriot rearranges chapters from his third and fourth British books—*Let Sleeping Vets Lie* and *Vet in Harness*—to focus attention on thematic concerns. In doing so, he also leaves out a number of chapters from the British books, including the story of Moses the Kitten that reappeared ten years later as an illustrated children's story.

Vet in Harness provides the framework of *All Things Bright and Beautiful*: the first two and last eight chapters of the British book are the first two and last eight chapters of the American one. The first two chapters focus attention on marriage, specifically on Jim and Helen's marriage as bringing changes in their relationship and a new dimension to Jim's life as a vet. These chapters also deal with the pressures that change creates—as illustrated in the story of Jock the sheep dog. The final eight chapters lead up to Jim's departure from Darrowby for military service and include his first encounter with the new drugs that would revolutionize veterinary medicine. The intermediate chapters—taken from both Herriot's third and fourth British books—explore relationships, especially marriage and human-animal relationships, and the challenge of dealing with change.

Like Herriot's other books, *All Things Bright and Beautiful* has an episodic structure. (See Chapter 3 for a more detailed discussion of this type of structure.) Once again, the typical chapter handles one or more complete incidents and has features common to short stories: it has a single aim, it limits details and development to what supports its aim, and it often ends with a striking conclusion that provokes thought about its aim. Once again, Herriot links chapters to avoid a sense of fragmentation. He carries incidents over two chapters in a row more frequently than in his previous book. He also brings back characters from earlier chapters for new adventures, in order to provide a unifying effect. In this volume that effect may be stronger, however, because he brings back fewer characters at more regular intervals. In *All Creatures Great and Small*, he gives considerable attention to Siegfried, Tristan, Helen, Miss Harbottle, Angus Grier, and Mrs. Pumphrey. In *All Things Bright and Beautiful* he gives comparable attention to only one new character, Granville Bennett, as well as to the already familiar Helen, Siegfried, and Tristan. Bennett's vivid appearances at roughly the book's quarter marks—in Chapters 16–17, 23–24, and 37—produce the impression of a consistency of focus and maintain continuity in major characters throughout the book.

Once again, Herriot also sets up connections between chapters by presenting similar situations and issues, which invite readers to notice points of comparison and contrast. The story of Jock the sheep dog in Chapter 2, for example, offers several points of connection. Mrs. Jock's occasional running with her husband just to humor him points back to Helen's insistence, earlier in the chapter, on pampering Jim with the only comfortable chair at breakfast. Later, Helen's humoring of Jim by accepting his whims about fat and by tolerating his wasting their money on absurd house sale bargains may recall Mrs. Jock's humoring of her husband. In addition, the desperate competition between Jock and his younger, stronger sons, which is at the center of the incident, is comparable to Jim's later competition with Richard Carmody, his extraordinarily intelligent and mature veterinary student. Many other chapters offer similar points of comparison and contrast, but the story of Jock is notable for bringing together the book's thematic concerns with marriage, career, and the challenge of dealing with change or, in other words, keeping up and keeping on top.

An interesting feature of *All Things Bright and Beautiful* is its reminding readers of its roots in *All Creatures Great and Small*. The continuing characters provide, of course, an unavoidable link between the two books. But Herriot emphasizes the connection. When he features Joe Mulligan and Clancy in Chapter 4, he is bringing back a colorful pair originally introduced briefly on Jim's first day in Darrowby in the earlier book. Similarly, the memorable comparison of Jim to Mr. Broomfield in Chapter 1 of the earlier book is repeated in Chapter 33 of *All Things Bright and Beautiful*, where Mr. Broomfield is again cited as the perfect vet by a character questioning Jim's competence. Flashback chapters featuring dates with Helen and Jim's experience at the Darrowby Show also point readers to the earlier book as a continuing context for the present one.

By positioning *All Things Bright and Beautiful* in the broad context of the earlier book's concerns, Herriot is able to build on them without spending much time reestablishing them. Essentially, he encourages readers to carry over secondary themes from *All Creatures Great and Small* regarding the experience of veterinarians in the 1930s. These themes include the harshness of a vet's life as well as its joys, contrasts between country practice and small animal practice, black magic versus science, and variety as a constant feature of the job. These secondary themes provide some linkage between episodes, as they do in the earlier book. Here, however, these matters are less important in themselves than as ways to illustrate the difficulty of adjustment to change.

NARRATIVE POINT OF VIEW

All Things Bright and Beautiful is a first-person narrative, as are all of Herriot's books. Once again, Jim is the main character in the book and the teller of the story. As a first-person narrator, he is limited to telling what a real person involved in a situation might be able to know and to tell others at the time.

Once again, however, a double narrative perspective emerges. A second narrative voice tells readers what Jim cannot know and tell as a character involved in the action, thus introducing an element of third-person narration. This second narrative perspective is again that of an older James Herriot who knows something of the future. And again, because the book is autobiographical, readers are inclined to accept the double narrative perspective as an essentially unified, first-person narrative. They generally equate character and author, younger and older narrative voice, and consider the narrator as simply James Herriot providing first-person narration, whether from his perspective at the time he was living the events or at the time he is writing about them. (See Chapter 3 for a more detailed discussion of narrative point of view and Herriot's double narrative perspective.)

Herriot's use of double narrative perspective and his handling of time, though effective, are limited and tentative in *All Creatures Great and Small* compared to *All Things Bright and Beautiful*. While in the earlier book there are few comments setting events of the 1930s in their later historical perspective, here such comments are quite frequent. The narrative perspective shifts regularly from about 1940 to about 1970. The narrator repeatedly makes brief references to "then" and "now," "those days" and "today," "at the time" versus "nowadays." He often comments, looking back from some thirty years in the future, to the effect that Jim and other vets had no treatments then for diseases curable now, that what was a major ailment then is no longer seen, that an effective treatment is still twenty years away, or that a breakthrough is around the corner although the characters cannot foresee it. He invites readers to travel for a moment many years into the future to see the outcome of Mrs. Donovan and Roy's story and of Mrs. Dalby's story, as well as to see the future Richard Carmody. He briefly draws readers ahead some twelve years in observing that his dog Sam will be his companion to age fourteen. He also remarks that Siegfried will look no older some thirty years later, and urges modern vets not to criticize him for the state of the profession in the 1930s. He uses Granville Bennett's example to observe that even country practices will eventually be well equipped for small animal surgery, in spite of the 1930s devaluing of small animal work. These looks into the future contrast the book's present with the future and focus attention on that contrast.

In addition, Herriot compares the time before and after his marriage and partnership, both by informing readers that his life has become more comfortable than he imagined and by providing four chapters of flashback. These flashback chapters shift to the past from the narrative present of Jim's first year of marriage, in order to relive situations in his courtship of Helen (two separate chapters) and in his veterinary experience before his marriage (two successive chapters). While the earlier book had only one brief flashback chapter—about Jim's encounter at seventeen with a horse and the value of humility—these flashback chapters are a more substantial part of *All Things Bright and Beautiful.* Together with the more extensive use of double narrative perspective, they emphasize the changes that time brings and, thus, help to call attention to change itself as a central concern of the book.

CHARACTERS AND CHARACTER DEVELOPMENT

Chapters featuring animals as distinctive individuals appear regularly throughout *All Things Bright and Beautiful.* Only three animals in *All Creatures Great and Small* stand out as having stories and, to some extent, personalities of their own—Tip, Tricki Woo, and Nugent the pig—although a number of other named animals also appear. In contrast, more than a dozen animals in *All Things Bright and Beautiful* have stories and personalities of their own. Many more named animals also appear here, and on a more equal footing with the human characters.

Partly as a result of this shift of attention to his animal patients as interesting individuals, *All Things Bright and Beautiful* seems to present a smaller number of human characters. In actuality, the number of human characters remains very high, with well over 125 distinct persons introduced and many others mentioned. Fewer human characters, however, receive extended attention in *All Things Bright and Beautiful.* Some major characters from the earlier book do not return, and only one new minor character, Granville Bennett, makes his presence felt beyond a single chapter or one short story carried over several chapters. Because the major Yorkshire types have already been illustrated—the rugged but generous farmers, the quacks and their believers, etc.—and because many major and some minor characters have already been introduced, Herriot has less need to give extended attention to as many characters here as in the earlier book. Because more attention is given to the animal patients, their human owners can often stay in the background. The result is an impression of a smaller number of human characters, and consequently greater focus.

Here again, Herriot's characters begin as types. Whether they are human or animal characters, they begin as belonging to recognizable categories of individuals. Instead of changing as a result of their experience, they become more individualized as their unique personal qualities are revealed in the emerging situations, dialogue, and details. Character development in Herriot's books is the gradual revelation of a more complete and complex personality. Once again, Herriot usually follows a "tell, then show" pattern, although he frequently alters or even reverses it. He generally begins depicting characters with a physical description and a brief personality description or label that identifies them by type. He then follows up by showing the characters speaking or acting. Often he plays with stereotypes concerning links between physical features and personality traits. (See Chapter 3 for a more detailed discussion of Herriot's methods of depicting and developing characters.)

In spite of Herriot's greater interest in animals as distinctive personalities here, he remains concerned primarily with reading human qualities into animal behavior and finding instructive parallels between animal and human situations. While in the earlier book Jim generally only identified animals as good-natured or not, he sees more specific qualities in them here: competitiveness and pride (Jock), adaptability and the will to live (Herbert), dignity and trust (Roy), meanness and bullying (Boris), bonds of affection and family (Gyp), and so on. Unlike Tricki Woo in *All Creatures Great and Small,* however, none of the animals in *All Things Bright and Beautiful* makes extended or repeated appearances. As a result, they do not really have the same opportunity as Herriot's more notable human characters to become more than types; they merely emerge as distinctive types from the crowd of animals Jim encounters.

Once again, the most significant characters can be divided into those who become a focus of attention through a large part of the book (major characters) and those who become a focus of attention only for a small portion of the book (minor characters). Generally, major characters figure directly in Jim's story, while notable minor characters are the leading characters in the shorter stories, which are part of Jim's experience as a vet. These notable minor characters are distinct from the many, relatively insignificant, minor characters who are known only by name or who make brief supporting appearances as part of the general background for the action.

Major Characters

James Herriot. In this volume Jim is more certain of his ability, of his affection for the Yorkshire Dales, and of the rightness of his having chosen to be a country vet and to marry Helen. Otherwise, he remains the same person readers met in *All Creatures Great and Small*. He continues to recognize in himself a tendency to take the role of an observer of life, to pause for a moment as "an uninvolved spectator" (45). He continues to undervalue himself, while also presenting a balanced, honest view of his successes, failures, insights, mistakes, strengths, and limitations. He continues to approach people and animals with empathy—here animals especially. And, as the narrator, he continues to distance himself slightly from the immediate action by avoiding a play-by-play description of his thoughts and feelings in favor of offering a commentary based on thoughtful reflection concerning the situation and everyone in it. Once again, he carefully limits and controls what he permits readers to see of himself and other characters, while also maintaining an aura of openness and honesty. (See Chapter 3 for a more complete discussion of his character.)

While *All Creatures Great and Small* focused on internal change, as Jim underwent a process of self-discovery and growth, *All Things Bright and Beautiful* is concerned with how Jim deals with external change. He faces here a test of character as much as an opportunity for further development. His marriage requires adjustment, since it is new both to him and to Helen. What precisely are their roles, now that they are married instead of dating? Will the strains of their new relationship, new responsibilities, and new financial burdens as a married couple damage what they originally found in each other? Similarly, progress is transforming the profession and the Yorkshire world that Jim has come to love. Will he be losing all that he has come to hold dear?

Jim does not really undergo conventional character development here, in the sense of changing as a result of his experience, but he does observe the challenges that change poses for others around him. He recognizes how they can be enthusiastic about change, as Siegfried and Cliff Tyreman are, or resist change, as Arnold Summergill does in refusing to use telephones. He recognizes how they can triumph over catastrophic change, as Mrs. Dalby does, or be defeated by it, as Frank Metcalfe is. He also finds much to value in his marriage and in new breakthroughs and opportunities in veterinary medicine.

He himself promotes change repeatedly, when it promises to help animals and people alike. For example, he arranges for Olive Pickersgill to take over the milking from her father to save their cow from mastitis. He admires Granville Bennett's state-of-the-art surgery, and tries an operation that he has never tried and never seen in order to save Harry

Sumner's bull. In a last effort to save Penny the poodle, he tests his chance discovery of the therapeutic value of sedation. And he nearly begs Mr. Clark to let him try the latest medicine on his dying calves for twenty-four hours before sending them to Mallock for slaughter.

Essentially, by the time his call-up arrives at the end of the book and he must face this change that threatens to tear him away from everything he loves, Jim has reason to believe it is possible to take courage and face it. He is pessimistic about what the future will bring, but optimistic about being able to deal with whatever it brings. If his experience has actually changed him, the change lies in his having gained the courage and confidence to deal with change. The more sweeping optimism about the future that emerges at the end of the book is not really his, but the older narrative voice's optimism of hindsight. Jim sees only loss in his departure from Darrowby, but he faces it with courage, in deciding to keep his veterinary expertise fresh by reading and in resolving never to be torn away from Helen again.

Helen Alderson Herriot. Helen is never far from Jim's—and the reader's—attention throughout the book. But here again it is very difficult to gain more than a sketchy impression of the real Helen behind the image of her that Jim sees and presents. Jim has been mistaken about Helen before (see Chapter 3). He also admits here to some difficulty understanding her. Thus, readers have reason to be more cautious about accepting his view of her than about accepting his view of other characters.

Although Jim, as the narrator, controls what readers are permitted to see of all the characters, he usually allows readers to confirm his impressions by judging for themselves when he shows the characters speaking and acting. In contrast, he regularly offers his interpretations of Helen's words and actions as he presents them. Frequently he provides only his summary description of her words and actions rather than allowing them to stand on their own. Few of Helen's specific words or actions actually appear in the book, and those almost always concern her interaction with Jim, not with other characters. Even when Helen's presence is strongly indicated, it is a nearly unseen and unheard presence, or one known only secondhand. This is especially evident in the flashback account of Helen and Jim's first kiss and their subsequent visit to the Chapmans. It is also quite clear in the closing chapter, where readers see no more of her farewell to Jim than his last glimpse of her waving, smiling, and crying in their upstairs window at Skeldale House. As a result, some ambiguity continues to surround her character.

Difficult as it is to see the real Helen behind Jim's image of her, readers, however, do get enough information to form an impression. The real Helen seems as strong-minded, capable, generous, responsible, and progressive as she was in *All Creatures Great and Small*. Her strong-mindedness is evident in her firm, unshakable refusal to give Jim the awkward chair in Chapter 2 and in Jim's recollection of another occasion when she held her position to the point of wrestling with him and nearly winning by physical strength. Helen is clearly the product of rugged farm life, as her first meeting with Jim suggested. She also seems to share the Dales farmers' hard-working ethics and cheerful attitude toward dealing with whatever life sends her way. Although her reaction to Jim's outrageous house-sale buys is sometimes a tactful suggestion that they have more pressing needs, she mainly displays a simple acceptance of fate. She seems to accept Jim's foibles as an unfortunate but unchangeable part of him, just as Jim accepts the positive and negative aspects of individual animals and people, or as the Dales' farmers accept disasters with the observation that such things happen.

Helen's domestic accomplishments emerge as further evidence of her strength of character and ability to succeed; they are more than just the expected activities of a woman in 1940. Having stepped in to run the Alderson household after her mother died, she has clearly made the effort to do it well. She has become highly skilled at handling cooking, sewing, and other domestic responsibilities. As the visit to Sunday tea recalled in Chapter 7 shows, by highlighting her cooking ability, she is more than a pretty face. She is more than the friendly smile that often sums up her personality for Jim, more than the good looks and class that Tristan finds in her, more than good company. When she capably sets up housekeeping on Jim's small income, she manages to produce a level of comfort and organization that Jim had not known in the Farnons' bachelor household, even with the efforts of the excellent Mrs. Hall. Even her pampering of Jim testifies to her domestic abilities; seen in connection with his wish to pamper her, it suggests love rather than the self-effacement that Jim fears it may be.

Although Jim's interpretation of the evidence conceals the real Helen, she is more than a typical housewife here, just as she was more than a typical romantic heroine in the earlier book. She is a little too complex a personality, a little too independent, a little too strong and determined to be reduced to a one-dimensional stereotype. She stands up well in comparisons with farmers' wives like Mrs. Horner and with the other veterinarian's wife, the elegant Zoe Bennett.

Siegfried Farnon. The Siegfried of *All Things Bright and Beautiful* is a kinder, mellower version of the strikingly complex person introduced in *All Creatures Great and Small* (see Chapter 3). This dimension of his personality is not new, since it could be seen earlier, for example, in his generous treatment of children, especially the withdrawn gypsy children whom he thaws with candy, kind words, and responsibility. It was less noticeable in the earlier book, however, because the focus of attention for both readers and Jim was on puzzling over Siegfried's character in an effort to understand it. Herriot now needs only to remind readers in Chapter 4 that Siegfried is "unpredictable, explosive, generous" (46), as well as smart and skillful, to recall that earlier picture. In part, the softer side of Siegfried emerges more clearly here because his peculiarities are already familiar, so both readers and Jim can look more closely at the rest of him.

Siegfried is still a man of rapid decision, as the report of his attempt to examine Clancy in Chapter 4 shows. He is still impatient, as his trip with Jim to the Dawson farm in Chapter 15 testifies. He is still ready to slip into a lecture when he feels others may be taking advantage of him or when the profitability of the practice may be in jeopardy. A bad night on calls, in combination with evidence that Jim and Tristan, in contrast, may have been slack in examining Clancy, prompts his lecture on giving every patient a full examination. Concern about the expense of replacing lost instruments prompts his lecture in Chapter 6 on concentration as the key to remembering to return with every instrument used on a case. Of course, the lecture sets up another demonstration of his own amazingly poor memory. His commanding and attractive personality is also displayed once again in his intimidating crusade against smoking, which causes him no resentment among farm workers and even brings some successes.

What is different in this volume is his more understandably human motivation and some humility. After exploding at Jim over the cost of lost instruments, he actually apologizes for shouting and admits "there's none of us perfect" (48). Sensitivity to the feelings of others, which had not appeared to be a strong trait in him earlier, is evident here along with a more obvious generosity. Knowing Helen is pregnant and they are badly in need of money, Siegfried gives Jim £50; but, to avoid embarrassing him, he does so under the pretext of having forgotten to pay him for testing work done before he became a partner. Siegfried's generosity is also evident in his having given the newlyweds free use of the third-floor rooms in Skeldale House as living quarters. His attitude toward his brother also becomes more understandable here, as the product of a conflict between his sense of responsibility as surrogate parent and his sense of decency and fair play. As James observes, these conflicting principles push him to try ineffective argumentation and nagging to stop Tristan from smoking, when he might have succeeded with the forceful threats that make some of the farm laborers stop. Even his consistently calling his junior partner James rather than Jim may be an indication of his generous treatment of others as well as his charming, elegant manners.

Tristan Farnon. Tristan also is a more mature version of his earlier self. Jim reintroduces him as "a rum lad as they said, but very sound" (46), but here an emphasis on his soundness replaces the earlier emphasis on his oddity. He is less the clown and more the competent vet who appreciates the humor in life and the challenge of a match of wits. He continues to be interested in enjoying life, avoiding hard work, playing practical jokes, and outwitting tough opponents. At the same time, however, he shows more interest in the profession. He offers to take the unusual tumor from Mr. Kendall's cow back to the college for identification. He is shown being involved in cases rather than avoiding them. His unusual career as a reluctant student receives only a passing mention and concludes with his becoming a qualified veterinarian. Tristan even shows an unexpected capacity for physical exercise when his pastime of chopping logs is revealed. Perhaps the strongest testimony to his soundness is his acceptance as a vet by the Yorkshire farmers.

Part of his success with the farmers comes from his system for impressing them while doing his job. He accomplishes by design what Siegfried accomplishes by chance with Mr. Kendall in Chapter 6. When the bull's tumor suddenly disappears up his sleeve, Siegfried conceals that fact in order to present Mr. Kendall with a cure mysterious enough to shake him from his habit of calmly accepting even outstanding veterinary work as routine. In contrast to Siegfried's downplaying that situation to make it mysterious, Tristan exaggerates the challenges posed by the most routine veterinary work to convince farmers that even his routine work is outstanding. He draws on his dramatic abilities to convince them that he is putting forth superhuman effort on their behalf, although the jobs really require far less effort.

Tristan's system is another form of his practical joking. Both the system and the jokes are a contest of wits in which success depends on a knowledge of psychology. The one major practical joke in this book, the Raynes Ghost scare, makes this clear. As Tristan tells Jim, he gains from the joke only the satisfaction of producing a predictable response from his victims, of "just getting the timing right," and of getting "a kick out of hearing" his victims race away (147). When the Raynes joke turns on Tristan, his failure to anticipate the unusual personality of Claude Blenkiron is what makes his getaway plans useless and brings him to the brink of disaster. Tristan's system for impressing the farmers is a similar contest of wits that relies on psychology. He relies on the Dales habit of being undemonstrative to predispose the farmers to accept his exaggerated display of effort at face value. Essentially, he tricks them into acknowledging his good work. Like the practical jokes, the system is basically harmless since his work is good; his dramatic efforts are more entertaining than ordinary efforts, and his performance puts something farmers can understand behind the bill for veterinary services.

Minor Characters

Among Herriot's many minor characters are those that stand out strongly and often serve as major characters within individual chapters in the book, although they remain minor characters in the overall book. These notable minor characters and their stories focus attention on aspects of the situations or concerns facing Jim in the book as a whole. Frequently they serve to make these clearer by offering a range of parallel but somewhat contrasting illustrations. Thus, a high proportion of the minor characters who stand out in *All Things Bright and Beautiful* are married couples and individuals faced with the need to adjust to abrupt, threatening changes in their lives. The married couples include the Ingledews, Crumps, Bennetts, Kirbys, Bonds, Peters, Horners, Chapmans, Hodgsons, and many others. They cover the spectrum from traditional rural to contemporary urban couples, from happy to strained relationships, and are meant to help to clarify the status of Jim and Helen's relationship. The characters dealing with catastrophic change include Mrs. Dalby, Cliff Tyreman, and Frank Metcalfe. Many of the characters also offer insights into human values and gender characteristics. The animal characters stand out in particular, because Jim reads them in terms of human values, often with the implication that we can see in animals better examples of the values and virtues that we should be able to find in human beings.

Among the minor characters who have a significant presence in *All Things Bright and Beautiful* are Granville and Zoe Bennett and the first of

what will be, in later books, a series of veterinary students at the Darrowby practice, Richard Carmody.

Granville Bennett and Zoe Bennett. Granville Bennett is a larger-than-life
character. He throws himself wholly both into his work and into play,
seeming to switch from one personality to another. His capacity for daring, even reckless risk taking is equal to his capacity for food and drink.
He is extraordinarily generous, but also shrewdly practical in business
matters. His veterinary hospital demonstrates a degree of specialization
and technical advancement that many human hospitals of the time
would have found difficult to match. He is part caricature, in his exaggerated traits, and part symbol of the future of veterinary medicine as
both a business and real medicine. But Bennett emerges as more than
just a caricature or a symbol; he is not just a one-dimensional set of
exaggerated, seemingly contradictory traits. Herriot makes him into a
believably human, if unusual character.

In part, Herriot accounts for Granville Bennett's exaggerated qualities
by identifying him as "a legend in northern England" (158), essentially
as someone in whom exceptional qualities would be expected. He also
partly accounts for Bennett's larger-than-life quality by making him literally larger than life: Bennett is an unusually large man, not fat but
massive and solid. His astonishing capacity for food and drink and his
physical daring are less astonishing because of his size. Similarly, his
generosity seems more reasonable when his means are taken into account. His impulsive gifts to Jim of some expensive tobacco and an expensive shirt, for example, are extravagant only from the viewpoint of
Jim's limited income. He can also afford occasionally to take a difficult,
unusual case free for people too poor to pay, given his successful practice
and his speed as a surgeon. Moreover, generosity and practicality come
together in these opportunities to add to his experience and skill by
treating these unusual cases. His generosity also enhances his reputation
for friendliness, which makes people more comfortable about coming to
him as a specialist. Clearly that friendliness makes Granville seem ap-
proachable to Jim, who sends him patients that cannot be helped in Darrowby.

Above all, Herriot offers a reasonable basis for seeing Bennett's qualities as interrelated. Although it repeatedly strikes Jim that Bennett does
everything to extremes, Jim also sees this as a function of Bennett's capacity for concentration and his resulting ability to compartmentalize his
life in a way that Jim cannot. Bennett focuses his attention and effort
exclusively in one area at a time and consequently gets impressive re-

sults. Having decided to go into small animal medicine, he not only focuses on it exclusively, but also pursues a level of modern procedure far in advance of the rest of veterinary medicine. Having decided to go to a meeting at the other end of a snowdrift-filled highway, he so focuses his attention on driving as to take full advantage of his skill and get through. In surgery, he seems all efficiency without human feeling, whereas outside surgery he shows his human side clearly in greeting his dog Phoebe with all of the sentimental foolishness of any other pet lover and in offering soothing affection to some of the animals recovering from surgery.

Zoe Bennett is the opposite of Jim's image of a wife living in the shadow of a great man as "domesticated, devoted, homely . . . [a willing slave in the background] . . . a plain little hausfrau" (167). Instead of being overshadowed by the impressive Granville, Zoe is a match for him. She is strikingly attractive, elegant in tweed suits, active in the community, and seldom at home. Essentially, she is the picture of the elegant wife of a prosperous, prominent citizen, who can lead a life independent of her husband's business, unlike the wives of country vets or the wives of the Dales farmers more familiar to Jim. Despite this difference, however, Zoe has much in common with her country counterparts. She is also an extremely accomplished cook, and she pampers Granville as much as Helen pampers Jim or the farmers' wives pamper their husbands. To some extent, this similarity to Helen and the farmers' wives invites reading some of their traits into Zoe to provide some substance to what is really a very sketchy depiction of her. Working in the other direction, the qualities that seem to set Zoe apart from her country counterparts may help readers to recognize similar qualities that separate them, or at least Helen, from Jim's negative image of the exploited wife. Zoe and Helen share not only their domestic accomplishments and their fondness for their husbands, but also a striking attractiveness, friendliness, and a strong, independent personality.

Richard Carmody. The first of a series of unusual veterinary students "seeing practice" in Darrowby in Herriot's books, Richard Carmody is a "great man" in the making. He has the poise and knowledge of an established vet rather than a student. Above all, he has what Jim recognizes as "a truly scientific mind" (277) and "a cold, superior intellect" (277). Carmody's time with Jim calls attention to the contrast between the more scientific practice of the future and the primitive nature of country practice at the time, much as Granville Bennett's veterinary hospital does. Carmody, however, differs from Bennett and affects Jim differently. Although both Carmody and Bennett are scientific and highly focused, Carmody makes Bennett's humanity more visible and valuable by his inability to relax and display some warmth. In fact, it is only at the end of his story that Carmody finally shows one brief flash of self-deprecating humor, almost to confirm that he is human. Carmody's is not the inviting face of change. Jim feels threatened by Carmody and compelled to compete with him, in contrast to feeling drawn to Bennett and inspired by him. Their rounds together become similar to the races between Jock the sheep dog and his sons, down to the relief over the competition's departure. Given Carmody's future success as a researcher writing "unintelligible article[s]" (277), the cold and threatening element in him may be due to the distance between theory and application. Unlike Carmody the researcher, both Jim and Bennett are practicing veterinarians who have to adapt science to fit human capabilities and to achieve desired results.

A FEMINIST READING

As a form of sociological criticism, feminist criticism views literature in relation to its societal context, starting from the assumption that authors and their literary works are shaped by their society. The feminist critic is concerned with how society defines male and female in contrast to how biology defines sexual differences. Feminist critics analyze the images of women in literary works, explore the options available to women as readers of sexually biased works, and try to identify a specifically feminine sensibility and tradition in literature. Feminist criticism is concerned with looking at how literary works reflect and contribute to society's understanding of what it means to be male or female.

All forms of sociological criticism, including feminist criticism, see society as a product of competing social forces and unequal power relationships between groups of people struggling for dominance. Feminist criticism focuses on unequal power relationships between the sexes and generally envisions a struggle between men and women that centers on gender ideologies. Feminist critics view Western societies as essentially patriarchal or male-dominated, setting men as superior to women and valuing traits identified as masculine more highly than traits identified as feminine. They believe that the impact of commonly accepted ideas about gender are visible in literary works, whether individual authors support or criticize these ideas. Essentially, authors reflect in their work the social conditions, values, issues, and practices of their upbringing and adult experience, whether they wish to do so or not and whether they realize it or not.

In patriarchal societies, women are often defined in terms of their being not male, as lacking male attributes or otherwise falling short of the male ideal. Masculine traits are generally identified as active, rational, independent, aggressive, tough, and creative. Feminine traits are generally identified as passive, emotional, dependent, timid, soft, and conservative. Patriarchal images of women emphasize their subordination and usefulness to men as helpmates, sexual objects, and sources of male offspring. Women are not viewed as equal, able to exist independently, or capable of individual development and achievement. Moreover, in their upbringing women are taught to see themselves as inferior to men, to accept their own subordination as right, and to reject any other possibility as unthinkable. Feminist critics believe that patriarchal assumptions are embodied in literary works.

A feminist reading of *All Things Bright and Beautiful* promises to be fruitful for two reasons. First, agrarian societies have been strongly patriarchal throughout the history of Western civilization. Second, Herriot focuses special attention in this book on marriage and on gender roles in marriage. The farming society of the Yorkshire Dales is quite clearly patriarchal. Males are the inheritors and workers of the land. Women are the keepers of home and hearth. Farmers work for their sons, who are expected to take an active part in running the farm and eventually to take over its operation. Males are exalted in family life, either as providers or as a promise for the future. Women have second-class status: they play a supporting role and add touches of comfort or grace to family life. As in all patriarchal societies, daughters are valued less than sons. In *All Things Bright and Beautiful,* Jim frequently identifies patriarchal assumptions and gender attributes while he tries to understand the people of the Yorkshire Dales, as well as the nature of human and human-animal relationships. He also directs attention to gender stereotypes as he recalls his experience of his first months of marriage and his uneasiness about the roles that he and Helen should adopt as married people.

The patriarchal nature of Yorkshire society is strongly evident in the story of Mrs. Dalby in Chapters 12 and 13. The sudden death of her farmer husband, Bill Dalby, leaves her in a position that emphasizes her dependency and vulnerability as a woman. She is left entirely alone, with no obvious means of support and the difficult burden of caring for three small children. The small Dalby farm has poor soil. She has no knowledge of farming and is physically very small. Charlie, the hired worker, is too unintelligent to run the farm, although he can follow directions well enough. As Herriot observes, everyone thought that her only option was to sell the farm because "a woman would never make a go of it" (111). Even her name emphasizes her second-class status, since it identifies her only in relation to her dead husband. She alone in these chapters does not have a first name, a name of her own.

When Mrs. Dalby refuses to act as expected, conventional gender expectations are called into question. She has a strong, independent turn of mind, physical endurance, and solid determination. Having decided to run the farm herself, with Charlie as a full-time worker, she pitches into the farm work as well as the housework. When she runs into a serious, avoidable problem with parasitic worms in her young cattle, the problem is the result of inexperience, not gender. To underscore that point, Charlie, who is familiar with the problem, neither foresees it nor recognizes its symptoms. Mrs. Dalby, after having gained experience, avoids the same problem the next year. Her only additional major problem is with copper deficiency, which would challenge even an experienced farmer, since Jim has some difficulty recognizing it. Mrs. Dalby clearly proves that she has the ability and the attitude necessary to succeed as well as her husband did in running the farm, once she has the opportunity to gain the knowledge and experience that was denied her as a woman.

This point is emphasized when Herriot moves some twenty years into the future to a time when she has raised three strong, successful children. She has not only made a living from the farm, but also expanded it by buying a better neighboring farm. Later, in Chapter 38, Frank Metcalfe's contrasting failure at farming serves as a reminder of the difficulty of her achievement. Even with his advantages of being male, having farming in his blood, and approaching it with intelligence and planning, he ends up losing his farm. Many other *men* also failed this way, as Herriot points out twice in four lines before concluding the episode by characterizing Frank's failure as the ruin of "a man's dream" (357).

At the same time that Mrs. Dalby's story demonstrates that women are actually as capable as men, however, it also maintains some gender stereotypes. Mrs. Dalby's three small children are three sons who grow up to be large, strong farmers, which suggests that the patriarchal objective of passing land on to sons may also be behind her determination to succeed in keeping the farm. In addition, Mrs. Dalby is identified with her tea tray throughout. As a symbol of graciousness and as the focus of her concern during at least part of Jim's every visit to the farm, the tea tray has two contradictory effects. On the one hand, it emphasizes the contrast between the conventional image of women and what Mrs. Dalby has actually demonstrated of her capabilities in running the farm. On the other hand, it also shows that she may still define herself according to the conventional image of women and, perhaps, even that Herriot himself is uncomfortable about departing too decisively from the conventional view. Similarly, by making the concluding line a question about tea instead of Jim's expected comment about her successful struggle, Herriot leaves readers with the impression that, in spite of Mrs. Dalby's strength of character, her rightful place is in the domestic sphere. Jim's early idea that her eight-year-old eldest son William has decided to be the man of the house also suggests that Herriot may be trying to have it both ways.

The later example of the two Misses Dunn in Chapter 42 presents the same difficulty. Like Mrs. Dalby, the Misses Dunn have no first names. Just as Jim introduces them by describing their marital status as ''maiden ladies'' (388), their name only identifies their marital status. They are distinguished from one another simply by size, as the big and the little Misses Dunn. They also are small farmers who do their own farm work successfully. They are viewed as unusual both for this reason and for their farming methods. They pamper their livestock as pets, and much of the episode where they appear concerns their use of biscuits to manage a spoiled and uncooperative pig. While their methods clearly work and may suggest that women do not have to behave like men to run a farm, Herriot makes it difficult to take them seriously as positive female models. Big Miss Dunn is stereotypically squeamish despite her muscular build—a problem that Jim elsewhere has recognized as common also to large men, although he offers no reminder here. Both Misses Dunn giggle. The entire episode is basically presented as a humorous break in a stressful afternoon.

Herriot calls attention to gender stereotypes more strongly when he recalls his first months of marriage and his uneasiness about the roles that he and Helen were expected to adopt as married people. Jim does not view his relationship with Helen in terms of conventional patriarchal conceptions of marriage. His first observation about marriage at the start of Chapter 1 concerns affection—simple closeness—as being the comfort and pleasure that marriage has brought into his life. Again in Chapter 39, he observes that loving and being loved would be enough to make marriage wonderful. This emphasis on feeling and relationship rather

than possession or self-indulgence is more nearly a conventionally feminine viewpoint than a conventionally masculine one. It might, perhaps,
be more accurately seen as a heartfelt view undistorted by societal conceptions of masculinity. The basic equality that Jim sees in his relationship with Helen is clear when they argue in Chapter 2 over which of
them will take the awkward chair at breakfast to spare the other discomfort. Their equality is also highlighted when Jim yields to the strength
of Helen's determination and when he mentions their having tried to
settle a disagreement with a wrestling match only to discover that neither
has a clear edge in physical strength.

Although he enjoys being pampered, Jim worries that Helen is slipping into the role of submissive wife. Where is the active, independent,
modern woman he courted? He sees the answer in her relationship with
her father. She pampered and catered to her father after her mother's
death, treating him according to the patriarchal principle that "the man
of the house was number one" (359). Now she is treating Jim in the same
way. The equation of husband and father clearly expresses the power
relationship between sexes in a patriarchal society, while also suggesting
that it is an unnatural power relationship.

Herriot backs away from the issue after drawing attention to it. Plead-
ing his inability to change Helen, he accepts her indulgence of his whims,
just as he accepted her refusal to complain when he bought impractical
house sale treasures instead of needed furniture. He enjoys being pampered, although he realizes it makes him seem like a "selfish swine"
(358). The flashback in Chapter 7 to one of his early dates with Helen
also shows the conventional side of Jim's attitude toward his wife. On
that date he was stunned by the realization that Helen is a very good
cook—one of the defining qualities of the perfect wife in a patriarchal
society. In Chapter 39, however, he recognizes that Helen's pampering
him with good food is not good for him even on a physical level, since
he is putting on weight. Shortly after, he elaborates on his negative picture of Walt Barnett by pointing out that Barnett has a "downtrodden
little wife" (368). Thus, Herriot draws attention to conventional gender
roles and their shortcomings, but does not rise above them. Even the
circumstances of the book's conclusion repeat the conventional patriarchal situation of the male leaving his pregnant wife to go to war. But
Jim's resolution never to let anything take him away from her again is
in contrast to the conventional masculine image of enthusiasm for battle.

Herriot also draws attention to the drawbacks of the conventional definition of masculinity as tough and unemotional. A notable example is

Sep Wilkin's inability to admit that he is so attached to Gyp, the epileptic sheep dog, that he wants to keep him as a pet. Wilkin has the reputation and appearance of a hard man to cross. To admit that Gyp has charmed him would be a sign of weakness, and weakness is not masculine. Jim explains that Yorkshire farmers in general do not willingly admit to keeping dogs because they like them; they are always kept as working dogs, although few are actually given work to do. A more vivid example of male refusal to admit affection appears in Bert Chapman. Large and rugged, he regularly worries about his dog Susie, while insisting that he is bringing her to the vet on behalf of his wife. Bert is embarrassed, apologetic, and completely obvious in his concern, but to admit his concern would be to identify himself with conventional feminine traits, to be seen as weak in society's view. The situation illustrates how the dominant class in society, the oppressor, can itself be oppressed to some degree by the system that ensures its dominance.

Even the animal stories frequently shed light on this aspect of the human condition, especially since Jim tends to compare animal and human behavior. The story of Jock the sheep dog, for example, points to the stresses of male competition and to the potential threat that coexists with the promise when sons are groomed to take over from their father. The story of Ted Buckle's bull says more about society's conceptions of motherhood and the image of woman than it does about social relationships among animals. The story of Roland Partridge's dog Percy demonstrates how societal concepts of gender are often at odds with biological realities when the chemical side effects of Percy's treatment convince male dogs from miles around that he is a female dog in heat. Roland himself challenges the conventional image of masculinity and society's expectation of sons succeeding fathers in running the family farm. He has not only rejected and sold the family farm, but also rejected conventional masculinity in his choice of a sensitive, refined, artistic lifestyle.

Throughout *All Things Bright and Beautiful,* Herriot draws attention to society's understanding of what it means to be male or female. In doing so, he challenges conventional gender ideologies, whether intentionally or inadvertently. His habit of ultimately backing away from gender issues, blunting their impact with humor, or shifting attention to quirks of character can be viewed in conflicting ways. He may, for example, be trying to keep gender issues nonthreatening to encourage a thoughtful response from his readers. He may be seeking a sympathetic acceptance of the way things were by projecting a 1970s consciousness of gender issues onto the unliberated 1930s. He may even be trying to trivialize gender issues in support of traditional patriarchal concepts. From the viewpoint of feminist criticism, Jim's ambiguous position in noticing, disliking, but ultimately accepting much of the status quo illustrates the powerful hold that upbringing has on individuals. Many sociological critics hold that ingrained biases are not entirely escapable even when recognized and rejected, because the individual remains, in some degree, the product of his or her society.

The end, or the beginning? The closing lines of *All Things Bright and Beautiful* focus attention directly on the issue of how best to view and respond to change. Jim confides to readers that he could see only end and loss as he left Darrowby. At the same time, however, he recognizes from hindsight that it was "only the beginning" (438), thus bringing the book to a close on a strong note of optimism and confidence.

What Jim has been discovering throughout the book is that one's response to change can make all the difference. His final call to Arnold Summergill illustrates this point emphatically. Arnold found on his only visit to a town larger than his local village that it is necessary to walk differently in towns than in open country. Arnold concluded that he "couldn't walk" (434) in towns and withdrew to his isolated farm. Although Jim shares Arnold's sense of the difference between town and country, he has no doubt of his ability to walk on the street in London. Jim does not like the thought, but he sees himself taking there the "big steps and little 'uns" (436) that Arnold considers impossible.

The same Jim who described himself in *All Creatures Great and Small* as resistant to change, especially in contrast to Siegfried's infatuation with innovation, shows himself throughout *All Things Bright and Beautiful* ready to embrace advances in his profession. Although he recognizes that the coming of effective medicines for old diseases means the loss of an element of mystery and art in veterinary practice, Jim embraces those changes because they enable him to save animals and help their owners. In this respect he is like Cliff, who accepts the passing of his life centered on workhorses because he recognizes the new opportunities that the tractor is opening up.

All Things Bright and Beautiful offers an affirmation of the human ability to handle change constructively. It is not a blind optimism that all will turn out for the best. Sometimes it does not, as Jim recognizes in Frank Metcalf's ruin and in countless other misfortunes that crush the undeserving. Nor is it a pessimistic expectation that all worth valuing will be lost. Despite Jim's feeling of loss at the end of the book, he is determined to face change, to handle it as best he can, and to affirm the values that matter most to him—his love for Helen and his love for working with animals.

5

All Things Wise and Wonderful
(1977)

All Things Wise and Wonderful is more conspicuously crafted than Herriot's earlier books, and its issues are less comfortable. His method of construction is much the same, as are his general themes and his perspective on life, but here the way Herriot has constructed the book calls attention to itself. Here Jim's stories of his veterinary experiences are clearly separated in time and place from the challenges facing the narrator. So it is easier to see how the stories that he shares with his readers and the progress of his life are positioned to relate informatively to one another.

What makes *All Things Wise and Wonderful* less comfortable from a thematic point of view than Herriot's earlier books is its questioning of the values and vision that have come to be at the center of Jim's life. Against the background of a world turned upside down by World War II, Jim's personal world is turned upside down as well. He is separated from all he felt certain about and is left beset by doubts. Now a trainee in the Royal Air Force (RAF), he is no longer a veterinarian. About to become a father, he is unable to be with Helen and uncertain about the future. Having entered the war effort out of lofty motives, he has encountered only rough, belittling treatment and the constant threat of failure. From the start, Jim is plagued by doubt. The world of the RAF is not what he expected it to be. Has he been more broadly mistaken about human nature and life?

Ultimately, however, *All Things Wise and Wonderful* affirms the values of the earlier books. Herriot expands on the central importance of social relationships, continuing to define his own identity through his relationship with others. In *All Creatures Great and Small,* he found his professional identity and a mature philosophy of life through his working relationship with the Farnons and the farmers of the Yorkshire Dales. In *All Things Bright and Beautiful,* he came to terms with issues of individuality and mutual dependence through adjusting to his own marriage and encountering mutual dependence and adaptability in a wide range of other relationships. In *All Things Wise and Wonderful,* Herriot affirms the fundamentally social and mutually dependent nature of human beings.

THEMATIC ISSUES

The beginning of *All Things Wise and Wonderful* focuses attention on a breakdown of social relationships. As the broad context for events, World War II itself stands essentially as a breakdown in international social relationships, especially since the causes of the war remain as distant from the book as its battles. On a more local and personal level, the breakdown of social relationships is painfully evident in the strain between the drill corporal and the recruits, in Jim's separation from his family, community, and career, and in Chapter 1's emphasis on homesickness. So pervasive is the breakdown and so disillusioned is the homesick narrator that the beginning of the book indirectly questions whether humankind genuinely values social relationships.

The rigors of basic training lead Jim to this issue, as he ponders his treatment and how his position as a trainee has redefined him as a person. The sense of social obligation that moved him to serve his country seems violated when he finds himself abused by the military instead of thanked for serving. Initially he sees his treatment as harsh and feels a loss of individual freedom and a loss of community. He must do as he is told, no matter how physically punishing, absurd, or demeaning it seems to him. Being under pressure in a strange place without friends, he feels isolated. He also feels a loss of identity: he is now just one among many lowly recruits rather than a respected professional. In his homesickness for Helen and Darrowby, he thinks about how responsibilities and hardships at home are compensated with appreciation, comforting gestures, and personal respect. In contrast, he sees his new life in the

RAF as one of dehumanizing abuse, and he questions the basic decency of human nature.

Jim's sudden uncertainty about life is mirrored in the book's unsettling mix of the humorous and the serious, the sentimental and the pragmatic, the heroic and the antiheroic. A similar mingling of irreconcilable elements characterizes popular treatments of the irrationality of war, such as the novel *Catch 22* and the movie *M*A*S*H*. Herriot's book shares with them an emphasis on the comic absurdities of military life, which are at once amusing and disturbing. It does not share, however, their antiwar focus. World War II remains for Jim unquestionably a worthy cause, and his most immediate concern lies in making sense of his personal experience as he seeks to make his contribution to that cause. In this respect, Jim's misadventures are more strictly related to black comedy and the theater of the absurd, which challenge traditional assumptions about the human condition and argue that life is without meaning and purpose. The conspicuously artless aspects of the book's plot and organization may also suggest a connection with absurdist literature, which often adopts an inconsequential and irrational form to match its philosophy.

Although he ultimately rejects the absurdist view, Herriot is interested in raising the same issues. Unlike Herriot's earlier books, which constantly affirm the value of life, *All Things Wise and Wonderful* repeatedly questions it before ultimately affirming it. By calling attention to the nightmarish confusion of elements in life, Herriot prompts his readers to join Jim in pondering life's meaning and purpose. The uncertainties at the center of *All Things Wise and Wonderful,* however, remain primarily personal rather than philosophical.

In relation to Herriot's earlier books, *All Things Wise and Wonderful* represents a midlife crisis for Jim—a time of rethinking his most basic values and the course of his life. Since Jim is only in his twenties at the time of his military service, it may seem early for a midlife crisis. But he thinks of himself from the start as a settled, married man with family responsibilities. Surrounded by fellow trainees who are mainly in their late teens and free of commitments, he later describes himself as "a comparatively old man" (131) and as both "elderly" and "old in their company" (196). Unlike them, he has already defined the future course of his life by choosing to be a country vet and by marrying Helen. When Jim simultaneously experiences the military trainee's complete loss of freedom and worries about the upcoming birth of his first child, he becomes more aware that his civilian life is marked by a narrowing of options, a loss of freedom. As a result, he finds himself beset by second thoughts, both about the wisdom of joining the RAF and about his life in general.

For Jim, the way to resolve this crisis is through reconciling the troubling conflict he sees between the worlds of the RAF and Yorkshire. The surface differences, of course, must remain. But, beneath them, can he find the same human nature and fundamental values? To this end, he seeks connections between his experiences in the RAF and in Yorkshire. The forced nature of the transitions from the RAF frame to his Yorkshire stories underscores the extent of the differences between the two worlds as he initially sees them and the difficulty of bringing them together. Gradually, however, more of the complexity of each world is revealed, and similarities emerge.

Jim's view gradually changes as he recalls events in his earlier life and bonds with other trainees on the basis of their shared experience. He recalls occasions when he was not appreciated for his good work as a vet, as well as incidents of inhumanity in Darrowby, such as the rash of dog poisonings and the parental neglect of young Wesley Binks. Since many of his stories, especially early in the book, concern his days in the Farnons' bachelor household and his dealings with the mainly male Yorkshire farmers, Jim's fond recollections turn out to be as predominantly male as his experience in the RAF. Furthermore—despite his very conventional assertion that women are generally mysterious and refined while men are typically rude and crude—his stories of both the Dales and the RAF feature examples of male generosity, sentimentality, and nurturing support. Conventional gender stereotypes simply do not hold true and do not account for the characteristic qualities of the two worlds. Men and women, the RAF and Darrowby, are undeniably different, but it would seem that they are actually more alike in important ways than not. The camaraderie Jim finds with fellow trainees is little different than the camaraderie he found with the Farnons, the solidarity he felt with the Dales farmers, and even the companionship he values in his more complex relationship with Helen. Male society emerges as very similar to Tristan's relationship with his cat: "a typical relationship—they tease each other unmercifully—but it is based on real affection" (426). Despite the mask of misleading teasing, the affection is nevertheless genuine. If it is not already clear, the parting gesture of Jim's fellow airmen in Chapter 40 reveals the strength of the bond formed among the trainees beneath their surface of rough camaraderie.

Jim also comes to recognize reasonable justifications for the RAF's training methods. Standing back from his rigorous training, Jim recognizes even in the first chapter that he has grown physically soft in his comfortable life in Darrowby. Later, he finds that he has become quite fit as a result of the training. Near the end, he even discovers that all the discipline and drill now "seemed good and meaningful and I missed it" (410). Like Jim, readers may find themselves revising their earlier views in retrospect. Jim's unhappiness in Chapter 1 encourages readers to see sadistic sarcasm in the cheerful, kind-looking drill corporal's putting raw recruits through punishing drills while smiling "affectionately" and insisting "you'll thank me for this later" (3). In light of Jim's later experience, however, the drill corporal's behavior reveals genuine concern over the recruits' welfare. Similarly, Jim finds himself forced to revise his negative view of Woodham, his flight instructor. Once Jim solos successfully, Woodham begins to relate to him on a friendly basis. Jim then suddenly realizes that he was "a very good teacher" working under conditions that permitted "no time for niceties" and demanded "get[ting] green young men into the air on their own without delay" (345). What earlier seemed harsh, uncaring treatment emerges as an effort to ready untrained men for service in record time.

A secondary theme involves teaching methods and the relative merit of a supportive, nurturing approach as opposed to a challenging, confrontational approach. Jim contrasts Siegfried's role as his teacher in his early days in the Dales with his flight instructor's methods. He provides a further contrast in recalling his own role as a teacher when showing practice to high school students interested in becoming veterinarians. His early theme of the variety of veterinary practice makes a brief reappearance here, with the unusual repetition of the same condition serving as an exception that proves the rule. This may also recall his role as a teacher with visiting veterinary students in the preceding book. Jim's willingness to share his knowledge as a vet—including trade secrets learned by experience—with others outside the profession is demonstrated repeatedly in the book, and serves as an additional example both of teaching style and generosity.

Herriot also develops the basically libertarian and anti-industrial subtheme evident in his earlier books, where Jim rejected the routine rut of a desk job and the blighted life of the smoky factories in favor of the country vet's independence, self-direction, and close interaction with people and nature. All of that seems lost to him now, as the mindless routine and discipline of basic training leads him to think of himself as a pawn. True, since he enjoyed seeing himself in *All Creatures Great and*

Small as part of the larger enterprise of British agriculture, he might be expected to enjoy becoming part of the larger enterprise of the British war effort. But for Jim serving a larger enterprise has always been a secondary effect of his conscientious independent activity. He saw himself as serving British agriculture because he did his best as a vet, not because he did only what British agriculture directed him to do. Consistent with this view, he volunteered to serve his country in what is popularly considered the most individualistic and independent of capacities: pilot. Military discipline, however, subordinates the individual to the larger enterprise. While Jim regularly takes a very positive view of people working together to achieve a common goal, he also dreads any loss of individuality in the process. His initial negative reaction to the RAF is directed against its subordination of the individual, in this respect a reaction that is more antibureaucracy than antimilitary. This becomes clearer when he presents the bureaucracy of official British agriculture (the Ministry of Agriculture) as just as pointlessly complex as the bureaucracy of the RAF. In both cases the bureaucracy essentially cancels out the humanity not just of underlings, but also of the individuals in charge. This is demonstrated by the contrast between the on-duty and off-duty personalities and by the off-the-record kindnesses of Charles Harcourt at the Ministry of Agriculture and of the RAF's Scottish corporal in Chapter 10, Flight Sergeant Blackett, and Flying Officer Woodham. Herriot's negative view of bureaucracy is also shown by its occasional harboring of such incompetents as the Butcher and Corporal Weekes and by its vulnerability to the display of powerful individuality as in the Cromarty example in Chapter 15.

Although *All Things Wise and Wonderful* revisits some earlier themes, such as experience versus book knowledge, medical science versus black magic, and the variety of veterinary practice, Jim's stories mainly show—and help him to recognize—the social nature of human beings and animals. Among these, the book's concluding story of Oscar the cat stands out. Oscar elicits an affectionate response from everyone he encounters and prompts all onlookers to explain his behavior as the product of a social urge. Similarly, the hardened vets and the burly Police Constable Phelps are attracted to the helpless and affectionate dog found mangled by a car. Jim is drawn to support old Mr. Potts with friendship, as he is drawn to try to help Andrew Vine escape depression by emphasizing his dog's dependence on him. Even Wesley Binks is almost saved from juvenile delinquency by experiencing love and responsibility for another for the first time in his life. Jim himself demonstrates the commanding power of love and responsibility for others in a strikingly opposite way by risking prison to visit his pregnant wife without official leave. Perhaps the most telling episode, however, is Jim's account of working on the Edwards farm while in the RAF. Here in Chapter 26 everything of concern to him comes together in mutual support—the worlds of the military and rural farming, his military and veterinary identities, brawn and brain, men and women, obligation and affectionate regard. The episode provides a neat resolution of doubts raised by his early military training, in preparation for his plunging into new doubts at flight school and struggling further to make sense of "how my thoughts had been mixed up by the war" (218). Ultimately, Jim's time in the RAF proves an unexpected confirmation of the characteristically social nature of human beings and of their mutual dependence.

PLOT DEVELOPMENT

All Things Wise and Wonderful follows the sequence of events in Herriot's military service in World War II, from his induction into the RAF to his discharge. This includes several visits to Helen in Darrowby and the birth of their first child. Into this context of events in the early 1940s, Herriot inserts stories remembered from his early years in Darrowby. Because they are separate in time and place, the stories seem subordinate to the unfolding events in Jim's military career. As a result, Jim's pursuit of his goal of becoming a pilot more closely resembles a conventional plot than the treatment of his life in the earlier books.

The plot centers on the physical and psychological challenges to his becoming a pilot. Both basic training and pilot training combine extreme physical demands with a high-stress instructional method of shouting and criticism. As a result, Jim's determination to reach his goal is tested, and part of his growth in this situation involves learning to deal with discouragement. This serves him well when he finally solos and qualifies as a pilot only to lose his eligibility on medical grounds. His ability to handle that disappointment emerges as a more significant success than his completing his first solo flight. Ultimately, it gives a heroic quality to his brief military service, despite his never seeing combat, and it supports the confident determination that he expresses on his return to Darrowby to take up the challenges of life.

All Things Wise and Wonderful is the last of Herriot's books to be produced by combining two earlier British books. While Herriot revised extensively for *All Things Bright and Beautiful,* his anticipation of the combined version is evident here. The two British books present two major stages in Jim's military career. *Vets Might Fly* covers his basic training in the RAF in London, additional physical training in the Initial Training Wing in Scarborough, physical conditioning in Shropshire, and departure for Flying School at Windsor, as well as his visits to Helen and the birth of their first child. *Vet in a Spin* covers his time in Flying School, his operation and convalescence, his wait for discharge, and his return to Darrowby. These two English books are set one after the other in *All Things Wise and Wonderful* with a minimum of revision. The opening or closing sentences of chapters are occasionally reworded, and two successive chapters are merged into one. Only three chapters are omitted: two that emphasize Jim's unhappy frame of mind and one that was too similar to the story of Gyp the sheep dog in *All Things Bright and Beautiful.*

The chronology of Jim's life in the early 1940s provides some overall structural coherence, which Herriot strengthens through an ordered arrangement of events. Jim's getting into flying school divides his military career into two phases, which constitute two major sections of *All Things Wise and Wonderful.* In the first, Jim overcomes obstacles to get into flying school, and in the second, he overcomes obstacles once he is there. Each of these two sections, moreover, is marked by a climatic event at roughly midpoint: the birth of Jim's son in the first and his solo flight in the second. Alternatively, the book as a whole can be seen as falling into roughly four major sections of nearly equal length, each ending with a significant accomplishment or turning point for Jim—the birth of his son in Chapter 13, his posting to flying school in Chapter 27, his solo flight in Chapter 35, and his return to Darrowby in Chapter 48. Superficially, Jim's progress from one training location or military posting to another and from one service level to another also suggests rough sectional divisions and an underlying structural plan operating in the book. Many of these moves are marked by short transitional chapters: half of Chapter 8, Chapter 18, Chapter 27, portions of Chapters 40 and 46, and Chapter 48. Whether readers notice the larger or the smaller of these basically compatible sectional divisions, Herriot is clearly going beyond reliance on chronology and formal chapter divisions to establish a sense of structure and coherence.

While the progress of Jim's military career is presented in a more continuous and less digressive fashion than the portions of his life covered in Herriot's earlier books, the structure of *All Things Wise and Wonderful* in general remains episodic. The typical chapter features a complete short story focused on Jim's prewar days in Yorkshire, with its own characters, plot, and theme. Jim's military experience itself is often presented in terms of separate incidents with their own sets of characters, issues, and resolutions, although the incidents frequently stretch over several chapters. Moreover, the juxtaposition of the separate worlds of Jim's RAF present and his Yorkshire past in nearly every chapter produces a impression of discontinuity and digression consistent with episodic structure.

In each chapter, Herriot bridges the worlds of the RAF and Yorkshire in a way that calls attention to itself. Instead of presenting substantial connections between the frame and stories, he relies on association of ideas. A small thing observed—the fog, a wall, inhibitions, noisy shouting, even a sense of humor—serves to trigger Jim's memory of one of his veterinary experiences and to introduce a story. Frequently, the detail that triggers Jim's memory has little significance in the story. It merely sets the narrator's subjective thought process in motion.

Association of ideas is an element of the elaborate stream-of-consciousness technique popular in modern fiction, and it invites readers to witness the narrator's mind at work. Thus, *All Things Wise and Wonderful* calls more attention to Jim's inner consciousness than Herriot's earlier books. The connections between frame and stories based on association of ideas become almost formulaic, however, with repetition from chapter to chapter. In addition, the triviality of the points of connection makes them seem increasingly forced and artificial. As a result, Herriot's bridges themselves reinforce the impression of a gulf between the worlds of the RAF and Darrowby.

As in Herriot's earlier books, nevertheless, the frame and the stories are set informatively against one another. What is difficult to recognize in one context often appears more clearly when encountered in other contexts. Animals' lives, human lives, and different realms of experience suggest insights when considered one against the other and viewed with an openness to comparisons as well as contrasts. More clearly than in Herriot's earlier books, Jim's stories of his veterinary experiences serve as plot development, exploring issues and concerns in alternative forms. The story of Blossom the cow in Chapter 1, for example, serves as a projection of Jim's homesickness, offering an opportunity to explore its depths without making Jim appear whining. In a more complex way, the stories of Paul Cotterell's and Andrew Vine's battles with depression explore in advance and without direct self-analysis Jim's situation of losing his hard-won qualification as a pilot. Jim's stories essentially stand in place of extended self-analysis. In the telling, they allow him to deal with his current concerns by recognizing underlying, universal truths—principles of human nature, experience, life.

NARRATIVE POINT OF VIEW

Like Herriot's other books, *All Things Wise and Wonderful* is a first-person narrative. Jim is both the teller of the story and the main character. Here his role as narrator is more obvious, however, because the stories of his veterinary experiences are presented explicitly as stories. They interrupt his account of the progress of his life in military service in the early 1940s. They are introduced as remembered experiences from an earlier period in his life. They concern his veterinary career rather than his military service, and they shift location from the military to the civilian world. As a result, the stories stand apart from the ongoing narrative of his life in a way that they do not in the earlier books, where both usually seem to be happening at roughly the same time. Thus, Jim begins to take on the identity of a storyteller beyond what might come from simply performing his function as narrator.

This complicates the narrative perspective to a greater extent than in the earlier books. There a double narrative perspective emerges when Jim speaks both as a character involved in the action and as an older man seeing events with some knowledge of the future. As a first-person narrator, Jim is limited to telling what he would be able to know and tell while involved in the situation. When he briefly speaks as an older man adding comments from hindsight, however, he introduces a knowledge of the future, which is an element of third-person narration. The conventional lines between past, present, and future blur when what was presented as present action briefly becomes past action. The line between character and author also blurs, especially since autobiography supports the natural tendency of readers to equate first-person narrator and author.

The narrative perspective in *All Things Wise and Wonderful* is further complicated by Jim's narrating both the experiences of his first years in Yorkshire and his experiences in the military in World War II as if they were present action. While the stories of Jim's early years are flashbacks to his pre-RAF days, they are told in present tense following their introduction, and they account for more than half the content of the book.

Thus readers are asked to accept several time frames as present and to accept at least three slightly different narrative perspectives as versions of the same narrative voice. The perspective of the young James of the stories is nested in the context of the perspective of an older Jim in the RAF, and both are nested in the context of the perspective of a still older James Herriot who can view events from the time when he is writing about them, which is closest to the readers' present time.

As in Herriot's earlier books, the multiple narrative perspective serves to call attention to elements that change over time, whether these are now outmoded veterinary instruments and medicines, vanished social customs, or even distant personal qualities, acquaintances, and challenges. In doing so, it also makes possible the recognition of whatever remains true over time. In *All Things Wise and Wonderful,* with not only the contrast between time periods but also the additional contrast between the worlds of the RAF and Yorkshire, the multiple narrative perspective encourages discernment of what remains true beyond altered circumstances as well as time.

Jim's story of his visit to the Blackburn dairy farm in Chapter 36, at a critical point just before his operation, is a good example of the multiple narrative perspective. It begins by emphasizing the contrast between the anxious farmers in old, primitive cow byres and the aloof, bustling workers in Blackburn's big, modern, mechanized dairy. This antiseptic environment, however, is not as dehumanizing as it seems. Although the workers are so busy that Jim is left to deliver a calf entirely unattended, one worker takes a moment to clean and dry Jim's back after a cow fouls it, and Mr. Blackburn displays the familiar Yorkshire generosity, pleasure over new life, and appreciation once the frenzied activity of milking is past. The story also offers an unexpected parallel between the worlds of Yorkshire and the RAF. Jim has repeatedly lamented being made a pawn in the RAF and has even observed in Chapter 15 that officers are pawns of the system. Mr. Blackburn turns out to be the pawn of another system: he and his men must work with frantic concentration to finish milking in time to meet the inflexible deadline of the collection truck for the dairy company. In this situation, they have as little control over their own lives as the recruits have in the RAF. Jim's concluding observation applies equally well to technological and social change in Yorkshire and to a comparison between the worlds of Yorkshire and the RAF: "Systems may be changing, but cows and calves and Yorkshire farmers were just the same" (323). Throughout *All Things Wise and Wonderful,* Jim discovers that things are not as different as they may appear to be on the surface.

CHARACTERS AND CHARACTER DEVELOPMENT

Characters familiar to readers from Herriot's earlier books join new examples from the range of Yorkshire citizenry and a very large, often nameless, cast of RAF officers and trainees. Herriot relies on his readers' past acquaintance with Helen, Siegfried, Tristan, and the Bennetts to make extended characterization of them unnecessary; he simply recalls and builds on their earlier characterization. Some minor figures, such as Boardman, Mrs. Hall, the Rosses, and Miss Harbottle, also return for brief appearances or brief mention, largely to help evoke the earlier time depicted in earlier books. The new characters from those early years provide readers an excursion through the familiar range of Yorkshire types.

Typically, Herriot begins by depicting characters through a physical description and a brief sketch of personality that play on popularly accepted stereotypes. He then follows up with speech and action that either confirm aspects of the stereotype or move a character beyond the confines of the stereotype.

The many RAF characters are treated somewhat differently, however. Only a few are individualized to any degree. The officers tend to blend into the representative RAF officer, developing the attributes of the drill corporal Jim encountered in Chapter 1. Only Corporal Weeks and Simkin, as negative types, stand apart from the rest in personality and action. Similarly, the trainees blend into an unindividualized mass of humanity, giving a universal quality to aspects of Jim's experience as a trainee by sharing resentment, fatigue, doubt, and ultimately supportive fellowship.

Usually Herriot's characters begin as members of recognizable categories of individuals who share common qualities. Instead of changing as a result of their experience, they become more individualized as ongoing situations, dialogue, and details gradually reveal personal qualities and more complex personalities. Here, however, the RAF characters and a few others, such as Charles Harcourt and Police Constable Phelps, seem to become representative of a class of characters. As they become slightly more individualized by revealing an unexpectedly human side, they serve to soften the reader's perception of that class. Repeatedly, the RAF officers unexpectedly reveal a human being behind the harsh surface of military discipline. Similarly, Police Constable Phelps reveals behind his facade of impersonal legal authority the soft-hearted devotion of a father of two little girls and a sense of humor. Charles Harcourt also ultimately reveals a human dimension in the impersonal bureaucrat.

Many distinctive animal characters also appear among the typically large number of individual characters—more than 150. The animal characters are distinguished from one another not so much by unique personality as by the special circumstances affecting their lives and especially by their essentially good- or bad-natured response to these circumstances. Again Herriot does not anthropomorphize his animal characters. Jim and the other human characters are inclined to sentimentalize and to read human attributes into the actions of animals—seeing homesickness in Blossom the cow, nursing duty in Judy the sheep dog, social flair in Oscar the cat, or mourning in Nip. But the animals themselves are presented simply as acting by instinct or habit in accordance with their basically friendly or unfriendly nature. Thus, Blossom returns to her barn by a familiar path because the barn offers food and security, Judy's nursing is an extension of her maternal nature, Oscar gravitates to social gatherings because they are typically comfortable in a physical as well as psychological sense, and Nip suffers from a break in routine and loss of companionship. In contrast to Herriot's earlier books, here the animals are uniformly good-natured.

Repeatedly, the human and animal characters in *All Things Wise and Wonderful* offer testimony to the importance of companionship, needing another and being needed, giving and receiving love for its sake alone, or making a difference for another simply for the satisfaction of doing so. This theme appears in Wesley Binks's brief discovery of responsibility and love in his relationship with his fatally ill dog and in Johnny Clifford's reliance on his guide dog Fergus. It appears in the pub crowd's collection to cure Albert Close's Mick and in everyone's willingness to recognize Oscar as a social cat. It appears in Paul Cotterell's inability to cope with life without his dog and in Andrew Vine's finding in his dog's dependency a reason to go on. It appears in Roddy Travers's making Jake his family and in Nip's need for company after Mr. Potts's death. It appears in the supportive relationships that form among the RAF trainees, in the comradeship of the Darrowby vets, and in the capacity for kindness and warmth that Jim finds not just in Darrowby but also in the slums of Hensfield, in bureaucrats, and in RAF officers.

Here again Herriot's more significant characters can be divided into those who are prominent in a large part of the book (major characters) and those who are prominent only in small portions of the book (minor characters). Major characters generally play a role directly in Jim's story of the progress of his life. Minor characters generally are the central characters in Jim's stories of his experiences and are distinct from the many characters who appear in supporting roles, whether in Jim's life or his stories.

Major Characters

James Herriot. James continues to grow in terms of developing a more mature understanding of life and of what is genuinely important to him. He remains essentially the same person as he was in the earlier books, except that he becomes more fully and confidently so. He continues to approach people and animals with empathy, to view his abilities modestly whether as a vet or as an airman, to observe life closely, to ponder over his observations, to value relationships, to wish to be liked, and to find satisfaction in helping others. As the narrator, he continues to present events filtered by thoughtful reflection rather than offering play-by-play descriptions of events and sharing his unfolding responses. He also continues to limit narrowly what he permits readers to see of his inner self, despite this book's using association of ideas to connect frame and stories, a method that would seem to promise more intimate insight into his character. As in the earlier books, Jim's development is more a matter of degree than difference. Instead of suffering reversals that foster alteration, he is tested and emerges the stronger for it.

Here, however, Jim is tested severely. To a certain extent, he experiences a version of midlife crisis, a time of dejection in which roads not taken seem more attractive than those taken and in which values of central importance in earlier life suddenly become uncertain. His heroic vision of becoming a dashing RAF pilot has led him to volunteer for the RAF and removed him from his comfortable life in Yorkshire. But the far from heroic realities of military life produce immediate disillusionment and regret. More than just homesick, Jim recognizes in Chapter 1 that the better road was his in Yorkshire. Worse, the impersonal and dehumanizing nature of military training causes him to question whether he has been mistaken in his vision of human nature as well. What makes Jim's situation seem most like a midlife crisis is not his leaving everything to pursue an heroic dream, but his finding himself suddenly doubting the values that have been central to his life. For Jim, the outcome of this experience is not ultimately world-shattering, but a gradual rediscovery and reconfirmation of his values and the rightness of his having chosen to become a country vet and a family man. This becomes clear when he faces one final test—a turning point—and rejects its invitation to renewed disillusionment and depression. The decisive, potentially shattering development comes right after he has apparently achieved his dream by becoming a qualified pilot: he undergoes an operation and becomes physically ineligible to fly. Jim's response to this crushing blow is acceptance, and the foundation for this response lies in the Yorkshire stories interwoven at this point, especially in his instructive encounters with depression in the stories of Paul Cotterell and Andrew Vine and with the satisfaction of helping others in his fond recollection of Mr. Potts.

Several aspects of Jim's character that were present in the earlier books are also revealed more clearly in *All Things Wise and Wonderful*. Among them are a daring and impulsive side of his personality, his persuasive ability, and his imagination. His military service itself is the result of his impulsively volunteering for the RAF. More striking are his boldly risking imprisonment to make two unauthorized trips to visit his pregnant wife and, later, his revelation that he has pursued his goal of flying despite a history of suffering from vertigo. In addition, a surprisingly bold, impulsive move produces his encounter with the Scots corporal in Chapter 10; Jim's handling of the corporal also reveals an astute persuasiveness that he usually downplays modestly. His persuasiveness is again emphasized in Chapter 25, when his arguments convince an unwilling Siegfried of the advantages of injecting cows in the neck rather than rump. Even more impressive is his persuasiveness in Chapter 38, when he talks Andrew Vine into taking the course of action that leads him out of suicidal depression.

The quality that this book most strongly emphasizes, however, is Jim's imagination. Repeatedly, *All Things Wise and Wonderful* presents situations when Jim is carried away by his imagination or, as he says, by his emotions. As the narrator, Jim regularly calls attention to his imagination by leaping from frame to stories on the basis of association of ideas, introducing the stories as essentially his reveries or daydreams while serving in the RAF. The very predicament in which Jim finds himself at the start of the book is the result of his having been carried away by his imagination to pursue a Walter Mitty-like heroic vision of himself as a dashing RAF pilot. In contrast, he found happiness in *All Creatures Great and Small* when he abandoned a similarly heroic vision of himself as a state-of-the-art veterinary specialist in favor of becoming a country vet in Yorkshire. Another striking example of Jim's being carried away by his imagination occurs when, thinking about Helen at home and pregnant without his supporting presence, he not only feels guilty and homesick, but also experiences symptoms of sympathetic pregnancy.

He is also uncharacteristically misled by his imagination when he envisions what others think and feel. In the earlier books Jim is only rarely mistaken about other people's feelings—the most notable case being his misreading of Helen in terms of romantic heroines of popular fiction during their courtship. Here he is greatly disturbed by the negative vision of human nature that comes to him when, feeling unappreciated and misused, he imagines all of the RAF officers responsible for his training, from his first drill corporal to F. O. Woodham, to be essentially sadists and maniacs. His misreading is unmistakably clear when several—including the Scots corporal, Blackett, and Woodham—reveal unexpected streaks of humanity. The most striking misreading of another, however, is his imagining Paul Cotterell's weakness to be strength. The decisiveness, cool rationality, and manly acceptance of reality that he sees in Paul and laments not having himself are exposed by Paul's suicide as the emptiness of depression and despair. Repeatedly, Jim is badly served when he is carried away by his imagination.

Jim's imagination is, nevertheless, one of his greatest strengths. Here and in Herriot's other books, one of Jim's most attractive qualities is his empathy—his ability to use his imagination to project himself into others to envision what they must feel and think. This use of imagination serves him well, by promoting rapport and an insightful understanding of the world around him. Despite occasional misreadings and sometimes becoming too personally involved with cases, it helps to keep his thinking down-to-earth. This is particularly clear when he recognizes his intense satisfaction from observing in others the difference that he has made to their lives. When he is attracted by visions of acclaim for achieving miraculous cures, this helps him to remind himself that acclaim is not what is important. As he points out throughout this book in recalling his Yorkshire experiences, what matters is the satisfaction to be found in relieving pain, helping another, saving a life. This lesson relearned and the lesson that Helen and his son are central in his life are what set him back on course at the end of the book.

Helen Alderson Herriot. Once again, readers see Helen largely through Jim's eyes. This indirect depiction fits the situation in *All Things Wise and Wonderful* particularly well. Hers is the conventional role of the soldier's sweetheart left behind, typically either the focus of his homesick longing or the inspiration for his heroic efforts. Hers is also the conventional role of mother-to-be in an era when husbands were regularly barred from the delivery room and when women viewed maternity almost as a secret society whose mysteries they alone might share and understand. Something of this last element is evident in Helen and Nurse Brown's shared, smug amusement over Jim's reaction to the red and swollen appearance of his newborn son Jimmy. Even on occasions such as this, when Helen is a participant in the action, however, she is still seen largely through Jim's eyes. As in the earlier books, she is shown speaking and acting less often than many minor characters, in spite of her frequently being the focus of Jim's thoughts.

Readers are likely to have the impression that Helen is a strong character, although certainly not the liberated woman of forty years later. The impression of strength may be partly the result of Jim's viewing her more as an equal and independent-minded person than as an extension of himself or a delicate creature on a pedestal. In addition, his noting that Helen held a job as secretary to a miller in the early years of their marriage suggests an identity beyond her role as his wife. An impression of her strength also grows from Jim's mentioning the stiff competition he encounters in contests with Helen. When they play children's games in the evening, Jim must struggle to win, and he regularly loses at the game of push-ha'penny that Helen has had years of experience playing. Even on a physical level, Helen occasionally outmatches him, since she never has colds while he does regularly. Helen's strength may also be a matter of firmness, practicality, and unwillingness to complain. In her appearance shortly after childbirth, tired but happy, she limits her description of the experience to the single word "awful" (115). She regularly urges Jim not to let his problem cases get to him or to blame himself when his best efforts fail.

Siegfried Farnon. The several episodes from Jim's early days with Siegfried essentially survey the unusual character traits presented more extensively in the earlier books. Siegfried reappears as a brilliant vet, full of restless energy, embracing change, making decisions and launching plans with great speed and minimal forethought, reversing himself just as quickly when prompted by hard reality or by his own generous nature, occasionally concerned about finances, and uncomfortably irritable in the role of his bother Tristan's keeper. As they were in *All Things Bright and Beautiful*, Siegfried's traits are presented as human foibles.

A strong impression of comradeship is maintained in Siegfried's clashes with Jim and with Tristan. Siegfried here reverses himself by adopting one of Jim's techniques, criticizes Jim only mildly for providing a poor pensioner with free services and medication, and seems restrained or perhaps wearied in his calling Tristan to task for carousing instead of studying. The easygoing domestic relationship of the Farnon brothers and Jim emerges in Chapter 6, with Siegfried's plan for Tristan to substitute for Mrs. Hall as housekeeper. Siegfried remains tolerant throughout the ordeal of repeated meals of sausages and mashed potatoes. His relatively restrained suffering seems more genuine and sympathetic than his dramatic pose of martyrdom in earlier books. Similarly, when he abandons the Hunt Ball in Chapter 33 to operate with Jim on a badly hurt stray dog, the emphasis is more strongly on their close, comfortable working relationship and Siegfried's affection for animals than on his shifting position on keeping pets. Essentially, Siegfried's familiar inconsistencies and occasional dramatic outbursts emerge as more understandable and comfortable than the inconsistencies and outbursts Jim is encountering in the RAF.

Tristan Farnon. Tristan is depicted in a lighter vein than in the earlier books. Although Jim observes that Tristan jokes to cope with the pressure of veterinary practice, he focuses entirely on the joking. Tristan's pranks also hold less potential for harm. They are exclusively mild schoolboy pranks: foreign accents when answering the phone, a nudist magazine placed among the usual reading matter in the waiting room, and his driverless car trick. The consequences of his actions are never potentially more serious or of more lasting concern to him than the pratfalls of slapstick comedy. Tristan is thoroughly the high-spirited student, drinking and chasing girls with the same lighthearted spirit as his clowning and without the suggestion of meanness that such activities would suggest in a more mature person. In addition, the touch of dignity that he maintains through the sausages and mashed potatoes episode as well as at the end of his pursuit of Deborah and his soft concern for Oscar the cat's terrible injuries reinforce the impression of Tristan as a sympathetic character. He emerges as a counterpart to Jim's younger, bachelor comrades in the RAF flying school, who can escape the pressures of training in the evening in similarly lighthearted girl-chasing and partying.

Minor Characters

F. O. Woodham. Flying Officer Woodham, Jim's flight instructor, is one of the dashing young pilots who fought fearlessly in the Battle of Britain before, according to Jim, experiencing true terror in trusting their lives to raw pilot trainees. In at least one respect, Woodham may remind readers of Siegfried as Jim first knew him. Both men are subject to abrupt changes in personality. The resemblance is especially noticeable because they both play the role of teacher—or mentor—to Jim, despite being approximately his age. Jim puzzles over Woodham's changes from quiet patience to frantic shouting and his barrage of seemingly conflicting advice much as he puzzled over Siegfried's outbursts and reversals of position in *All Creatures Great and Small.*

Unlike Siegfried, however, Woodham never offers encouragement and praise, only criticism. Flight instruction is an intensely discouraging experience. The flight instructors bemoan their students' ability, and the trainees begin to despair of ever becoming pilots. Only after he has become convinced that "whatever I did was wrong" (312) is Jim invited to make his first solo flight. And only after that flight does Woodham reveal his confidence in Jim's ability to be a pilot and become friendly. Siegfried's approach is to build confidence, while Woodham and the other flight instructors reduce confidence. As Jim suggests repeatedly, overconfidence may be the greatest danger student pilots face, and the instructional approach of the RAF flying school valued results over people: to win the war, the RAF "had to get green young men into the air on their own without delay" (345). For those who succeed, like Jim, the result is confidence firmly grounded in ability. Like basic training, flying school is dehumanizing but effective. Turning from Woodham's teaching to speak of his own in Chapter 39, however, Jim clearly rejects the RAF's end-justifies-the-means approach in favor of following Siegfried's friendly, supportive approach.

Granville and Zoe Bennett. Granville Bennett is the same generous, larger-than-life specialist and Zoe the same striking, confident woman as in *All Things Bright and Beautiful.* In their brief appearance here, however, the Bennetts emerge as a little more fully human and more like the Herriots than not.

Their first evening with Helen and Jim as newlyweds is not only another occasion for Jim to embarrass himself, but also an occasion for Granville to embarrass himself. In contrast to Granville's ability in the earlier book to consume great quantities of alcohol and still conquer a blizzard with his expert driving, here fog and drink defeat him. He damages the front and rear of his car without succeeding in leaving his driveway. His befuddlement in the situation is as obvious as Jim's more extreme incapacity at the end of the evening. In fact, Jim's alcohol-induced confidence that he can triumph over saveloy sausages echoes

Granville's earlier confidence that he can triumph over the fog. While Granville reveals his human weakness, Zoe reveals her strength in patiently insisting that Granville recognize their precarious situation in the fog. Her action is reminiscent of Helen's patient tolerance of Jim's foibles in the earlier book, and similar in its positive effect.

This episode emphasizes the basic similarity of the Bennetts and Herriots despite their very obvious surface differences. It also develops Jim's observation that Helen and Zoe, although different in coloring, are much the same: both attractive and "both of them warm and smiling" (199).

Stewie Brannan. Advertising himself as a canine specialist in the slums of Hensfield, Stewie Brannan stands on the opposite end of the economic spectrum from that other small animal specialist, Granville Bennett. The two could not seem farther apart, yet both men have a larger-than-life quality and a similarly friendly, gentle, generous nature. Jim's time in Hensfield emphasizes the value of seeing beyond surface differences. More specifically, Stewie Brannan serves as a reminder that happiness is more important in life than material success, both by his example and by his giving Jim the opportunity to see that happiness as a vet comes from the satisfaction of helping others.

If Stewie's appearance in the earlier book raised any concern that he might be too improvident a fellow to avoid disaster, his appearance here with his happy family suggests that he has had the right idea about life. His family is clearly thriving, not torn by financial worries. The children are high-spirited, and Stewie and his wife Meg are obviously in love. Meg seems to share his view that all is well as long as the bills are covered. The Brannans are clearly content, although worn with hard work and with the messy pandemonium of living with six young children. In fact, Jim sees in them a picture of conventional family bliss. He describes their seaside family photograph as the image of the typical British family on vacation and Stewie as the "archetype of the British father on holiday" (179).

While filling in for Stewie, Jim finds that the satisfaction of helping people and animals can be found not just in the idyllic Yorkshire Dales that he loves, but also in the typically dirty, industrial, urban settings that he has always despised. Stewie's surgery is dingy and ill-equipped, but this aspect quickly begins to seem less important to Jim. His attention is drawn instead to Stewie's gentle treatment of the animals, to his consideration for their concerned owners, and to how clearly his clients like Stewie. Soon, with the arrival of the Gillards and Kim, Jim is in the familiar situation of fighting for a well-loved animal's life. The odds are against him, not because Stewie's supplies are limited and his faulty table is inconvenient, but because the antibiotics that Kim really needs belong, as the older Jim observes, to the future of medicine. Similarly, the sharp characters that Jim meets at the greyhound track seem very much like the unscrupulous horse and pet owners he has encountered at Yorkshire fairgrounds in earlier books. In his time at Hensfield, Jim begins to see more clearly that the satisfaction he finds in being a vet is not just a matter of lifestyle, but a feeling of making a difference to animals—and people—who need help. Stewie himself serves as a model in providing low-cost care for animals in the poorest part of Hensfield. By replacing Stewie for a time, Jim finds that he could be happy as a vet in Hensfield as well as Darrowby (or Devon, as he finds later in the book), although he prefers being able to enjoy the Yorkshire countryside.

A DECONSTRUCTIONIST READING

Deconstruction has become the most influential form of poststructuralist or postmodern criticism. In sharp contrast to earlier structuralist, formalist, and new critical approaches, it rejects the possibility of finding just one "correct" reading, one fixed meaning, for a literary text. Deconstructionists view text as unstable, that is, as supporting multiple, often contradictory readings, and not providing a reliable guide to an author's intention. Deconstructionists argue that texts invite readers to go in many directions and that it is impossible to decide which is more "correct," because language itself is arbitrary and invites multiple interpretations.

Deconstructionist criticism is an outgrowth of the complex theoretical work of the French philosopher Jacques Derrida, who was influenced by the linguistic theories of Ferdinand de Saussure. Credited with founding modern linguistics, Saussure established the concept of language as a system of arbitrary signs. Words, as signs, are separate from the concepts they describe; their meanings depend on the people using them and on the context. Meaning is not contained in the words themselves, but is produced by how each word differs from all other words in the language. Thus, meaning flows from a network of difference. This concept became important in the development of structuralism and semiotics as well as deconstruction, but these earlier critical approaches view meaning as having firm existence independent of words. They view words as arbitrary signs, codes, or tools for conveying a pre-existent meaning. In contrast, Derrida views meaning—and, by extension, human consciousness—as a product of language. Essentially, human beings think in words. Without words, we might feel sensations and even act on them (as in the stimulus-response sequence of hunger-eating), but we would be unable to reflect upon and make meaning of our experience. Derrida argues, therefore, that meaning is as unstable as words themselves.

Derrida's primary interest lies in challenging the basic assumption of Western philosophy concerning the central position of human consciousness as an absolute. This includes challenging how human consciousness is represented in language as well as examining the nature of the relationship between consciousness or language and everything else in the world. Derrida argues that Western logic works through exploring differences. We think in terms of paired opposites, such as self and other, existence and nonexistence, up and down, masculine and feminine, speech and writing. Moreover, Derrida argues that these opposing pairs or dichotomies embody hierarchies in which one term is always seen in Western culture as superior or preferable to the other. Given his interest in Western philosophy's assumptions about the relationship between consciousness, language, and the world, he is especially concerned about the privileged position of the spoken word as opposed to the written word in Western culture. Derrida wishes to break down such dichotomies, first by reversing the hierarchy to expose it and to question the values it implies and then by positioning both the original and the reversed hierarchies as undecidable alternatives. They are undecidable in the sense that neither can be determined with certainty to be more correct. *Deconstruction,* the term Derrida coined for the middle ground of the opposing pair *construction/destruction,* represents this effort to level the hierarchies and to move beyond dichotomous thinking to explore the space between two equal, undecidable opposites.

Applying Derrida's ideas to literary criticism, deconstructionists seek to demonstrate that literary texts themselves work against the establishment of a single, fixed meaning and that they support many, often contradictory readings. Deconstructionist criticism does not claim, however, that literary texts are impossible to interpret or that all readings are equally valid. It recognizes that text/language exists to be interpreted and that readings will differ in whether or how well the text supports them. But deconstructionists view all readings as provisional (temporary and conditional). They insist on the impossibility of being certain that any one good (supported) reading is the only correct reading, thus rejecting the assumption of structuralist, formalist, and new critical readers that close analysis can show that a text's parts work together to form a unified whole with a single, fixed, correct meaning. Instead, deconstructionists frequently use close analysis to show how, as writers use language to create meaning in a text and readers reconstruct the meaning, language sends the text's meaning in more than one direction.

In practical terms, deconstructionists approach texts in a variety of ways depending on the nature of the text. With classic texts, deconstructionists use close analysis to show that the texts support contradictory alternatives to widely accepted readings. With less familiar texts, they show the texts at odds with themselves, often saying one thing and doing another, or they draw out of the texts' gaps and inconsistencies a systematic pattern of contradictory meaning. They often search out dichotomous thought patterns in order to expose, reverse, and invalidate the hierarchies those dichotomies imply. They may seek to question figurative language, showing that language purporting to be literal is actually metaphoric or that metaphors embody forgotten literal rather than imaginative relationships. They frequently seek to undermine the privileged status of the literary text as an independent entity in Western culture, by considering how readers become writers of the text as they reconstruct a meaning for it, developing that meaning from their process of reading and their social and cultural context as much as from the text.

Although deconstruction remains a difficult approach practiced by a relatively small number of readers, it has encouraged wider discussion of literary texts by breaking the monopoly of skilled readers—especially trained literary critics—on determining the "correct" meaning of literary works. When certainty about the correct meaning of a text is seen as impossible to achieve, all choices of one reading over another are exposed as determined by personal preference and subject to change. Thus, deconstructionists have opened new opportunities for all readers, to contribute to the discussion of texts.

Herriot's books exhibit many of the qualities that deconstructionists believe characterize all texts. In fact, despite his firm commitment to traditional values (fixed truths), his books seem to encourage a deconstructionist reading. Herriot's mixture of autobiography with features of the short story, for example, blurs the conventional separation between fiction and nonfiction, between art and life. Similarly, his handling of narrative perspective and time undermines the conventional compartmentalization of experience in Western culture. His handling of narrative perspective shows events, in essence, to have an evolving rather than a fixed meaning. His handling of time reveals the arbitrary nature of conventional time divisions and draws readers beyond dichotomous thinking about time (past-present, present-future, past-future), to a middle ground in which past, present, and future intertwine. Above all, Herriot's books may be seen to encourage readers to entertain multiple, often conflicting, interpretations of the same textual material and to become receptive to thinking in terms of *both . . . and* rather than *either . . . or.*

Since *All Things Wise and Wonderful* is not a text with a widely accepted, critically established, "correct" reading, Jim as its narrator provides a convenient standard reading of events and their significance to use as a reference point in a deconstructionist reading of the book. Jim's interpretations of events as the narrator are quite reasonable, but they are also often at odds with what readers are shown of the events. As a result, Jim's reading becomes one among a number of provisional readings of the text.

He repeats near the start of Chapter 25, for example, one of his most familiar pronouncements from the earlier books, namely that he and Siegfried are *opposites.* Once again, Jim reads Siegfried as restlessly embracing change and constantly generating new ideas. In contrast, he reads himself as ploddingly resistant to change and never having an idea. Jim clearly values these contrasting qualities differently, since he contends that Siegfried outshines him. Whether modesty, admiration, or something else underlies his seeing Siegfried's qualities as superior to his own, the opposing qualities that he mentions reflect the privileging in twentieth-century Western culture of change or progress over perseverance, imagination over imitation, individual over group, action over contemplation. But when he immediately afterward introduces three incidents that he says illustrate conflict between the two vets, his readings of the incidents and the vets do not hold.

The first incident apparently shows Siegfried arguing for change and Jim against change as represented by disposable, sterilized, plastic syringes. But the promised conflict of opposites fails to materialize. Both men agree on the value of the promised medical advantages of the plastic syringes. The issue for Jim is one of practicality, not resistance to change. He simply cannot make them work as well as his old apparatus, and he even concedes that the problem may lie in his mechanical aptitude rather than the design of the syringe. Moreover, he readily agrees to try again at his next opportunity, making it difficult to see in him a strong resistance to change as such. Jim's next opportunity brings the disclosure that the plastic syringes have worked just as poorly for Siegfried, despite his continued insistence that they are "foolproof" (209). Not only is Siegfried's blind spot exposed, but his arguments for the syringes are effectively undermined by Jim's having to repeat Siegfried's earlier injection in order for the patient to get a full dose of medication. What appeared to be a conflict over change turns into a conflict over good medical practice, with both vets being right. The advantages that Siegfried sees in the syringes and the practicality that Jim demands are both desirable, even necessary, and the vets are not really given a choice between the two. Instead, they are faced with alternatives that offer a mix of trade-offs. The choice is more difficult than a choice for or against change, for or against good medicine, and the stakes are high in terms of the patient's health.

The second illustrative incident revisits the competing demands of generosity and anxiety about maintaining financial stability that figured in Herriot's first book. Wisdom rather than resistance to change is the apparent focus of difference in this clash between the two vets. Jim improvidently allows his emotions to overcome his reason in providing free treatment to poor Mr. Bailey's dog, while Siegfried argues for the necessity of subordinating emotion to reason in order to survive in a hard world. The incident reproduces the conventional privileging of reason over emotion in Western culture, with Siegfried again associated with the superior quality. But, in doing so, it attributes to the two vets aspects of personality that are curiously at odds with what the first incident revealed. Formerly practical Jim is now offered to readers as impractically generous, and rash Siegfried is now cast as coolly deliberative. This alternative version of their personalities is then debunked when Siegfried concludes the incident by outdoing Jim in generosity. At the same time, the opposition between reason and emotion, self-interest and generosity, Siegfried and Jim, is undermined. This second incident actually shows both vets spontaneously acting with generosity toward Mr. Bailey, thus responding in exactly the same way in the same situation.

The third illustrative incident recalls the first in focusing on change and good medical practice. Jim and Siegfried prefer opposite ends of cows—neck versus rump—as the best location for injections. In its insignificance, this disagreement resembles the disagreement in *Gulliver's Travels* over opening eggs on the little versus the big end. In actuality, this incident shows both vets as equally resistant to change, equally blind to opposing arguments, and equally inconsistent in deciding to try the other's method in spite of previous arguments against it.

Overall, the incidents in Chapter 25 show that Siegfried and Jim do indeed differ in personality, but are hardly the opposites Jim claims. In fact, they are as much alike in significant ways as they are different. They are essentially opposite and not-opposite at the same time. Jim's reading is a reasonable interpretation of events, but it is neither complete in itself nor the only reasonable interpretation.

Chapter 39 similarly invites alternative interpretations and works against dichotomous thinking. This chapter revisits the theme of variety originally presented in Herriot's first book. Here it is, in part, an extraordinary lack of variety that demonstrates that variety is a feature of veterinary practice. While showing fifteen-year-old David a day in the life of a vet, Jim encounters two dogs and a sow suffering from false pregnancy, a rare and largely psychological rather than physiological illness. Jim reads this situation as a fiasco: he sees the reappearance of the same illness as an embarrassing lack of variety, and he repeatedly promises David that the next case will show *real* veterinary practice. What is real practice? In his apologetic comments, Jim makes it clear that he has been thinking in terms of rough, demanding working conditions, mundane physical ailments, and the challenging scientific nature of diagnosis and treatment. From that viewpoint, neurotic ailments are not part of country practice any more than reappearance of the same ailment is a demonstration of variety.

What Jim ignores here is the strong interest he has shown elsewhere in the personalities of animals and the emphasis he places on behavioral and psychological factors—especially an animal's fear—in diagnosis and treatment. What Jim also fails to notice is how each owner's reaction to the false pregnancy must remind David (and readers) of how extraordinary it is to encounter even one case of this ailment, much less several. In the context of these cases, the chapter's final case is a striking example of encountering variety, although Jim refuses to see it that way because it too is psychological rather than physiological in nature. Called to assist at a calving, Jim finds a cow without a calf. The prospect of another false pregnancy is dashed, however, with the revelation that the cow has delivered and hidden her calf, perhaps to avoid having it taken from her as in the past.

Thus, variety both emerges and—as Jim contends in focusing on the psychological nature of the cases—does not emerge in Chapter 39. At the same time, the serious and unglamorous side of veterinary medicine that Jim wishes to emphasize emerges only in the repetitiousness of these unusual cases. Instead of providing a serious and stuffy lesson, the cases show how the unexpected and unusual enliven the profession. At the end, David makes that point when he answers Jim's comment that vets do encounter "funny things" with his own observation that the vet's life is "a funny life altogether" (355). By "funny" Jim obviously means "strange" or "unusual," and it is easy to see how that meaning also applies to David's comment. But the chapter's humor—luring a poodle with a squeaking doll, the repetitive diagnoses as a running joke on Jim, the punctured expectations—suggests a different and equally valid meaning for "funny" in both comments. Moreover, a third meaning of "funny" as "deceptive" is also possible. The symptoms are deceptive in false pregnancy. Appearances can be deceptive, making it difficult to know why the cow hid her calf. And, of course, impressions of the vet's life can be deceptive. The point of bringing teens on rounds is to remedy misconceptions of the vet's life. Here, events have not only changed David's concept, but also challenged the narrow concept Jim apparently intended to emphasize.

While key terms such as "funny" reveal an aptness beyond what Jim sees, the figurative language in the book breaks down to reveal itself as less imaginative and much closer to ordinary speech than it first appears. Figurative language plays on analogy, speaking of one thing in terms of another basically different thing, and literary criticism has placed higher value on those analogies in which imagination, not common experience, is the basis for the association of one thing with another. Deconstructionists, however, see all figurative language as presenting associations that originated in experience, with the apparently more imaginative associations simply being those where the original connection between the analogy's unlike things has been forgotten. Such is the case with two important figures of speech in *All Things Wise and Wonderful:* Jim's conventional metaphor of the "pawn" in Chapter 15 and his smile "men are like animals" in Chapter 29.

Throughout the early chapters, Jim laments his loss of freedom and self-direction as a trainee. Required in Chapter 15 to follow orders that seem ridiculous, he speaks of himself as a "pawn" (131). Then, when events show vividly that his physical training (PT) sergeant also lacks autonomy, Jim declares him "a pawn too" (135). So commonplace is this metaphor that being a "pawn" seems literally to mean being used for another's advantage. But behind this meaning lies what was once a more imaginative relationship between apparently unrelated things, between a human being and a game piece. The pawn is the least valuable piece in the game of chess. Numerous and limited in ability, pawns are usually moved and sacrificed to gain an advantage for more valuable pieces. Metaphorically, Jim and his PT sergeant are no more than minor pieces in someone else's game. But chess is not just any game, since it began as a exercise in military strategy, and the pieces themselves originally represented opposing military forces, with the pawn as the game's stand-in for the lowest-ranked or foot soldier. To say that military trainees are pawns is thus not so much a metaphoric statement as ultimately a factual one, expressing the close, direct link between chess pieces and soldiers. It is not simply literal in being metaphoric, and in being metaphoric it is essentially literal.

The simile "men are like animals" (240) also reveals a far more complex system of relationships than appears at first. Western philosophy has sought historically to present human beings as different from and superior to all other animals despite their close association. Thus, Jim's statement functions as a simile—a comparison of unlike things—only by suggesting similarity where Western philosophy argues difference. In other words, it is more than a commonplace statement only as long as readers believe that humans and animals are quite unlike. It begins to break down not only because humans and animals are actually closely related living things, but also because the simile simultaneously undermines the belief that they are different. Herriot then hastens the breakdown by backing away from this simile's apparently direct challenge of humanity's special and superior nature. Jim quickly explains that he does not mean to say that humans have the inferior—and detestable—qualities usually attributed to animals: "I don't mean men are 'beastly.' The fact is I don't think animals are 'beastly' " (240). He explains the simile as simply an assertion that humans and animals alike display a range of personalities rather than a single, standard, human or animal personality. He, in fact, inverts his original simile to a more attractive, yet also subversive, assertion that animals are like humans. In doing so, he returns to an idea that pervades Herriot's books. Repeatedly, characters read human traits and personality into animals and Jim finds instructive parallels between animal and human behavior. The inverted simile describes what he has been doing. On the other hand, the original simile also is widely in evidence in this book, since the stories presented show that some men are indeed capable of detestable behavior, and Jim has essentially made such behavior his running complaint about life in the RAF. Curiously incompatible, the inverted simile flirts with sentimentality, and the original simile flirts with cynicism or misanthropy. Of course, neither extreme holds. Both similes, as they enter Chapter 29 and mark the rest of the book, direct readers into the uncharted middle ground where humans and animals are both undecidably the same and different, superior and inferior, attractive and repellent.

In *All Things Wise and Wonderful* as a whole, the dichotomy that Jim initially sees between military and civilian life, between his negative and positive visions of human nature and human values, breaks down into similarly undecidable alternatives. As circumstances lead him to reread his experiences in the RAF and those he recalls from his earliest years in Darrowby, it becomes clear that his interpretations are provisional, each conditioned by his perspective of the moment and subject to change. By the time he leaves the RAF, Jim can find much to appreciate in military life, and he has recalled that civilian life also has its bad moments. When he steps off the bus on his return to Darrowby, he steps with an optimistic determination to unite what he values from his military experience with what he values in his civilian life. Whether Herriot intended so or not, his treatment of his wartime experience is distinctly postmodern in character and open to deconstructionist readings.

All of Herriot's books have a slightly bittersweet quality—a positive emphasis and an optimism about life combined with at least a passing recognition that the world is also an imperfect place where the good can suffer unfairly and a happy ending is not always possible. What has probably made *All Things Wise and Wonderful* less attractive to many readers than Herriot's other books is the stronger presence of that painful side of life. In part, this presence is stronger because Jim goes beyond his usual, modest doubts about his own capability and direction to doubt the values that have supported and guided him in the past. In part, it is stronger because the stories go beyond common mishaps, natural deaths, and economic distress to include examples of malice, depression, despair, and suicide. The contrast is more remarkable, perhaps, as it is at the start of Chapter 16, where Jim admits to taking a "rosy" view (136) of his experiences in Darrowby just before telling of a series of malicious poisonings of dogs there.

The presence of the painful side of life is not entirely compensated even by the presence of intensely heartwarming stories—such as those of Mrs. Ainsworth's Christmas kitten, the Sander's Skipper, the begging market day dog, Judy the nurse dog, and Oscar the cat. The bittersweet quality of this book as a whole is very much like that of two of its stories, which end happily but with some uncomfortable questions lingering. After a lifetime of joyless existence waiting for something special to happen, Ned Finch finds love at first sight and a happily-ever-after marriage featuring the appreciation and comfort he has never known. But does the happily-ever-after ending cancel out entirely the bleak picture of some sixty years of emotional and physical deprivation? Roddy Travers's story also ends happily when Jim saves his only family, his dog Jake, with an emergency operation. Roddy's lifestyle is attractive, featuring healthy habits, nomadic freedom, and a warm welcome awaiting him at every farm he visits. But Jim's glimpse of the old photograph of a young woman among Roddy's few possessions gives an inescapably poignant quality to what seemed earlier a wholly idealistic choice of lifestyle. As in these stories, readers of *All Things Wise and Wonderful* are likely to have experienced a more challenging journey than in Herriot's earlier books while working around to the book's closing reassertion of Herriot's usual, upbeat view of life.

The Lord God Made Them All
(1981)

The Lord God Made Them All is unique among Herriot's books in venturing outside his special, well-loved corner of the world and outside England. Herriot's Yorkshire often seems a type of utopia, a world set apart from the troubles of modern life. In part, this book tries to place his Yorkshire back in the context of the larger world, and to recognize that people have much in common despite obvious differences in circumstances and culture.

Attractive as this aim may seem, it helps to make this book weaker than his others. Here he weaves journal accounts of brief trips in the 1960s to the Soviet Union and to Turkey into the account of his experiences in Yorkshire in the late 1940s and early 1950s. In these journal accounts, he continues to take what he called in *All Things Wise and Wonderful* his usual "rosy" view, which consists of an occasional recognition of the ugly side of life and a strong, continuing emphasis on all that is positive. Unfortunately, here the result is a bland view of life in the Soviet Union and colorful Istanbul. Except for his traveling companions, the people he meets remain largely nameless and indistinct. They do not become centers of attention in individual stories, as people and animals in Yorkshire so frequently do. Only Herriot's mishaps serve to enliven these travelogues, which seem unusually drawn out in comparison with his more typical Yorkshire stories in the rest of the book.

Since the installments of his travelogues account for more than a quarter of the book's chapters, they greatly reduce the overall number of stories. In comparison with Herriot's other books, *The Lord God Made Them All* simply does not offer as much to command his readers' attention, leading to some measure of disappointment and dissatisfaction.

THEMATIC ISSUES

One of Herriot's aims here is to give a universal dimension to his positive vision of life, but this thematic concern emerges primarily in the chapters on his travels and is not notably present in the rest of the book. Thus, the idea that people have much in common despite political and cultural divisions remains only a secondary theme. Similarly, *The Lord God Made Them All* is not the story of Jim's re-establishing himself in Yorkshire, which readers of *All Things Wise and Wonderful* might expect it to be. In that earlier book, Jim's anxiety about whether he really will be able to return to his profession and to the special world of Yorkshire after serving in the RAF is left unresolved at the end, when he marches homeward with determination to meet the future. *The Lord God Made Them All* does take up the issue, but Jim's anxiety is effectively resolved in the first chapter, when he finds that it is almost as if he had never left.

Other portions of the book raise alternative issues, many recalling thematic concerns featured in Herriot's earlier books, but they are not pursued either. Here, for example, advances in treatment are changing his profession more rapidly than ever before, but Jim is too caught up in the momentum of change—and too happy with its benefits—to be troubled by it, as he was in *All Things Bright and Beautiful*. Nor does the birth of his second child and his experience of parenthood raise for him new questions of adjustment and identity resembling those he faced as a newlywed in *All Things Bright and Beautiful*. Even when he once again impulsively seeks adventure, leaving his family behind, as he did before in volunteering for the RAF, he faces on his brief trips none of the doubts and anxieties that troubled him throughout his RAF adventure in *All Things Wise and Wonderful*. Nor do the trips, treated as brief holidays, do much to suggest that Jim is having any regrets or second thoughts about the choices that he has made in his life. As the obvious possibilities fall one by one, the thematic focus of *The Lord God Made Them All* begins to seem unusually elusive.

Readers may find that it remains elusive far into the book, perhaps even until the end, largely because this book, unlike Herriot's earlier ones, does not present a time of notable challenge, adjustment, doubt, or decision in Jim's life. No personal or professional issue preoccupies him. He negotiates no obvious turning point in his life. He struggles to no realization marking significant personal growth or the passage into a new level of maturity. Instead, *The Lord God Made Them All* presents Jim living through a period in his life that, although eventful, is neither very dramatic nor easy to label. It shows him finding his life wonderfully rewarding; he observes repeatedly that his life, both in its joys and in its trying moments, is intensely satisfying. Then, at the end of the book, Jim and Siegfried emphasize this view by together declaring this period their best time of life, professionally and personally.

Thus, *The Lord God Made Them All* is focused thematically on an affirmation of the goodness of life and, more specifically, the values that prevail in Jim's life. Essentially, it is the story of Jim's recognizing, more and more clearly, that this is a special, richly happy, and satisfying period in his life. To this end, the book becomes almost a survey of sources of satisfaction. Jim rediscovers the beauty of the Yorkshire countryside, the engaging hospitality and quirks of the citizenry, and the feeling of being an accepted and valued member of the community. He experiences again his comfortable friendship with his partner Siegfried and the sparkle of Tristan's carefree approach to life. He finds increased pleasure in helping animals now that new medicines and procedures are resulting in successful treatment and prevention of disease, producing a new reliance on vets among farmers, and causing the Darrowby practice to thrive. He finds the comforts of married life gaining a new dimension with the poignancy of parenthood and the discovery of his young children as people with distinct personalities. He even finds reaffirmation when he seeks adventure in travel to the world outside his immediate experience. Ultimately, this adds up to a very strong picture of well-founded satisfaction and contentment in the life that he has chosen to lead in Yorkshire.

Within this larger picture of Jim's happiness with his life in the 1950s, three strong secondary themes emerge: the potentially dangerous nature of impulsive behavior, the necessity of steering between the extremes of oppression and anarchy to find the right degree of order or structure in life as a foundation for happiness, and the value of generosity as a form of compassion and tolerance.

Impulsive behavior has figured in Herriot's earlier books, especially as one of Siegfried's defining characteristics. Jim himself has occasionally acted impulsively in spite of seeing himself as slow to act without first thinking things through (see the discussion of his character in Chapter 5). But here Herriot emphasizes the more serious, potentially dangerous nature of impulsive behavior. The humorous examples of Siegfried's impulsiveness take a more threatening turn. His wild test drive in Chapter 3 badly shakes the imperturbable Mr. Hammond's nerves, and the hedge clippers he tests in Chapter 33 come terrifyingly close to ironmonger Albert Kenning's fingers.

Examples of Jim's impulsiveness multiply and take a similarly dangerous turn. Jim's humorous first experience with bovine artificial insemination in Chapter 26 is the result of his impulsive actions. Eager to try the new method and equipment, Jim seizes his first opportunity without really knowing what he is doing, botches it badly, and escapes injury from an enraged bull only by beating the bull's nose with his equipment. It is a humorous version of the very tense situation in Chapter 8 where Jim tries his first cesarean delivery of a calf without knowing how it is done. Relying entirely on his veterinary student Norman's ability to guide him through, Jim discovers too late that Norman had been able to see very little of the only cesarean that he had witnessed at school. Even the cow's miraculous recovery does not compensate for the tension of the operation.

More obviously dangerous are Jim's impulsive actions that place him in serious and easily foreseen danger. The most notable is his attempt in Chapter 16 to reach the isolated Kealey farm on skis during the great snows of 1947. Having overconfidently promised to try, Jim sets out on skis despite "a twinge of misgiving" (147) and finds himself frighteningly lost in a sudden snow shower. Although he has the wisdom to turn back when it stops, he should have foreseen the danger, recognizing with Bert Kealey that "Fellers have got lost and died in the snow up here" (148).

Jim's two foreign trips are similarly impulsive and dangerous. Both times he makes a sudden decision to seize the opportunity to travel, substitutes enthusiasm for practicality, and finds himself in unexpectedly difficult situations. The stormy voyage to and from Russia is dangerous, and the plane trip to and from Istanbul is even more dangerous. In fact, Jim has to sign away his right to death benefits in order to fly back right away instead of waiting for safer transportation. His cargoes also prove more difficult to deliver successfully and in perfect health than he expected. Moreover, impulsive actions in port bring Jim into an encounter with vicious Russian guard dogs, a near miss of arrest for invading a Russian school, and the embarrassment of mistaking a Turkish wedding reception for a bar. Despite the generally slapstick, comedy of errors nature of Jim's mishaps, the undercurrent of danger remains strong. The cowman's warning before his Russian trip, "One wrong word and you'll find yourself in t'nick" (34), nearly proves true. Reports that the Russian POWs he had met in Yorkshire "went home to death or captivity" (56) should have made him more wary of danger. The genuine danger of his return flight from Turkey is underscored by his hearing that, shortly afterward, the same plane "plunged into the Mediterranean with the loss of all her crew" (342).

A secondary theme concerning the necessity of having order and structure in life as a foundation for happiness also emerges in the book. As a parent, Jim finds that he must exert a degree of control over his children to prevent them from injuring themselves and to channel their energies positively. But he also worries about doing the right thing, about steering between too little and too much control. He recalls in Chapter 5 how his son Jimmy at four struggled to establish his identity by helping on rounds, by getting his own pair of hobnailed boots, and by testing his father's rules. Jimmy's fall while climbing the forbidden wisteria clearly shows the value of the rules, and Jim's reaction shows him to be more "old hen" (47) than dictator. In Chapter 22, he treats his daughter Rosie at three in much the same way. But he has greater doubts about having done the right thing when, in her teens, he played the "heavy father" and talked her out of becoming a country vet, instead of holding to his belief that "children should follow their inclinations" (210).

Jim's parental concern about maintaining the right degree of discipline finds its counterpart in other areas of his experience in this book. In his veterinary experience, he sees the effect of too little discipline in the horrible Muffles and Ruffles in Chapter 36. Products of a complete lack of discipline, the two dogs are unusually mean-tempered. Later their replacements also change from amiable to nasty in a matter of months, as a result of the same lack of discipline. As Siegfried explains it, dogs need to obey to feel secure and happy; they become insecure and unhappy when forced to be the boss by owners who spoil them. On his Russian trip, Jim finds the opposite of this anarchy to be equally unfortunate, when he observes the effect of oppressive governmental control on the people he meets. He finds the soldiers unfriendly, the officials cordial but suspicious, the people drab, the shops dingy and dirty. But

he also finds himself feeling secure and confident with the firm leadership of Captain Rasmussen and again later in the commanding presence
of Captain Birch on his Turkish trip.

The secondary theme of generosity is most explicitly presented in
Chapter 10, in the example of Robert Maxwell's charitable behavior toward people who have harmed him through their shortcomings. From
Maxwell's generous treatment of him when he was responsible for the
unnecessary death of a cow, Jim found that he "learned more on that
farm about the way to live than . . . about veterinary science" (91). He
learned the value of responding with generosity when he "found people
at fault and at my mercy if I wished to make trouble for them" (92). And
the chapter concludes with his declaration that Maxwell became his
model of "a standard of conduct to follow" (92).

This point is especially striking because it explicitly identifies a quality
that Jim demonstrates in several earlier chapters, especially in Chapter
8, where his veterinary student Norman leads him into doing, unexpectedly blindly, his first cesarean on a cow. After his initial irritation
with Norman, Jim makes a special point of apologizing, recognizing his
own greater responsibility, and thanking Norman for his help in a difficult situation. Similarly, he responds with generosity to Humphrey
Cobb's inconvenient, alcohol-induced, false alarms in Chapter 2 and to
the damage he suffers in Chapter 1 from Mr. Ripley's procrastination.
The same generosity or charity on a broader scale is also evidenced in
Chapter 6 in the Yorkshire farmers' friendly treatment of POWs serving
as farm help at the end of the war. The theme of generosity toward the
feelings of others continues throughout the book, most notably in Jim's
not telling Josh Anderson the details of his dog's cure in Chapter 13 and
in Jim's toasting a quack vet with the Cundalls in Chapter 25 because
he recognizes their happy ending as more important than accuracy about
its means or any damage to his pride.

More than in Herriot's earlier books, the thematic focus of *The Lord
God Made Them All* is fully revealed in the last chapter. Grandma Clarke's
platitude that the best time of life is when your children are young becomes something more with her explanation. Too often just a way of
saying "you'll regret having children when they're teenagers," she
makes it instead a celebration of having your children "growin' up
around ye" (369). She has a shrewd idea that Jim knows the value of
being close to his children and nurturing them, since, with a "sideways
smile," she observes to him, "You allus seem to have one or t'other of
your bairns with you on your calls" (370). In the scheme of good times

past and to come, Jim and Siegfried agree with Grandma Clarke that this may well be the best time of their lives, not just because both of them have their children growing up around them, but also because their profession is similarly growing up around them. New advances have brought improved care for animals and new respect for vets. Their practice is booming with extensive Ministry work. It is a richly satisfying time of life for them, and for both it is reason to look with enthusiasm to what the future will bring.

PLOT DEVELOPMENT

The Lord God Made Them All is the first book Herriot wrote to be published at the length of the American edition. Previously, Herriot had approached writing as a series of smaller-scale projects, regularly writing two shorter books for British publication and then combining and revising them to make a larger book for American publication. Here he faces the challenge of working directly on a larger-scale project. He clearly tries to meet this challenge by adapting the approach he used in *All Things Wise and Wonderful,* which had required very little revision. There he used the continuing, chronological story of his military career as a frame linking independent stories of his earlier veterinary experiences. Here he interweaves installments of his journal or diary records of two working trips outside England in the early 1960s. Unlike the earlier story of his military career, however, the story of these trips is outside the period in Jim's life at the center of this book. *The Lord God Made Them All* concerns the period in Herriot's life following World War II, roughly from 1946 to 1955, when the emergence of modern veterinary medicine was well under way and his two children traveled, in turn, on calls with him through their preschool years.

Because *The Lord God Made Them All* is not concerned with following Jim's progress to a decisive moment in his life but aims, instead, at establishing a strong impression of the quality of his life, readers who look for elements of a conventional plot will be disappointed. In the book as a whole, as opposed to individual chapters, incidents and actions do not build on one another to suggest movement forward to a concluding action or to a revelation of character. Even chronology, simple sequence over time, is not strongly in evidence in the book as a whole, except across the travelogue chapters. The Yorkshire chapters skip forward and backward through the postwar years, building an impression of Jim's leading a fulfilling life.

Herriot compensates for the lack of conventional plot in the book as a whole by using the interwoven travelogue chapters as a frame serving to impose a sense of structural coherence and forward direction on the book. As journeys, the travelogues have a built-in plot in the sense that both trips have a beginning and an end, with an ordered series of incidents between them. Both trips also provide a degree of suspense, not so much over whether Jim will survive since the book is autobiographical, but over what disasters short of death might befall him. Readers are encouraged to carry over an impression of plot development from the travelogues to the book as a whole, since installments of these travelogues appear regularly throughout the book at intervals of one to four Yorkshire chapters apart.

Herriot used a similar technique in structuring *All Things Wise and Wonderful,* where the progress of his career in the RAF formed a framework for stories recollected from his earlier years as a vet. There, however, the recollected stories served as an elaboration on the process of growth that Jim was undergoing in his RAF career. In other words, the plot provided the framework for the introduction of additional stories. In contrast, this relationship is reversed in *The Lord God Made Them All.* The book's center of interest is in the stories of Jim's postwar years. Its plot, if it had a conventional plot, would also be centered in the postwar years, not in the progress of two trips a decade or so later. Neither trip is presented as having a significant impact on Jim's life and personal development. Moreover, the travelogue chapters are set apart from the postwar stories as self-contained, dated, journal or diary extracts, in contrast to *All Things Wise and Wonderful's* complex connection of RAF stories and Yorkshire stories through association of ideas. Thus, the travelogues have a supplementary relationship to the stories of Jim's postwar years and merely superimpose a frame on them, giving the book as a whole the appearance rather than the substance of structural coherence.

Like Herriot's other books, *The Lord God Made Them All* is basically episodic. The typical chapter is essentially a short story, presenting an independent and complete incident with its own major characters, plot, and theme. Even the travelogue chapters generally follow this pattern. As installments of a continuing story, they closely resemble an extended version of Herriot's practice in his first two books of linking chapters by occasionally carrying action over two or more chapters. Although the travelogue chapters are surprisingly colorless, many of the Yorkshire chapters stand out as among Herriot's most vivid and effective short stories.

NARRATIVE POINT OF VIEW

The Lord God Made Them All continues the first-person narration found in Herriot's other books. Here too Jim is both the main character in the book as a whole and the teller of the story. As a first-person narrator, he is limited to telling what a real person in a real situation might be able to know and to tell others at the time.

Once again, however, Herriot complicates ordinary first-person narration by blurring the reader's sense of time divisions. The episodes from his life in Yorkshire do not follow chronological order, although he makes them all seem to be taking place in the book's present time by drawing readers into each chapter's unfolding action and dialogue. Jim, as the narrator, again seems as much an observer as a participant, since he comments at a slight distance from the action instead of sharing his thoughts as events unfold. He also comments more regularly in past tense here, which suggests that he is speaking somewhere between the time of the action and the reader's present. As with the entries from the travel journals, which similarly combine unfolding dialogue and action with the diarist's narrative commentary in past tense, the impression is one of a narrator reflecting on events very shortly after they happened.

As a further complicating factor, a double narrative perspective again enters with very frequent, brief, narrative comments offered from the perspective of an obviously much older James Herriot who is looking back on his early experience from twenty to thirty years in the future, at the time of the book's writing. This much older Jim can reveal glimpses of the distant future when offering comments from hindsight. Since autobiography generally equates author with first-person narrator, readers will be likely to accept this multiple narrative perspective as essentially a unified, first-person narrative. As a result, Herriot approximates the informative power of third-person narration without violating the strict limitations on the first-person narrator's knowledge.

CHARACTERS AND CHARACTER DEVELOPMENT

Here again, Herriot's more significant characters can be divided into those who become an important part of Jim's life over several chapters (major characters) and those who become the focus of attention for a small portion of the book (minor characters), usually as the leading characters in stories of Jim's veterinary experiences. Many additional, relatively insignificant characters also appear in supporting roles throughout the book.

Among many new additions to Herriot's standard cast of interesting Yorkshire characters and animals, only a few familiar characters reappear, and few of them at any length. Only Siegfried and, more briefly, Tristan and Helen are returning major characters. Only Nurse Brown, her husband Cliff, and Walt Barnett return briefly as minor characters. Mrs. Hall is merely mentioned in Chapter 11. Jimmy and Rosie are established as new major characters on the strength of two chapters each. New minor characters appearing in more than one chapter are limited to those in the travel stories, where only Captain Rasmussen, Raun, and Nielsen stand out among the many lightly sketched and often nameless characters. Unlike the nameless RAF officers and trainees who fill the background in *All Things Wise and Wonderful,* many of these travelogue characters are more directly involved in events, but they never move beyond being broadly representative types. Colorless similarity often seems to be Herriot's objective in depicting them.

As a result of the space given to the travelogues, the book seems to offer a smaller, less interesting cast of characters. The overall number of characters, however, is nearly as large as in Herriot's other books. In addition, many of the Yorkshire stories and their characters, human and animal, are among Herriot's best. The memorable human characters include two procrastinators in lazy Mr. Ripley and penny-pinching Mr. Biggins, two drunks in guilt-ridden Humphrey Cobb and Jim's psychic-fingered barber, and several scoundrels including the insurance-milking Hudson brothers and the hard but unexpectedly human Walt Barnett. Notable human characters also include the goat-obsessed Miss Grantley, Jack Scott who farms with a loving heart, banker Andrew Bruce who loses his interest in country life, and roadman Lionel Brough who has the wisdom to return to a life of contentment. Memorable animal characters include Myrtle the beagle of soulful looks, Venus the silky-haired mongrel, Amber the dog who broke Jim's heart, Tess Kealey's Polly the pig, Bramble the cow with the seductive wink, Brandy the dog with trashy taste, and the horrible Ruffles and Muffles.

As in his earlier books, Herriot regularly introduces characters by first offering details of physical description or a brief personality sketch to place characters in relation to popularly accepted stereotypes. Each character's subsequent speech and actions then confirm, refute, extend, or modify key aspects of that initial impression. As events unfold, those characters who remain most directly involved in the action gradually reveal more complex personalities and more distinctly personal qualities.

Major Characters

James Herriot. In the postwar years, Jim experiences something new and unexpected, security. Instead of finding it difficult to resume his veterinary career, to find reacceptance in the community, and to be part of his family after missing so much of his son's first year, he finds a degree of success and acceptance beyond what he had known before the war. Although he feels that veterinary science is moving forward so quickly that he might be left behind, he rushes forward with it. Quick to try the new medicines and surgery, he finds it possible to do more for animals than ever before. Some cases are still failures, but far more of them are successes. Instead of the old battles to win the farmers' trust and to discredit quack cures, he finds vets respected and sought for help and advice. He finds himself greeted as a familiar part of the community. He also finds himself closely involved in Jimmy's and then Rosie's up-bringing, spending more time with his preschool children than most men of his time. Traveling with them on his rounds, he experiences the joy of seeing the world anew with them and discovering their distinct personalities. He finds parenthood is as good as he found marriage, not without trials—such as the children's brushes with injury and the anxiety of Jimmy's piano recital—but on the whole immensely rewarding. Having a family becomes another source of happiness and security for him.

Jim remains the same modest, empathic, generous, and reflective person he has always been. He is different here only in showing more clearly and more frequently the impulsiveness that has always been part of him. He is also more willing to admit to this part of his personality, which is at odds with his basic conception of himself as steady and unimaginative. As he puts it while introducing one foolishly impulsive mistake on his Russian trip, "I believe I am fundamentally a fairly solid citizen, but every now and then I do something daft" (129). His moments of daftness include not only notable cases, such as his trips and the risks he takes on them, his ski adventure in 1947, and his "blind" first cesarean operation, but also moments of quick medical decision, such as when he dashes outdoors to resuscitate Josh Anderson's Venus by swinging her through the air. His daftness also includes warning Lionel Brough, without waiting for the Ministry's diagnosis, to sell off his pigs at a loss rather than lose everything if the still unconfirmed swine fever should spread to them. The positive side of Jim's impulsiveness is as strongly evident throughout the book as the negative side, both in his readiness to try new medicines and procedures when an animal's life depends on it and in his readiness to respond supportively to the psychological needs of their owners.

Siegfried Farnon. Jim finds reassurance on his return from the war in those aspects of the Dales that have not changed and in his realization that "Siegfried hadn't changed either" (33). Siegfried remains the unpredictably impulsive fellow so puzzling to Jim in his first year in Darrowby. What is different is a lack of the reversals of view that so bothered Jim initially. In addition, Jim has come to accept and expect, even to enjoy, Siegfried's unpredictable flights of enthusiasm. Readers are also reminded that Siegfried is always not only enormously attractive to women, but also a man of "natural charm and commanding personality" (95).

Here Siegfried combines enthusiastic excess and the solid, dependable wisdom of experience. His excesses are vivid but comparatively mild: the wild test drive in Chapter 3, reminiscent of his first drive with Jim, and his flamboyant test of the hedge clippers in Chapter 33. His outwitting of stubborn Mr. Biggins in Chapter 19 relies on psychology rather than force of will. Married and living outside Darrowby, this is an older, more settled Siegfried. When Jim and Tristan celebrate Rosie's birth, Siegfried goes home early from the pub. When Jim wonders about Ruffles and Muffles, Siegfried shares his knowledge of dog psychology and speaks about the value of appropriate discipline. When Jim rails about the Ministry's caution in confirming his diagnosis of swine fever, Siegfried reminds him that the Ministry's reputation depends on its accuracy. In spite of his impulsiveness, Siegfried has always been, to some extent, a voice of reason and experience for Jim.

The two partners, however, are less like father and son here and more alike than in the earlier books. Both vets travel their rounds with dogs and children. Siegfried has both of his children, Alan and Janet, helping him in the closing chapter. Both vets turn to books that offer passages with a lulling succession of similar syllables when they cannot sleep. Both look to the past with affection, relish their engagement with the present, and look with optimistic enthusiasm to the future. In fact, here Siegfried substitutes for Jim in closing the book by embracing the future.

Tristan Farnon. In Herriot's earlier books, Tristan's carefree, comfort-loving life usually has a touch of complexity—a suggestion of repressed unhappiness beneath his cool surface, a tendency to get into scrapes with his pranks, a refusal to be serious. In the postwar years, Tristan is older, married, and presumably more serious as well as successful in his career with the Ministry of Agriculture. But here the purer essence of his good-humored approach to life is emphasized: Tristan is completely the fun-loving, girl chasing, sociable drinking companion of memory.

He makes three appearances in *The Lord God Made Them All,* and each recalls part of his basic personality as it was established in the earlier books. Chapter 11 revisits the prewar, bachelor days in the Darrowby practice, with Tristan in ever-hopeful pursuit of attractive young women. Here it is the beautiful Miss Grantley, who is uninterested in romance and completely obsessed with raising goats. Herriot regularly presents Tristan's chasing, win or lose, as humorously innocent in its outcome—a game simply of winning each girl's good opinion. Here Tristan wins Miss Grantley's favor in the form of goat pellets to test for parasites. Chapter 17 reasserts Tristan's affection for beer and pub companionship when he insists that Jim celebrate Rosie's birth properly. Tristan is at his best in assessing the quality of the beer available in the local pubs and in subverting the law in the person of Police Constable Goole. He not only talks the sternly upright Goole out of an arrest for after-hours drinking, but also manages to talk him into joining them, typically gaining a little more than he intended in a drunken and boisterous Goole. Finally, building on this foundation, Herriot brings Tristan back in Chapter 26. Amusingly typecast as the Ministry of Agriculture's fertility expert, Tristan helps to raise Jim's humorously ill-fated first efforts to do a fertility test on a young bull to an even more outrageous level of slapstick comedy. Tristan proves himself once more to lead to charmed life as, typically against all odds, he emerges by chance a winner.

Helen Alderson Herriot. As in Herriot's earlier books, Helen exists in that part of the author's life that he tries to keep private. She is a central figure in Jim's life, but readers rarely have an opportunity to see her in action. When key incidents in Jim's life bring her into the book with an active role in events, readers usually see her still at a distance, through Jim's eyes rather than directly in her own speech and actions. Here she rarely appears at all, except unavoidably in Chapter 17's account of their daughter's birth.

While Jim makes clear that he and his wife are close and happy together, he keeps her mainly in the background. She is a comforting presence in their home, whether delighting him with a traditional Sunday dinner of roast beef and Yorkshire pudding in Chapter 1 or caring anxiously for the children in Chapter 37. Attuned to his moods, she recognizes when he is upset, as in Chapters 16 and 37. And they know each other fully enough to communicate with glances in Chapter 22.

She is more visible in Chapter 17's account of Rosie's birth. Something of the strong and independent, yet conventionally home-oriented, woman of *All Creatures Great and Small* reappears here. Helen's bemused laughter echoes her laughter during Jim's disaster-plagued courtship. Now Jim's anxiety for her welfare during the pregnancy, his nervousness on their afternoon holiday before the birth, and his impulsively visiting mother and child too soon once again prompt a similarly patient amusement. Helen emerges fully confident and in control of the situation, while Jim plays the nervous expectant father. This is the same strength of character that readers have been permitted to glimpse in Chapter 5, when she succeeds against all odds in finding a tiny pair of hob-nailed boots for Jimmy.

Jimmy and Rosie Herriot. Although readers actually see very little of Jimmy and Rosie, the two emerge with somewhat different personalities. Both eagerly find ways to help Jim on calls, with Jimmy enjoying most shouting for unseen farmers and Rosie opening gates on the way to farms. As Rosie's encounter with the charging cow in Chapter 22 shows, she is inclined to remain obediently where she is told to play and to face problems with quiet patience. In a similar situation, Jim recalls, Jimmy and a cow ran screaming in opposite directions. Jimmy is presented as the more active and mischievous, and Rosie as the more careful and supportive. Jimmy's piano recital demonstrates more talent for prankish showmanship than feeling for music. It is a grander version of his needling his father by climbing the wisteria when he was younger. Rosie, in contrast, handles records and Jim's new player with extreme care, and she expresses herself readily in song. To some extent, their differences are those of age, birth order, and a general expectation that boys will be wilder than girls. Their common quality is an impressive loving regard for their father, most evident in their wish to become vets too.

Minor Characters

Captain Rasmussen and Captain Birch. As the captain of the animal transport ship for Jim's voyage to Russia, Captain Rasmussen is one of several figures Jim finds impressive for their ability to command both situations and respect. Jim occasionally describes Siegfried in similar terms, and he speaks of Captain Rasmussen's counterpart on the Turkish trip, Captain Birch, in the same way. Captain Rasmussen is small, gentle, courteous, and concerned about playing the attentive host to Jim as a guest aboard ship. He quickly proves himself also to be competent, decisive, and even daring in guiding his ship and men through whatever natural and human dangers arise. Captain Birch does the same, while having a more conventionally impressive physical appearance and being in command of a plane less modern and reliable than Rasmussen's ship. Both men provide firm leadership to crewmen who are remarkably happy and comfortable together. Both men serve to demonstrate, as Siegfried does also at times, that command is a function of personality and competence rather than force. This is especially clear in Captain Rasmussen's case, given his unimposing appearance and the sharp contrast offered by the oppressive conditions Jim sees in Russia and Poland.

Raun. The young Danish sailor in charge of feeding the animals aboard ship on Jim's voyage to Russia provides a demonstration of the human need for affection and its role in creating a bond between humans and animals. Huge and rugged in appearance, with a boxer's flattened nose, Raun tends the sheep with loving care. He is drawn to them, and Jim finds him hugging them "like huge teddy bears" (78). The fact that Raun has been at sea since he was fourteen, half his life, and is away from his wife and young children may explain his warm-hearted treatment of the animals in his care. When the sheep suffer stress from the rough seas, Raun strokes them, murmurs "endearments in Danish" (104), stays in the straw with them overnight, and is carried away with excitement over their recovery. Raun is a proof of the universal appeal of animals for humans, and he demonstrates that strength and rugged appearance can be joined with a loving, nurturing heart.

Nielsen. A large man in a tiny galley, Nielsen is remarkable for turning out gourmet cooking on Jim's Russian trip, regardless of weather conditions. The variety, quantity, and excellence of his cooking surprises Jim and keeps the crew content. Unlike the rest of the crew, who take Nielsen for granted, Jim applauds his "culinary genius" (107). As a result, Nielsen directs his efforts toward pleasing Jim, inviting him to try his most special dishes. Among these is a specialty popular with the poor in Denmark, called "Hot Love" (201). Nielsen's food in general serves as hot love for the crew, a solace for the loneliness of life at sea. Jim's praise is Nielsen's solace.

A FEMINIST READING

Feminist criticism is a form of sociological criticism that views literature in terms of gender issues. (See Chapter 4 for a more complete explanation of feminist criticism.) Typically, feminist criticism concerns itself with the male-centered or patriarchal nature of Western culture, in which highly valued traits are identified as masculine, less valued and opposing traits are identified as feminine, and women consequently are envisioned as inferior, subordinate, and deficient in comparison to men.

Readers may find *The Lord God Made Them All* an inviting prospect for a feminist reading, particularly when Herriot says that he talked his daughter Rosie out of her childhood determination to become a country vet on the grounds that it was an inappropriate career for a woman. This incident calls attention very strongly to gender issues, especially as a result of the defensiveness of Herriot's approach. He confesses to "sometimes wonder[ing] if I did the right thing" and rationalizes that "parents are never sure that they have done the right thing" (210).

The women's liberation movement of the 1960s and 1970s produced a sensitivity to gender issues that was virtually unknown in the unliberated, conventional 1950s, when Herriot dissuaded Rosie from becoming a vet. Writing at the start of the 1980s, he clearly recognizes that readers are likely to disapprove of his action. Perhaps defensively, he tries to present both conflicting perspectives. Taking the 1950s perspective, he explains why he honestly thought, at the time, that he was acting in Rosie's best interests. Taking the later perspective, he expresses some doubt and possibly regret over his fairness in opposing her goal largely on the basis of her gender. Similar second thoughts may have prompted him to mention the incident in one of his rare interviews a few years earlier (Green 95). Lingering doubts may also have led him to return briefly to the incident some ten years later, in his final book. He does not, however, renounce his action, and persists in seeing an essential rightness in it, despite his recognition of its gender bias.

The entire incident also has an ironic dimension. By 1950s standards— or even by 1980s standards—Herriot actually pushed Rosie farther beyond the conventional place of women in a patriarchal society. By encouraging her to become a physician instead of a vet, he encouraged her to enter a more prestigious, predominantly male profession. He did not press on her the conventional role of woman as homemaker in a patriarchal society. Faced with the autobiographer's commitment to speaking the truth as he sees it, Herriot presents several truths at once: his understanding of the incident at the time, his understanding of it now, and his inability to draw a definitive conclusion about which is right. He ultimately evades the issue of principle by turning it into an issue of practicality, observing that all is long past remedy and Rosie is happy as a physician. By refusing to draw a definitive conclusion about the incident, Herriot leaves the whole matter of gender issues an open question as unresolved as it is in society.

Once readers focus their attention on gender in *The Lord God Made Them All,* they may notice that this book is unusually male-centered and involved with gender issues. Strong female characters are noticeably absent throughout, even among the working women Jim finds in Russia. Although the veterinarians Jim encounters there are mainly women and he notices many other women doing work normally done by men in the West, it slowly becomes clear that communist society is still extremely patriarchal and exploitative. Jim notices that "women seemed to do a lot of the rough jobs" (169). Then his visit to a grammar school reveals an entirely female teaching staff, while the director, the deputy director, and the security officers who arrive to investigate his presence are all male. Even the female veterinarians must defer to male superiors. The rest of the book, however, focuses primarily on men. To some extent, all of Herriot's books are male-centered, since they concern life in a farming community—historically patriarchal in Western civilization. What is unusual here is the combination of the patriarchal agrarian society with the exclusively male society of seafarers and aviators.

Jim's trips to Russia and Turkey place him in the exclusively male society of seafarers and aviators engaged in the commercial freight business. The men on the cargo ship continue a pattern millennia old in leaving wives and families behind to earn a living on the sea. Jim too has left wife and family behind to join them, notably spending his wedding anniversary at sea. Readers may recall the exclusively masculine focus of most well-known stories of the sea, from the *Odyssey* to *Two Years Before the Mast, Mutiny on the Bounty,* and *Moby Dick.* Typically, such stories justify patriarchy by demonstrating the necessity of strong leadership and a hierarchical social structure. They define manhood as something to be tested and proven, usually by demonstrating such qualities as physical strength, courage, endurance, or mechanical ingenuity. And they feature a struggle to defeat the forces of nature in direct confrontation.

All of these features are evident in Jim's voyage to Russia. Captain

Rasmussen, with his innate authority, sound judgment, and quiet courage, stands as a positive example of paternal authority. He leads his crew through the dangers of storms, an incompetent port pilot, and Jim's brushes with communist authorities. Yet Captain Rasmussen, who has a limp, also resembles *Moby Dick*'s egomaniacal Captain Ahab in his fearless determination to battle the powers of nature by rejecting the harbor pilot's caution and choosing to sail directly into a Force Nine gale. In the male world of the sea, what separates a Captain Rasmussen from an Ahab, an admirable leader from a reckless despot, is his successfully concluding the voyage. Captain Rasmussen's actions are confirmed as justifying his crew's confidence and exemplifying experience, decisiveness, and courage when he brings his ship successfully to port in Stettin. The irrationality of this is similar to that underlying the crew's admiration and respect for Jim as, in the captain's words, "a very good sailor" (103) because he was born extraordinarily resistant to seasickness. Repeatedly, Jim marvels over this response to his chance inheritance of a strong stomach, especially because he remains acutely aware that his inexperience as a sailor makes it dangerous for him to leave his cabin in rough seas. Jim's strong stomach calls attention to the gap between the way things are and the way a patriarchal vision of the world insists on viewing them.

Several other aspects of Jim's account reinforce the impression that reality is more complex than the masculine ideal of shipboard life recognizes. Freedom from seasickness may be the mark of a sailor, but the captain tells Jim that the mess boy is "always ill in bad weather" (103), and Jim eventually finds many of the rugged, veteran seamen miserably seasick from the rough seas (217). Far from being rough, unsentimental individualists, the ship's officers hasten to show Jim pictures of their families, while the crew is friendly and all are courteous. Despite the captain's prominence, Nielsen the cook is also at the center of shipboard life. Although he is taken for granted by all except Jim, Nielsen attends to the human needs of the crew, maintaining their morale as well as their health. He may look nothing like the stereotypical, bounteous, nurturing mother who equates food with love, but this is the role Nielsen plays, as Jim discovers to his waistline's peril. Raun similarly emerges as an unexpectedly nurturing although physically rugged figure when he hugs, comforts, and fusses over the sheep. To various degrees, the seamen suggest by their example that qualities conventionally identified as feminine are actually indispensable, universal human qualities. In doing so, the seamen establish an interesting context for the role of nurturing father that Jim plays in the book.

Masculine idealizations of reality are more strongly challenged in Jim's trip to Turkey. Initially, the crewmen of the cargo plane appear to be modern, more independent counterparts of the seamen. Jim sees them as "carefree" (271). The unattached and footloose young Americans, Ed and Dave, in particular seem to be living the bachelor's dream of travel and excitement without entangling responsibilities. The trip is too short for Jim to know the crew better, but their attractive, near-heroic picture of masculine individualism is very quickly stripped of its glamour. Failing, obsolete equipment makes their lives far from "carefree." Even Captain Birch, as commanding a presence as Captain Rasmussen, clearly requires more than a little luck to defy gravity successfully with his decrepit aircraft. As the problem-plagued trip becomes increasingly nightmarish, Jim's expectation of an exotic holiday is shattered.

The only positive part of the trip, the Turkish wedding reception, is the antithesis of everything he initially saw in both the crew and the trip. When Jim and his two farmer companions blunder into the reception, their unexpected welcome serves as a reminder of the attractions of family life and of the social ties of community, which make the masculine ideal of independence seem empty. Jim and the farmers become so anxious to return home that they actually risk their families' security to return on the damaged plane, ironically highlighting the situation's conflicting values and their inability to escape their patriarchal mindset. The three men cling, as Jim points out, to an irrational confidence in the captain's ability to make the flight successfully. That same irrational confidence resurfaces as the chapter closes with Jim's reluctance to believe the news that plane and crew were lost a short time later.

Similarly, Herriot clings to patriarchal assumptions—women are inherently nurturing and men inherently autonomous—even as the book demonstrates that conventional masculine and feminine traits are not gender-specific, but shared human traits. The episode of Rosie's birth is almost a caricature of patriarchal stereotypes: the man wholly ignorant about the female territory of pregnancy and birth (despite Jim's being a vet experienced in delivery), the woman instinctively knowing when the time is right and confidently delivering her baby, the conspiratorial relationship of mother and midwife as sharers of secret knowledge exclusive to their sex, the expulsion of the father from the nursery, and his subsequent indulgence in celebratory male revelry. The chapter is as humorously artificial as Jim's certainty that, had fathers been allowed to be present at their children's birth back then, he would have fainted during the delivery. What makes Chapter 17 difficult to take as merely humorous exaggeration, however, is the scarcity of other depictions of women in the book. Helen is almost invisible outside this chapter. Grandma Clarke alone stands out, and she appears mainly to speak for the accumulated wisdom of motherhood in endorsing a close relationship between fathers and their young children. Patriarchal assumptions are also evident in Herriot's depiction of his children. Young Jimmy's episodes focus on activity and a challenging of authority, while Rosie's appearances focus on passivity and solicitude. For example, Rosie displays a natural affinity for music and brightens Jim's rounds with song, while Jimmy turns his piano recital into an occasion for mischievously exploiting dramatic suspense.

Nevertheless, Herriot never questions the ability of women, their strength or independence, and their right to a career (despite steering his daughter away from being a vet). Although *The Lord God Made Them All* fails to provide examples of strong women, it does challenge patriarchal assumptions by insisting that men share with women the same capacity, the same need, to nurture others. Jim even discovers a trace of this capacity in Chapter 31 in that most coldly self-sufficient of men, Walt Barnett. The final chapter's double example of Jim and Siegfried as fathers very closely involved with their young children speaks softly and eloquently for a rethinking of conventional gender stereotypes.

The period in Herriot's life covered by *The Lord God Made Them All* is not a dramatic period of challenge or change, but a period of fulfillment with promise of more to come. In a sense, it is the positive fruit of Jim's earlier decisions to become a vet, to settle in country practice in Yorkshire, to marry Helen, and to raise a family. Savoring the richness of that fruit, enjoying success and happiness in his personal and professional life, confirms the wisdom of Jim's choices and presents an attractively positive vision of life. Unfortunately, however attractive and incident-filled, the book shares the essentially static nature of any effort to expand on a "happily-ever-after" ending. It has nowhere to go because it has already arrived. In a sense, it can only look back with each new experience—just as Siegfried and Jim do at the end, when they sit in the garden at Skeldale House, recall their first meeting there, and conclude "we've come through a few things together since then" (371).

Every Living Thing
(1992)

Every Living Thing can be seen as a book with a mission. In part, its mission is to cap Herriot's series of memoirs with a farewell performance that crystallizes the special essence of his books—their vitality, skillful storytelling, and penetrating focus on life's most fundamentally important qualities. In part, its mission is also to prove, as perhaps all farewell performances try to prove, that the author's ability is genuine and undiminished by success or the passage of time.

In several respects, Herriot's previous book, *The Lord God Made Them All*, seemed to be his swan song. Despite his promise in Chapter 4 to write about John Crooks in the future, no new book followed in two years, as others had before. When none followed as a decade passed, it began to seem significant that *The Lord God Made Them All* had used for its title the last remaining line in the verse from the old Anglican hymn that had supplied the titles of his American books. The relatively disappointing nature of the book also suggested that Herriot might have exhausted his material. That impression found reinforcement as the passing years saw him recycling his previously published stories in new collections and in illustrated versions for children.

Herriot himself cooled expectations that another book would be forthcoming. He had always expressed mixed feelings about his part-time career as a writer, and insisted that his full-time career as a vet left him little time for what he saw as the very hard work of writing. In the decade after *The Lord God Made Them All* was published, Herriot spoke of preferring to spend his spare time enjoying his family, especially his grandchildren, rather than writing. Just attending to the republication of his stories, he suggested, took altogether too much of his time, even considering his gradual retirement from veterinary practice.

At some point, however, he began working quietly on his final book, while continuing to mine his earlier work for republication. Although writing may simply have gotten into his blood, the decision to write in secret a book that no one any longer expected suggests a strong personal stake in writing it. He may have felt it necessary to bring a sense of completion to the series, or to draw his writing career to a close with a flourish by producing a book equal to his extraordinarily successful first books. If so, he succeeded in both respects. *Every Living Thing* is a grand farewell performance that presents Herriot's vision of life anew, revisiting familiar situations and themes without merely retracing old ground. Undoubtedly, as the project moved forward, Herriot also enjoyed the prospect of surprising everyone—family, publisher, and readers—with the completed book. In that too he succeeded.

THEMATIC ISSUES

Every Living Thing briefly revisits some of Herriot's earlier themes, especially the ideas of variety and unpredictability that figure in his first book. Chapter 4 highlights the veterinary profession's "infinite variety" (35), while Chapter 27 recalls Siegfried's early observation that the profession "offers unparalleled opportunities for making a chump of yourself" (202). Siegfried's own changeability, absent-mindedness, and interest in innovations—which were emphasized in the first book—also reappear briefly, as does his quality of instant decision—which reappears here in John Crooks with a family focus. Jim's familiar recognition, when feeling depressed, that others nevertheless have it worse returns in Chapter 5, as well as his appreciation for the funny side of life. These are, however, secondary themes that serve mainly as points of connection with the earlier books, in much the same way as the reappearance of Mrs. Pumphrey and the Sidlows or the references to Tristan and Granville Bennett ground this book explicitly in what has come before it.

The dominant theme of *Every Living Thing* is the importance of discernment—seeing beyond surfaces to underlying realities, distinguishing between false impressions and truths, separating the trivial from the fundamental—to achieve happiness in life. The necessity of discernment is evident in Chapter 1, when Jim mistakenly jumps to the conclusion that his medical efforts have killed Mr. Kettlewell's impressive draft horse. Given his concern for helping animals, the situation seems to be his worst nightmare come true. Jim is immobilized with shock and guilt, until the horse suddenly recovers from fainting. This is the first of a superabundance of situations in which characters focus on appearances, draw hasty conclusions, and act on that basis for good or ill.

One of the most alarming situations involves Hugo Mottram's virtual declaration of war on Jim and Siegfried in Chapter 8 as unscrupulous competitors. Not only is Mottram mistaken in his hasty reading of events, but also insulting and arrogant in his refusal to consider that he might be wrong. Prejudging Jim's explanations as lies and cutting them off, he declares the matter and his mind closed. The situation would rapidly worsen if his hostility were answered in kind. Instead, succeeding events vindicate the Darrowby vets and ultimately enlighten Mottram. His embarrassed turnaround underscores his rashness in misreading his colleagues and in refusing, much earlier, to establish a social relationship with them.

Other situations are less extreme, but equally vivid in focusing on the deceptive nature of appearances. Wolfie surprises two burglars by wagging his tail in deceptive friendliness and attacking at the same time. Harmless Bernard Wain's masked defense against odors, forgotten in his haste to get to town, leads the police to assume that he is a criminal. The new-looking, shiny exterior of Jim's used car draws both good-natured and serious jabs at his prosperity at a time when he is uncomfortably short of funds. And the attractions of a cottage to be auctioned win such interest that it is almost instantly bid up beyond Jim's means. When Jim discovers, after the bidding, that the cottage actually has a stubbornly leaky roof, he is consoled, but also alarmed to find that he has had his second narrow escape from folly in pursuit of a dream house at auction.

Frequently characters are deluded by the way they envision things, whether or not the actual appearance of things is deceptive. Jim's image of a convenient house that will be easier on Helen than Skeldale House becomes an obsession even before it feeds his irrational bidding frenzy at the first house auction and his disappointment at the second auction. Denny Boynton's mental image of the most vicious horses as more foolish than dangerous is convenient for his work as a blacksmith, but as irrational as his fixed idea that even a docile, elderly dog must be a dangerously untrustworthy, savage dog. Similarly, Bob Stockdale is so frightened by the possibility of cancer, generally incurable at the time, that he assumes his dog's harmless tumor must be cancerous and refuses to have it examined. Jim's combination of real and mythical success picking winners in the pools suddenly leads Lord Gresham's farm men not only to envision him as admirable for that ability, but also to respect him as a vet. Mental images of reality, however mistaken, are powerfully influential in *Every Living Thing*.

In some cases, appearances prompt very positive results. The frequent presence of Mrs. Pumphrey's chauffeured limousine outside the new Chinese restaurant in Darrowby, for example, miraculously stifles local prejudice and boosts the struggling venture's popularity. Similarly, the quality of Jim's suit, courtesy of the late Mr. Pumphrey, speaks as loudly as his report in swaying the Milk Committee to approve Ted Newcombe's sorely needed Tuberculin Tested (T.T.) license. Another type of packaging is as important as the product in Geoffrey Hatfield's case. Hatfield's salesmanship rather than the quality of his candy makes his shop popular: people enjoy the show and personal attention, so they see his candy as special. John Crooks's bedside manner, the concern for owner as well as animal that he shares with Jim, wins him the regard of critical Major Sykes where his skill as a vet alone could not. Calum Buchanan's friendly personality and skill similarly win people over to him, despite the oddity of his carrying a pet badger on his shoulder.

Appearances, however, are not always deceptive—or, at least, not predictably deceptive. Precisely at the midpoint of the book, old Arnold Braithwaite draws jeers from the young men of Darrowby with his tales of close friendship with a wide range of leading sports figures of the day. He seems a classic example of the lonely retiree telling tale tales for attention. Jim sees him that way too, enjoying his stories and dreading with sympathetic concern the inevitable, painful outcome when they are suddenly put to a test. But the test shows his stories to be true, however unlikely. A few chapters later, Basil Courtenay's slightly exotic handsomeness, gracious manner, refined temperament, and conversational ability make him seem a misfit as a farmer—correctly, as Jim eventually discovers. They suit him perfectly, however, as a waiter in an elegant restaurant. Later in the book, Siegfried raises the issue of image directly: "being forgetful can project quite a different image. People can think . . . that you don't care" (230). When the perpetually forgetful Siegfried begins to lecture Jim in characteristic fashion on his methods for preventing absent-mindedness, Siegfried's deceptive self-image is more forcefully revealed—and pointed out by Jim—than it was on the memorable oc-

casion of a similar lecture in Chapter 6 of *All Things Bright and Beautiful.*
Siegfried's comment on image is underscored shortly after, when Mr.
Busby accuses Jim of not caring about his cow because he gave emergency treatment to a dog first and when Mr. Busby then accuses him a
few weeks later of not caring about his dog because he gave emergency
treatment to a bullock first.

Nearly every chapter presents readers with examples of conflicting
appearances and realities. Some are as obvious as the inflated positive
image Mr. Dawson has of Jim in Chapter 13, or William Hawley has of
Siegfried in Chapter 31. Others are as challenging for readers to discern
as for the characters. Even the vet's common activity of diagnosis develops this theme in *Every Living Thing.* Basically, diagnosis involves
seeing beyond symptoms, which are frequently misleading, to discover
the source of a problem in order to treat it successfully. In Chapter 7,
Jimmy at ten demonstrates his promise as a vet when he beats his father
at a diagnosis of mastitis by following Jim's own rule of testing the milk
for flakes instead of being misled, as Jim allows himself to be, by the
milk's perfect appearance. But what symptoms suggest can also be true,
however unlikely, as Jim's experience with Dick Fawcett's cat Frisk in
Chapter 14 demonstrates. Frisk's ailment is beyond diagnosis, because
his symptoms of drugged sleep prove, in fact, to be a drugged sleep
resulting from his occasionally finishing his master's milky sedative.
Near the end, when Jim fails to save Molly Minican's Robbie despite
repeated efforts at diagnosis and treatment, readers are reminded that
diagnosis is always more than a scientific exercise in Herriot's books: it
is a means of helping animals and the people connected with them. Jim
is troubled mainly because he sees himself as having failed Molly. His
discovery of Molly's contrasting image of him as heroic for his efforts
turns attention strongly once again to discerning what really matters in
life.

For Herriot discernment means recognition that relationships are of
paramount importance. The bonds of affection and mutual dependence
between human beings, between human and animal, between all creatures, form an enduring theme throughout his books. They lie at the
heart of Jim's choices in his professional and personal life. He enjoys his
work because, as he reminds his readers repeatedly, he finds regard for
the people of Yorkshire, inspiration in the rugged countryside, and satisfaction in helping animals. These intangible rewards far outweigh for
him fame and fortune as definitions of a successful life. In his personal
life, the first link between Jim and Helen was their shared love of the

rugged Yorkshire landscape. Their continuing relationship as well as Jim's relationship with their children are distinguished by a mutually dependent regard and understanding of one another, marked often by an amused appreciation of each other's eccentricities. To a great extent, each of Herriot's books chronicles Jim's growth in the insight that these bonds of affection and mutual dependence matter more than competing values in life.

Every Living Thing focuses on the elusive nature of this insight in its closing chapters, as Jim struggles to win the trust of Olly and Ginny. As descendants of a long line of wild cats, they are fearful of human beings and wary of confined spaces. In addition, they have a strong impression of Jim as a threat, based on his having captured and caged them for neutering and, in Olly's case, for grooming. Not only must Jim overcome their doubly negative impression of him to win their confidence, but he must overcome his own impression that they dislike him. Unlike all of Herriot's other books, which close looking toward a future rich with possibilities, *Every Living Thing* looks inward to a special moment when Jim, having won Olly's trust before his sudden death, has finally succeeded in winning the more timid Ginny's trust.

PLOT DEVELOPMENT

Every Living Thing may, at first, seem closely related to *The Lord God Made Them All*. Both were written from the start as a large-scale project rather than as two shorter British books to be combined later for American publication. Both focus on Herriot's experiences in the 1950s. Both emphasize the satisfactions of a happy home life and an established, progressive veterinary practice. But *Every Living Thing* more closely resembles Herriot's earliest books. Like them, it is more complex in its connections between his life and the stories from his experiences. It has a strong thematic emphasis. And its plot development parallels Herriot's life, progressing toward a new turning point. Here the plot carries his life forward toward retirement, despite remaining nominally focused on the 1950s, when he was still in his middle years. It concludes with a decisive moment that unites and transcends his professional and social lives—the modest victory that he finally gains in his intensely personal campaign to win Olly and Ginny's trust.

Although *Every Living Thing* nominally deals with the 1950s, the time period is unusually vague, and the events give the impression of being set in a later period in Herriot's life. *The Lord God Made Them All* emphasized Jim's role as the father of a young family and his close relationship with his young children as toddlers. In *Every Living Thing* the children are no longer toddlers: they are ten and six when they return in Chapter 7. As the book progresses without further mention of their age, they begin to seem even older and more independent. In school and developing friends of their own, they show at their last appearance, in the middle of the book, the interest in rock and roll music typical of teens of their generation. Then they disappear from Jim and Helen's daily life after the move to Hannerly, except for Jim's mentioning once that the wild cats accepted his children but rejected him.

Jim himself seems older and more confident in terms of his profession and his family. In fact, early in the book, he slips forward a generation from youth to age, learner to mentor. As he points out in Chapter 10, he suddenly finds himself no longer viewed as "t'yoong man" (82) in the practice, replaced in that role by younger assistants. To some extent, the reappearance in Chapter 4 of the Sidlows and of Mrs. Pumphrey and Tricki Woo from his first book recalls his early days in preparation for this moment. He now finds himself watching others undergo a process of growth similar to his own in *All Creatures Great and Small*, as well as playing the role of experienced and comparatively mellower, senior colleague to them. As John Crooks and then Calum Buchanan prove themselves, marry, and begin families, they recall the pattern of Jim's life in the preceding books and make that earlier part of his life seem increasingly distant. It seems even more distant when Jim mentions their later life: Crooks's progress to the presidency of the British Veterinary Association in 1983 and Buchanan's progress to the menagerie that his grown daughter describes in 1988. When Jim moves, near the end of the book, into the idyllic High Field House in Hannerly, this last home strongly suggests a retirement spot, not only in the apparent absence of the children, but also in his emphasis on quietly enjoying nature there in "heaven" (294) with Helen. His description of their first visit to the house even suggests the closing of a circle by its roughly paralleling his first meeting with Helen, sitting on a hillside behind a house, enjoying a magnificent view of Yorkshire together, and voicing their shared love of the countryside.

Every Living Thing has an episodic structure, as do all of Herriot's books. Chapters typically resemble short stories, each with its own localized characters, plot, and theme. Jim's presence in each chapter is their common thread, of course, and collectively they serve larger aims as the experiences that have shaped Jim's life and outlook. To avoid a sense of fragmentation, Herriot also links individual chapters by presenting similar situations and issues, which invite readers to notice points of comparison and contrast. In addition, as in his earlier books, he occasionally carries over the action of one chapter into following chapters, either in direct succession or as an interrupted series of chapters.

The progress of the two young veterinary assistants, John Crooks and Calum Buchanan, from their arrival in Darrowby to their departure form continuing stories of both types. Their parallel stories are essentially two versions of the same story, first in short form and then in extended form. Crooks's story is completed in two successive chapters (Chapters 10 and 11), while the parallel Buchanan story is interwoven through the rest of the book (at intervals from Chapter 15 to Chapter 51). In contrast to Herriot's use of the continuing story of Jim's RAF service in *All Things Wise and Wonderful* and the continuing stories of his two trips in *The Lord God Made Them All*, the stories of the two young vets do not function as framing stories. Because they are presented as happening at the same time as the other incidents interwoven with them, they provide a more subtle linkage, similar to Siegfried's ongoing skirmishes with Miss Harbottle in *All Creatures Great and Small* and Jim's series of encounters with Granville Bennett in *All Things Bright and Beautiful*. In other words, they do not stand apart in time and place from the other chapters near them. They simply form a pattern of connection to one another that is far more obvious, even predictable, than the patterns that other chapters might be seen to form. They also provide a sense of continuity that carries over to nearby chapters.

A second, easily recognizable pattern also emerges, providing an overall structural framework for *Every Living Thing*. The second pattern concerns Jim's house-hunting, which comes to the forefront at the book's roughly one-quarter (Chapter 12), midway (Chapters 21, 23, and 25), and three-quarter (Chapter 42) points. Immediately following Crooks's story, Jim recognizes the inconvenience of Skeldale House as a home for his family, searches unsuccessfully for a more practical house, falls for Mrs. Dryden's little house, and narrowly survives his first upsetting experience of a house auction. After Buchanan's arrival, Jim has his second unfortunate experience of a house auction, decides to build rather than buy, encounters frustrating difficulties building, and leaves Skeldale House for his family's new home at Rowan Garth. Finally, as Buchanan's departure nears, a dream house appears in Hannerly and Jim's last move proceeds with dreamlike ease. Together, the progress of the Herriots from Skeldale House to Hannerly and the progress of the two young assistants from their first professional case to marriage and setting out on their own establish an overall structural coherence for *Every Living Thing,* while emphasizing the sweep of time from youth to maturity.

NARRATIVE POINT OF VIEW

Every Living Thing is a first-person narrative. As in Herriot's earlier books, Jim is both the main character and the teller of the story, and is limited to telling only what someone in a situation would be able to know and to tell others at the time.

Once again, however, Herriot blurs the reader's sense of time. Is Jim speaking as events occur, after some events but before the concluding action, shortly after the episode concluded, or years after? The answer is all of the above at times. The narrative present, the spot in time from which the narrator views events, often changes. Jim alternates between speaking with the limited knowledge of a participant at the time and speaking with the slightly more informed knowledge of hindsight. The shift is unobtrusive, because Jim, as the narrator, often seems as much an observer as a participant. In fact, he mentions "contemporary note-taking" (139) as enabling him to reproduce Mr. Bendelow's nonstop chatter. Even when apparently presenting events as they occur, Jim speaks at a slight distance from the action, instead of sharing his tentative ideas as events unfold.

To encourage readers to accept this blurring of the narrative present, Herriot begins the first chapter of this book (as well as all his other books) in medias res. Starting in the middle of the situation and then going back to work through it chronologically makes viewing the situation from more than one perspective—with limited or slightly more informed knowledge—seem quite natural. In Chapter 1, he first depicts the situation and his actions as he sees them at his darkest moment, then returns to his innocently positive outlook at the start of the situation, and finally encounters a surprising revelation at the end that prompts a more complex view. Herriot begins later chapters in medias res as well.

Similar, but more extreme, is his use of a double narrative perspective. Occasionally, a second narrative voice enters and introduces an element of third-person narration: the ability to see the distant future. This second narrative voice is that of an older James Herriot, who is looking back on events from some thirty years in the future. Since the book is autobiographical, readers are inclined to accept the younger Herriot, older Herriot, and author Herriot as essentially one narrative voice, further blurring where the narrative present lies. The older Herriot's retrospective comments, which place events in the context of later developments or offer glimpses of the future, are especially frequent here. Herriot extends his use of the double narrative perspective in ways that contribute to making *Every Living Thing* unusually vague about its basic time frame.

While all of Herriot's books blur the narrative present, they usually provide a clear and consistent idea about a basic time frame. *All Creatures Great and Small* is centered on a two-year span in the late 1930s, from Jim's arrival in Darrowby to his marriage. *All Things Bright and Beautiful* is centered on the months between Jim's marriage and his call-up to military service in World War II. *All Things Wise and Wonderful* is centered on the time of his military service. *The Lord God Made Them All* is centered on his postwar years, roughly from 1946 to 1955. In contrast, despite Jim's several references to its being set in the early 1950s, *Every Living Thing* seems to fit that time frame uncertainly and to compress within it a far greater span of time.

This impression results, in part, from its overlapping the time period of *The Lord God Made Them All* while presenting what appears to be a very different world. In the earlier book Jim is caught up in an onrush of medical advances and new surgical procedures, while here much of that—especially the cesarean operations—is taken in stride. Among the first to try large animal surgery in the earlier book, here Jim has long delayed doing small animal surgery, in spite of his extensive experience operating on large animals. In the earlier book, Jim emphasizes having his children with him until they reach school age. Here the book starts with Rosie at age six and Jimmy at ten. Their toddler days behind them, they are soon shown having an interest in practical jokes and rock music. The impression that *Every Living Thing* focuses on a later period than the earlier book is inescapable for readers familiar with both books.

In addition, the nominal time frame of the early 1950s seems too narrow to contain the events presented in the book. The two veterinary assistants prove themselves, marry, and start their married life in Darrowby in the space of what Jim identifies as two years for Calum and perhaps three for Crooks. Little sense of haste or brevity marks either association, however. Moreover, Calum's two-year stay, spanning 37 chapters, seems far longer than Crooks's equal or longer stay, which runs only two consecutive chapters. Similarly, Jim's searching for an alternative to Skeldale House, building and moving into the house at Rowan

Garth, and finally moving to High Field in Hannerly might reasonably fit into five or six years, but the book suggests a longer period. Jim speaks of Rowan Garth's being home "for many years" (162), although Siegfried later speaks of it as a one-year stay when suggesting the move to Hannerly. Is the move to Rowan Garth in the early 1950s closer to 1950, as the reference to the postwar materials shortage suggests, or closer to 1955, as the reference to hearing Elvis Presley's early hits on their first morning there suggests? Whether or not the nominal time frame is correct, readers have ample reason to feel uncertain and to have the impression that it compresses within it a far greater span of time.

This impression is reinforced by the way Herriot uses double narrative perspective in *Every Living Thing.* Far more frequently than in any of the earlier books, the narrative voice of the author enters here to emphasize the time relationship between events in the book and when the book is being written. Repeatedly, the voice of the author enters to observe that thirty, forty, sometimes even fifty years separate then and now. When earlier books offer glimpses of the future, they usually speak of "now" broadly and focus attention on advances in veterinary medicine. Here, the passage of time in Herriot's life is the focus of attention, and mentions of "now" point more specifically to the time of writing. Typical are such references as "even now, fifty years later" (95), "now, more than thirty years later" (172), and "now, nearly forty years later" (267). Instead of offering glimpses into the future, such phrasing serves to recast events as glimpses into Herriot's past. As a result, readers are made strongly aware of Jim both as he is depicted in the book and as a much older man. As a result, they are also prepared to merge the two images when Jim's move to Hannerly begins to suggest retirement or sunset years, as the children leave the picture and Jim decides to slow down and enjoy life.

CHARACTERS AND CHARACTER DEVELOPMENT

Every Living Thing brings back from Herriot's earliest books two of his best-loved characters, Mrs. Pumphrey and Tricki Woo, and some of his nastiest, the Sidlows. But the displacement of familiar characters by new ones marks the book more strongly. Tristan is gone. Siegfried's appearances are few, with Helen taking a more prominent, active role in his place as a sounding board and source of advice for Jim. Above all, a new generation of vets turns attention from the regulars. A new assistant, either John Crooks or Calum Buchanan, appears in nearly a quarter of the chapters, spaced over most of the book. Both old and new characters call attention more strongly than ever to the bonds of affection and mutual dependence that draw people, people and animals, and even animals together. The characters and their situations also call attention to the importance of seeing beyond deceptive surfaces to recognize enduring values such as those bonds.

As in his earlier books, Herriot generally introduces characters by using a brief physical description or a comment on personality that initially identifies them as types, that is, as belonging to an easily recognized, popularly accepted category of people who share common qualities. Many characters simply remain types, especially those who make brief appearances; other characters move beyond, especially those who appear at length. Their subsequent speech and actions set them apart as individuals or even reveal them to be quite different from what they first appeared.

Here again, the more notable characters in Herriot's extensive cast can be separated for convenience into those who command attention in the book as a whole (major characters) and those who command attention within smaller portions of the book (minor characters). Major characters generally play a direct and continuing role in Jim's life, while minor characters are generally the central characters in Jim's stories of his experiences and are distinct from the many characters who appear in minor supporting roles in his life and his stories.

Major Characters

James Herriot. As in the earlier books, the people and situations that Jim encounters become a learning experience for him. Through observing them and reflecting on his own behavior, he grows more aware of the values central to his life and better prepared to affirm those values as he faces new challenges and choices.

Readers see a more mature Jim in *Every Living Thing.* Early in the book, he finds himself suddenly on the other side of a generation gap, not just as a father but in his professional life. When the Darrowby practice begins employing newly qualified young vets as veterinary assistants, Jim finds them assuming his accustomed status as the "yoong man" (82) in the practice. He finds himself playing the role of older mentor, just as the slightly older Siegfried played mentor to him on his arrival in Darrowby years earlier. As the actual age difference increases with successive assistants, this generation gap increases. Jim notes his growing distance from the assistants' world and speaks of his transformation to "ageing colleague, elder statesman, and finally to quaint old fossil" (91). At the same time, his children are growing up, and he exchanges his makeshift tenancy of Skeldale House for the more settled life of a homeowner.

Jim's greater maturity is primarily a matter of attitude, however. In addition to progressing from occasional mother hen in earlier books to mentor here, he shows himself now to be confident of his ability, comfortable with his daily routine, and secure in his relationship with his clients, partner, wife, and children. He does not interpret his financial pinch, his cases that prove resistant to diagnosis or treatment, and even his recurring bouts of brucellosis as evidence of some type of personal inadequacy. At frustrating moments such as these in the earlier books, he was inclined to doubt himself. Here, instead, he accepts these difficult circumstances as an inevitable part of life. Despite feeling mixed emotions about them, he recognizes that they are "just bad luck, nobody's fault" (162), as he says about losing the unsupported gable of his partly built house in a gale. Later, he assumes the same attitude of chagrined but resigned acceptance when the Hardwick's think him crazy as a result of an odd series of coincidences. Similarly, he makes light of the periods of genuine delirium that come with his brucellosis attacks, instead of indulging in self pity. Because the attacks are predictable in their course, he sees them as bearable small disasters, no worse than many other small disasters in life.

In situations that invite depression or self-pity, Jim is mainly concerned about letting other people down. His physical discomfort at the meeting of the Milk Committee, for example, is nothing compared to his anxiety over gaining approval for Ted Newcombe's T.T. license. His difficult veterinary cases find him concerned about what the loss of an animal will mean to its owner. He is spurred to exceptional efforts on behalf of his patients, not because he has something to prove to himself, but because he sees people badly affected by a pet's illness and he dreads even more devastating consequences from the pet's death. These difficult cases appear with notable regularity throughout this book. They include the cases of Geoffrey Hatfield's cat Alfred, Dick Fawcett's cat Frisk, Mr. Bendelow's dog Blanco, Arnold Braithwaite's dog Bouncer, Mr. Chandler's dog Don, Eugene Ireson's cat Emily, Molly Minican's dog Robbie, and Bob Stockdale's dog Meg. Hatfield and Bendelow, in particular, un-

dergo alarming personality changes when their pets become ill and return dramatically to themselves after their pets recover. The most
extreme case involves the death of Molly Minican shortly after Jim has
failed in his long series of efforts to help her dog Robbie. Molly's death
so depresses Jim that it begins to color his view of himself. He comes
close to wallowing in self-doubt before he admits that what is really
bothering him is not the failing, but the thought that Molly "must have
felt that I had let her down" (330). He finds comfort in the discovery
that Molly actually considered him heroic for his efforts to help.
Throughout this book, Jim's focus is on other people instead of himself—
even his house hunting is motivated by a desire to make Helen's life
easier.

In *Every Living Thing* Jim's attention is focused more strongly than ever
on the quality of relationships—to people, other creatures, community,
and countryside. In these relationships he favors what he calls the "fundamental things" (267) in speaking of Calum Buchanan or the "old values" (91) in speaking of John Crooks. These fundamentals are the
old-fashioned values of love, commitment, acceptance, unselfishness,
and such that lie beneath the surface of enduring relationships and cement them. Their presence—or absence—is more easily recognizable in
human-animal relationships than in more complex human relationships,
but readers are encouraged to experience each in the context of the other,
as Jim does regularly. This happens vividly, for example, in the short
space of Chapter 34. There the Birses neglect their dog Jet because everyone in the family is too self-absorbed to notice and to care for him. They
are also oblivious to Jim's presence, to each other, and to the condition
of their surroundings. In contrast, the Farrows actively nurse a sick calf,
and family members interact cooperatively while expressing warmth and
hospitality. Elderly Mr. and Mrs. Howell resemble the Farrows in showing more concern for Jet than the Birses, their neighbors. When the elderly couple happily wash Jet and care for him together, they exemplify
the same fundamental qualities in their relationship with each other and
with Jet. Four chapters later, Jim is probably thinking of the Howells'
long-term, caring relationship when he recognizes extraordinarily good
sense in Calum's marrying "the kind of girl any young man would be
glad to see [daily]" (267) rather then someone as exotic as his menagerie
choices.

The strongest example here of a solid, long-term relationship founded
on traditional values is Jim and Helen's relationship. Repeatedly, they
give evidence of knowing each other's minds even without speaking and

of accepting each other's foibles, such as her compulsive housekeeping and his impulsive buying. The quality of their relationship is especially clear in their decision to move to Hannerly and in their interaction with the wild cats, Olly and Ginny, at the end of the book. Jim's decision to slow the pace of his life and to win Olly and Ginny's friendship, as Helen already has, by taking the time to let them get to know him and develop trust is not really a change of direction. It is a decision he has made again and again in various forms from the moment he arrived in Darrowby—a decision to keep those fundamental values firmly at the center of his life. The closing image of vet and cat gazing deep into each other's eyes in friendship is a fitting image of the deep, inexpressible bond of affection and mutual dependence uniting every living thing.

Helen Alderson Herriot. Always a sketchy figure, Helen frequently disappears into that private part of Herriot's life which he does not discuss. Even when she is a key participant in the action, readers usually see her only at a distance, through Jim's eyes. In this book, however, Herriot allows readers to see more of Helen than in any of his other books since the courtship in *All Creatures Great and Small.* As on that occasion, readers have an opportunity to see a little of Helen directly through her own speech and actions as well as through Jim's eyes. Moreover, unlike during the courtship, Jim's view of her is not distorted by a lover's anxiety. When Jim speaks of Helen here, he speaks with an understanding and confidence born of their many years together. They communicate with a glance and voice each other's thoughts on several notable occasions, particularly when deciding to build at Rowan Garth, reacting to the house at Hannerly, and bearing the loss of Olly. Since Helen appears relatively frequently here, her picture is not only more consistent, but also more complete.

Many of the qualities that Helen seemed to possess in earlier books return more strongly here. Her enigmatic, twitching smile of suppressed laughter is back when Jim places himself in ridiculous positions (or in Mr. Pumphrey's ridiculously oversized suit), but now it emerges as both her effort to avoid hurting his feelings and her ability to approach small disasters with a sense of humor, recognizing them as less important than they seem. She overcomes her own anxiety at the second house auction, for example, to see the irony in Jim's never having had the chance to bid, and she helps him to get over the embarrassment of the flea episode by comically translating his lament into operatic form. Her domestic focus also returns as clearly her preference when she deals cheerfully with the demanding upkeep of Skeldale House, refuses to do less, and remains unconcerned about finding a smaller, more practical house. Like Jim, she has a mind of her own and a strong will to go her own way. Her refusal to listen to his pleas to stop wearing herself out cleaning find a parallel in his refusal to listen to her pleas to stop bidding at the first house auction. At the same time, Helen is quick to see the possibilities in a situation and to take the initiative when Jim is reluctant, most notably with the Pumphrey suit and the decision to view the house at Hannerly.

Helen's more active presence in this book brings her closer to the position Siegfried occupied in earlier books, as a visible participant in shared enterprises, as a partner of sometimes complementary and sometimes like personality, and as a sounding board for ideas or source of advice. Jim, however, is the more excitable member of this partnership and Helen the more deliberate. The two house auctions present a striking example of this, while the rug episode in Chapter 25 is the exception that proves the rule. Helen's good sense stands starkly in contrast to Jim's gullibility as he adds to his early history of inept purchases at house sales by being deceived into buying broken nets and impractical cloches for the garden. When Helen reverses the usual pattern by falling for a dreadful, obviously fake oriental rug, the turnabout is similar to those that often marked Jim and Siegfried's relationship in earlier books; but here it serves to emphasize, not to undercut, Helen's usual practicality, since Jim admits that the rug episode was "her only aberration" (181), the only instance he would be able to mention in future to defend his gullibility.

Perhaps Helen's most impressive quality here is her ability to give sound advice. In fact, Jim twice hails her insight as "prophetic" (294, 371) in its accuracy. When he regrets his inability to get near their cats, she points out what he has been unable to see for himself. She points out that he has not taken the time to let them get to know and trust him, because his life "is one long rush" (370). Her advice brings him to the realization that turns his life in a new direction and ultimately leads to the book's concluding moment.

Siegfried Farnon. Siegfried, like Jim, seems mellowed by time. Herriot provides brief reminders that Siegfried is still given to outbursts, infatuation with innovations, fast judgments and backsliding second thoughts, annoying lectures, and forgetfulness. But his warmth is also more evident. He is extremely kind to Mottram's young assistant under difficult circumstances, giving as much attention to Harry's well-being as to the desperately ill horse. When Mottram apologizes, he is also quick to defuse the tension by embracing him in friendship. Similarly, his attitude toward Calum is unusually generous. The siege he suffers by Calum's Dobermans turns into reality his certainty that he would regret allowing Calum to expand the menagerie. But the Dobermans stay, and he accepts the ever-expanding menagerie with no more than brief expressions of astonishment and protest, until, on Calum's departure, he admits that he will genuinely miss him. Siegfried also remains sufficiently attuned to Jim to call his attention to the Birrell obituary and the availability of the perfect house for him in Hannerly. Siegfried's mellowness may simply be a result of aging—he does attribute to being tired his giving in to Jim about the expansion of Calum's menagerie—but all of his activity here is on a more ordinarily human scale. That is what William Hawley discovers when Siegfried's requested string does not work medical magic, but simply keeps his coat out of the way while he gives an injection.

Tristan Farnon. Tristan is absent from *Every Living Thing,* making it the only one of Herriot's books in which he does not appear. There is a mention of his taking a job with the Ministry of Agriculture, but he does not visit in that role as he did in *The Lord God Made Them All.* No flashbacks return readers to his days in the practice. Jim does identify Tristan as having nicknamed Bernard Wain the Cisco Kid after "the famous bandit" (255), and he mentions Tristan in making the point that Tristan, Crooks, and Buchanan were all "different" (174) from each other, despite their common role as assistants, their youth, their quirks, and their likeability. Tristan's absence further distances events from Jim's earlier years in Darrowby, while references to Tristan highlight the difference between surface impression and substance.

Jimmy and Rosie Herriot. The strong attraction to veterinary work and the basic differences in personality that marked the Herriot children in *The Lord God Made Them All* continue here with very little elaboration. Chapter 7 reintroduces Jimmy and Rosie, at ages ten and six, as both still wishing to become vets. Both are now helping Jim on calls on the weekends, with the older Jimmy also helping in the evening before bedtime. Once again, Jimmy is described as calm and deliberate in his actions, even in moments of excitement, while Rosie is described as more likely to run than walk at all times and more solicitous of her father's welfare. Readers are also reminded of Rosie's concern about Jim's ability to manage without her and of Jimmy's contrasting confidence that Jim will manage without him.

In general, their personalities reflect the stereotypical, opposing male/

female characteristics of reason and emotion, independence and nurturing. As in the preceding book, Herriot uses these characteristics uncritically to differentiate the two children and raises the issue of gender bias only insofar as his efforts to prevent Rosie, but not Jimmy, from becoming a vet are concerned. He explains again briefly that the dangerous and dirty nature of the profession led him to view it as unsuitable for a woman, and he confesses that advances and changes in the profession subsequently proved him mistaken. While the incident clearly involves issues of fairness and gender bias, it stands here as one among many examples of people acting on misconceptions. In fact, at one point, Herriot speaks of it as a failure of vision: "Though I could imagine tough little Jimmy living my life I couldn't bear the thought of Rosie doing it" (54).

Jimmy and Rosie have more in common here than their wish to become vets. Both children are, like their parents, "besotted with animals" (49). And, like their father, both are keen observers, "taking in every detail of my diagnostic efforts and treatments" (49). Jimmy's besting his father in diagnosing mastitis serves as a proof of this keen observation, just as the incident of the milking lessons demonstrates his independence and determination. Both of these incidents also involve a contrast between mistaken ideas (Jim's taking clear milk at face value, parental visions of injury or worse) and reality.

In addition, Herriot's depiction of the children helps to establish the book's equivocal time frame of both no more than and far more than roughly five years in the early 1950s. Although described as ten and six near the start, the Herriot children seem increasingly grown up as the book progresses. The picture of their helpfulness as youngsters in Chapter 7 is replaced in Chapter 9 by mention of their tendency to find their father's actions amusing, especially the singing stage of his recurring brucellosis attacks. Chapter 18 finds Rosie playing piano and Jimmy, who played piano in the preceding book, now playing the harmonica. In Chapter 23, when they move to Rowan Garth, they are strongly interested in practical jokes and rock music. The typical generation gap between parents and teenagers would appear to have opened when Herriot speaks of being aggravated, as a lover of classical music, by their daily "blasting" (172) of Elvis Presley through the house and of finding their music "just a loud, unpleasant noise" (172). Later, both children slip out of Herriot's picture of his daily life with Helen after the move to Hannerly, as if they had grown up and left home. This impression of their growing up runs simultaneously with occasional narrative comments seemingly fixing their age throughout at ten and six and limiting the time period to roughly 1950–56.

Minor Characters

Mrs. Pumphrey and Tricki Woo. The passage of years has not greatly altered Jim's favorite refuge of his early days in Darrowby. Mrs. Pumphrey's hospitality is still offered as enthusiastically as Tricki Woo's greeting. Tricki himself is older and arthritic now, but still good-natured. The sullen gardener Hodgkin, Tricki's reluctant exercise partner, is also older and arthritic but unchanged in his distaste for dogs. Mrs. Pumphrey is still inclined to pamper and overfeed Tricki, although his good health suggests that she has achieved some moderation.

What seemed quite likely in *All Creatures Great and Small* becomes more certain when Mrs. Pumphrey and Tricki Woo reappear here. Far from being foolish or merely eccentric, wealthy Mrs. Pumphrey enjoys doing indirectly in Tricki's name whatever might prove awkward or inappropriate when done directly by a woman of her class and standing in the community. Her elaborate fictions starring the little Pekinese have the added advantage of providing an entertaining outlet for her imagination. Here again, Mrs. Pumphrey credits Tricki Woo when her generous impulses might produce either embarrassment or a sense of obligation in the recipient. She attributes to Tricki her own success in picking the winners of horse and greyhound races. She even identifies Tricki as complaining about Hodgkin's mean behavior, thereby avoiding the immediate, stern reprimand that her witnessing it would have required.

Mrs. Pumphrey's wish to avoid embarrassing anyone with her generosity—and risking their refusal of help—becomes clear in the one situation where she cannot present her generosity as one of Tricki's whims. When Jim's worn suit catches her attention, she thinks of her late husband's suits hanging unused in his wardrobe and offers one to Jim. Since the suit is previously owned, if unused, she cannot avoid making the offer directly; and, when he is briefly speechless, she cannot avoid voicing her worry that the offer might be embarrassing him. Even here, however, the offer is presented not as an act of generosity, but as a request for help in preventing waste.

Mrs. Pumphrey's intelligence and practicality, which Jim emphasizes in describing her, are exemplified not only in her delicate handling of the suit situation, but also in her approach to the situation with Hodgkin and in her efforts to combat ethnic prejudice. Recognizing that Hodgkin's ring tossing for Tricki has become difficult for both of them to continue as before, she enlists Jim's aid to find a way to return Hodgkin's long-standing resentment of his dog-care duties to a manageable level without ending Tricki's exercise sessions. The resulting advice to modify the sessions, on medical grounds, would defuse the worsening situation and work to everyone's benefit. Mrs. Pumphrey also works indirectly to combat local prejudice against a Chinese couple who have opened a restaurant. She recognizes that prejudice, not the quality of the restaurant, is the source of its difficulty in drawing customers. In order to ensure the restaurant's short-term economic survival, Mrs. Pumphrey counters negative rumor with positive rumor by frequenting the restaurant and fostering its image as a popular spot. Her approach is both nonconfrontational and effective.

John and Heather Crooks. The qualities Jim admires in the Darrowby practice's first veterinary assistant, John Crooks, are the forceful personality and quick decision that he had also found admirable in Siegfried in the earliest books. Otherwise, John most resembles Jim himself, especially as he appeared in *All Creatures Great and Small.* John follows the same pattern of starting his career under an established vet who can be both friend and mentor, except that Jim rather than Siegfried plays that role here. He too proves himself on a difficult first case and wins the trust of the Yorkshire farmers. He develops the self-confidence to argue with Siegfried and to give an ultimatum concerning the Inductotherm (an innovative electrical device similar to a heating pad for treating strained tendons in horses). He courts and marries Heather, a teacher, at the end of his first year in the practice. Then, as Jim did earlier, he begins his married life under Siegfried's roof. Like Jim, he is "sensitive and totally lacking in vanity" (91). Moreover, his wife Heather is reminiscent of Helen: both women are dark, attractive, relatively sketchy characters. Helen's familiar, politely suppressed smile of amusement even reappears on Heather's face in response to Jim's pratfall at their first meeting.

At the center of John's success in life—part of which is represented by his rise to the presidency of the British Veterinary Association—Jim sees a quality frequently recognizable in himself, an "uncanny ability to get through to people of all stations in life" (88). This quality appears in the brief account of John's inauguration, when his humorous quip unites and relaxes the audience. The account also portrays as the greater part of

John's success in life the proud, loving family—wife, children, grand-children—present to share his moment of fame. When Herriot cites as the secrets of John's success his devotion to his wife and his instant decision, he also carefully reminds readers about the abandoned car incident during John's courtship, where both qualities are exemplified simultaneously and nearly inseparably. As Herriot treats it here, an occasion that typifies worldly success, the inauguration, becomes a celebration of character and of essentially the same values that decided Jim on remaining a country vet. The description he offers of John, in the first of the two chapters in which John appears, could apply equally well to Jim himself, since both men display "an unshakable belief in the old values and a reverence for the beautiful county in which we worked" (91). Similarly, Jim's most extensive description of Heather could apply equally well to Helen: "cherished partner through life, staunch helpmeet, happy companion" (90).

Calum and Deirdre Buchanan. The Darrowby practice's second veterinary assistant, Calum Buchanan, also repeats Jim's pattern of development, as John Crooks did before him. Calum proves himself on a difficult first case, wins the trust of the Yorkshire farmers, holds his own with Siegfried, marries after a year in the practice, and begins married life upstairs in the Herriots' old rooms at Skeldale House. Like John Crooks and Jim, Calum is very good with people. But his personality is even more forceful than Siegfried's, and his skill as a surgeon extraordinary. Calum appears larger than life not because he possesses basically different qualities than the others, but because he possesses some of their key qualities in more extreme, concentrated form. In particular, their unselfishness and Jim's self-professed obsession with animals are carried to their logical extreme in Calum. As Jim realizes, Calum's spartan habits simply represent a lack of attention to himself because he is so focused on his work and his study of nature. Calum's traveling with a badger on his shoulder and gathering an ever-expanding menagerie seem strikingly bizarre because they are due to an obsession with animals.

Although Calum's badger initially gives people the wrong impression of him—as did the extremely youthful appearance of John Crooks—Calum's skill and personality quickly win everyone over to him. People get used to looking past the surface to the person and accepting him on his own terms. And he brings a new dimension to their lives. He prods Jim into doing routine operations on small animals. His Highland dancing club enlivens the social scene, drawing people together and shaking them—literally, in Albert Budd's case—out of their comfortable ruts into a dangerous world of new possibilities. When later he moves on, he has a similar impact on the settled lifestyles of the people in each locale. He wins acceptance in spite of his unusual ways because he shares, like Jim and John Crooks, many old-fashioned values. As Jim observes in endorsing Calum's wish to marry Deirdre, "with all his funny ways, he seemed to get the fundamental things right" (267). Even Siegfried becomes resigned to Calum's menagerie and seems genuinely sad to see him go.

Deirdre, described only as "tall," "kind," and "motherly" (267), is an even sketchier figure than Helen and Heather, but she too shares much with her husband in being similarly obsessed with nature. Calum and Deirdre's moving on to Nova Scotia and then to New Guinea seems the natural consequence of their mutual passion for unspoiled nature.

Olly and Ginny. After their move to Hannerly, Jim and Helen are adopted by a family of wild domestic cats. The initial situation resembles Herriot's sentimental children's story, *The Christmas Day Kitten,* adapted from Chapter 9 of *All Things Wise and Wonderful:* a wild mother cat, who is fearful of humans, nevertheless associates them with the means of survival and entrusts her offspring to them. But here the relationship between the kittens and adopted humans is more complicated. The scrawny mother cat and her two tiny kittens are willing to look to humans in time of need, but unwilling to trade their freedom for security. The kittens, Olly and Ginny, remain unalterably wild as they grow. They refuse to enter the house or any enclosed area without a clear route of escape, and they remain extremely fearful of humans, despite being basically friendly and affectionate. Even when terrified, brother and sister remain basically good-natured, limp with terror rather than ferocious. Helen soon succeeds in winning enough of their trust to be able to stroke them, but they permit Helen and other humans to get close to them only on their own terms.

Although Jim also becomes very fond of the two cats, his capturing them for neutering and treatment makes them even more wary of him as a human too ready to take away their freedom. A more serious barrier to friendship, however, is Jim's own conception of how they view him. In his mind, they have him "cast firmly as the villain of the piece" (304), and they immediately think "net and cage" (317) when they see him. He believes that he cannot change the situation, until Helen reminds him that he cannot expect them to trust him before he has taken the time to let them get to know him. He is a threat because he is a stranger. By working slowly and patiently to encourage them to accept him as a familiar and nonthreatening presence, Jim eventually succeeds in winning a friendly response from the less timid Olly. Then, after Olly's sudden death, Jim works even more patiently to overcome Ginny's timidity and loneliness and to gain her acceptance. Their close relationship at the end, representing a sacrifice as well as a gain for each of them, brings them together on an unusually equal footing. Their silent stare deep into each other's eyes signifies both continuing independence and a deep emotional bond.

A MARXIST READING

Marxist criticism views literary works as shaped by and, in turn, reinforcing the social forces that shape society. These social forces serve the interests of a dominant class in society by fostering an ideology favorable to it. An ideology is a complex of beliefs, values, and social structures that are accepted by members of a society as the prevailing way of understanding their world. Just as feminist criticism focuses on an ideology fostered by inequalities of gender, Marxist criticism focuses on an ideology fostered by inequalities of economic class. Drawing on the theories set forth in the nineteenth century by Marx and Engels, current Marxist criticism takes a variety of forms and encompasses a range of political views. In essence, however, it encourages readers to view a literary work in terms of the competing economic interests, conflicting economic classes, and unequal power relationships that shape society.

Any reader of Herriot's works quickly recognizes that they are almost self-consciously apolitical. His preference for traditional values does not translate recognizably to political issues and positions. His tendency to bow to social class distinctions is offset by his holding the common Yorkshire farmer and farm laborer in highest esteem. Personal relationships, not power relationships, seem to be at the center of his world. At the same time, however, he feels strongly the effects of the economic structure of society all around him, ranging from his own concern about being short of funds despite a prospering practice to his recognition of the dehumanizing effects of wealth. A Marxist reading of *Every Living Thing* offers an opportunity to consider how Herriot's progress to what he terms "one of my greatest triumphs" (374) is shaped by, and either supports or questions, the economic forces that have shaped society.

The book's most explicit criticisms of capitalism emerge in the contrast between Eugene and Cornelius Ireson in Chapter 40 and in Jim and Siegfried's encounter with Hugo Mottram in Chapter 8. Eugene Ireson resembles the Henry David Thoreau of *Walden* in choosing to live simply in a hut with his cat. He is educated, unworldly, and widely liked for his gentle personality. His millionaire brother Cornelius, in contrast, is hard and humorless, a powerful but hated man. Eugene, unlike his brother, has nothing materially, but actually everything worth having in life. Initially, Hugo Mottram has much in common with Cornelius. His vision of the world as profit-driven and marked by economic competition distorts every situation. It unjustly makes villains of the Darrowby vets and brings Mottram nothing but misery. Ultimately, Mottram begins to move toward Eugene's view and offers a powerful judgment against his original vision of the world by rejecting it at the end of the chapter.

Seeing a world of economic rivalry, Mottram initially believes that other vets cannot be friends and allies, but only "neighbours in opposition" (58). Their object is to maximize profits, but they can do so only at each other's expense. Much like modern corporations that compete for market shares in mature markets, neighboring vets compete for the same pool of potential clients and profit in proportion to their share of the pool. Since clients can obtain the same services from either vet, each vet inevitably deprives the other of some share of the pool. Thus, the very presence of each vet means business lost to the other. This is also the world of late nineteenth-century social Darwinism's "survival of the fittest," where the fittest of the great industrial barons survived by devouring their business rivals. In such a world, where the profit motive is uppermost, the vet's clients are not people with animals who are suffering and in need of help, but rather proprietary assets—potential sources of income to which a vet has staked a claim like a gold rush miner. Mottram takes this view when he insists that Jim and Siegfried's seeing several of his clients represents a deliberate plan to prosper at his expense, an undeniable effort to "steal" (59) his clients. Jim and Siegfried very clearly take the opposite view when, despite Mottram's insults, they hasten to help his assistant Lumsden to save his horse.

In contrast to the altruistic concern that the Darrowby vets display throughout their association with Mottram, his vision of a profit-driven world seems bleak and inhuman. It is not profitable either, since Mottram himself refuses throughout to engage in the cutthroat tactics that he believes so common, repeatedly judging such tactics "dishonest" (56) and all who engage in them dishonorable. More crushing is the suggestion that his view of the world has victimized him. Accepting economic rivalry as the norm, he has been unable to recognize any other possibility. As a result, he has created the negative effects of unrestrained competition, despite its absence, by repaying friendship with enmity and misinterpreting altruism as cutthroat tactics. In the end, Mottram's recognition that friendship is preferable to competition stands as a powerful rejection of his earlier capitalist vision.

The pursuit of profit, or a fixation on money, surfaces at intervals throughout the book as a dehumanizing and alienating force in society. It is blatant in the swindling salesmen that Jim and Helen encounter in Chapter 25. It is more subtle when Jim speaks in Chapter 4 of his lack of money as threatening his satisfaction in his work. He finds it a troubling "contradiction" (27) that he does not earn enough money to escape being permanently in debt, in spite of the practice's success and his love for his work itself. A similar contradiction arises when Lord Gresham's men gain respect for Jim not because he is a good vet, but because they believe he has the ability to win money at will by betting on sports pools. Social standing becomes a function of wealth or the ability to gain wealth readily. That is why the Sidlows, despite their affluence, are so resentful of Jim's new-looking used car. Whether the car represents genuine prosperity or just empty show, their own status is threatened by any real or imagined rise in his wealth or status. Money emerges as the center of social as well as economic competition and conflict.

The dehumanizing effect of a society's fixation on money arises from its displacing a wide variety of intrinsic values. Money is an extrinsic, artificial, societally defined value, while intrinsic values arise from the essential nature of a thing and are inseparable from it. The relationship between monetary and intrinsic values is arbitrary. This is especially evident in Jim's attempts to buy a home for his family at auction. Each time, the selling price is independent of the house's value as living space or shelter, and it rises far above what the house itself, or a comparable house, would justify. Seth Bootland, unlike Jim, does not want to live in the first house auctioned, but his wealth enables him to bid as much as necessary to get it. A leaky roof and hidden rot will make the second house a problem to live in, but its attractive appearance drives its price up. In idealistic contrast, the house that Jim and Helen build at Rowan Garth is designed to be unusually convenient for living and also affordable. Similarly, the house they buy later at Hannerly adds to these advantages the opportunity to live their daily lives in harmony with the

Yorkshire countryside that they love, and its price is settled by mutual agreement and a handshake, without the distorting effects of competition.

Monetary and intrinsic values are frequently in conflict, as Chapter 35 emphasizes when money is pitted against compassion and affection in asking how an animal is to be valued. When Mr. Busby's cow needs help, he asserts that an animal that has monetary value is more important than a pet. When his dog rather than his cow needs help, he reverses himself and argues strongly that importance cannot be measured in money and that his dog is priceless to him. His obvious self-interest gives another definition to importance, while medical necessity justifies the actual priority of treatment in both cases. As in the Mottram situation, self-interest and profit emerge as empty values in comparison to compassion and affection. When a society measures importance, as Busby does, in money and self-interest, that society's economic system reduces the means of production—animals, labor, equipment—to commodities and puts monetary value above other values.

Thus, when Jim's satisfaction in his work is threatened by anxiety over his poor finances, the value of the work itself is called into question. Quality, utility, and the worker's feelings of personal satisfaction or accomplishment become irrelevant and secondary to the wages paid in exchange for the work. If the wage paid defines the value of the work, however, workers become alienated from their work. Geoffrey Hatfield's experience demonstrates vividly how empty work becomes when a sense of its intrinsic value is missing. Because Geoffrey becomes preoccupied with his cat's illness, his level of attention and enthusiasm for his work plummets. He performs his duties in robot-like fashion. Geoffrey's passivity is one response to alienation; subversive resistance is another. Basil Courtenay simply lies about dosing the sick calves in his charge instead of doing it. Mr. Bendelow the tailor takes a more active approach. Money establishes not only importance, but also power. When the means of production are reduced to commodities, a power relationship is created between those who have money and those who must exchange their labor for money. Mr. Bendelow's repeated delays in completing his work emerge as a form of resistance against having his skill reduced to a commodity and exploited. In the context of his unending talk about frustrated quests for wealth and the miserly eccentricities of the wealthy, his delays leave him indisputably in control of his own labor despite his customers' demands and threats. Their economic coercion cannot prompt

Mr. Bendelow to action, although his respect for fine workmanship can, as demonstrated by his swift alteration of Mr. Pumphrey's suit for Jim.

In *Every Living Thing* the power relationship between the wealthy and the workers in society is given symbolic representation in the power relationship between humans and animals. At its most exploitative, the relationship is one of owner and animal, with the animal reduced to an object. It is a literal version of Marx's concept of the enslavement of labor in a capitalist system. The obvious example of animals treated as commodities would be farm animals raised for slaughter, but general acceptance of that practice as natural might support accepting exploitation of workers as natural. Herriot focuses here primarily on animals for whom better treatment commonly would be expected: pets. The most extreme example of a pet treated as an object is the Birses' treatment of their dog Jet as outdated and disposable property. Having lost interest in Jet, the Birses ignore and neglect him. They allow Jet's mange to reach an advanced state before calling a vet, and then decide to put Jet down rather than face the bother of giving him weekly medicinal baths and paying for his medicine. Only the opportunity to transfer his vet bills, not any regard for Jet, convinces them to give him to their neighbors.

By far the greatest number of human-animal relationships in this book, however, is not obviously exploitative. Human beings remain dominant—regulating their pets' lives, limiting their reproduction, and determining life and death when they are ill. At the same time, they frequently describe and treat their pets as friends and occasionally as workmates. Are these human-animal relationships symbiotic or something else in disguise? They have the same ambiguity one finds in human economic relationships. Is Jim's relationship with the assistant vets, for example, closer to the friendship he believes it to be or to the power relationship expressed in the half-serious, half-humorous line that Calum so frequently repeats, "Permission to eat, sir" (364).

Herriot departs from that ambiguous middle ground in his account of Olly and Ginny, who reject even the most commonly accepted forms of human dominance in their relationship with Helen and Jim. The two wild cats will accept help (food, medicine, and shelter), affection, and companionship from humans, no less than from each other, but not at the cost of their freedom. They refuse to be bought with comforts, shunning walls of any type and even a box of bedding. Rejecting anything that would restrict their ability to come and go at will, they refuse to be held—captured—although they enjoy Helen's touching and stroking them while they remain moving. For Jim this is an unusually difficult situation, because his views, as a vet, about what is best for their welfare often conflict with their views. Repeatedly, although well-intentioned, he captures and imposes his will on them: netting and examining them, caging and neutering them, handling them to treat their cat flu, drugging and grooming long-haired Olly. He cannot avoid feeling that his help should have given him a "right" (317) to their affection. To form a relationship with them, Jim must earn their trust that he will not infringe their freedom. When he eventually succeeds, his "triumph" is over his own inclination to establish a power relationship and assert dominance. In its place is an entirely voluntary relationship marked by mutual respect.

Despite the strength of this concluding triumph and the clarity of contrast between such opposites as the Birses and himself or Cornelius and Eugene Ireson, Herriot remains a product of his society. A reformer rather than a revolutionary, he presents social conditions as a function not of economic pressures, but of personality and choice. Even as he succeeded in reforming his relationship with Olly and Ginny, he suggests, it is possible to have wealth or power and be nonexploitative. But his examples can be, in part, disturbing. Mrs. Pumphrey's philanthropy is admirable but also manipulative, just as her relationship with Tricki Woo is many-layered. By giving Jim a suit, she helps both him and Ted Newcombe, but she still has more than a shopful of suits going to waste. If John Crooks shows the possibility of having both family and worldly success, he is only shown choosing family first. Jim himself must shift priorities to devote time to Olly and Ginny. Calum Buchanan, devoted as he is to nature in its most primitive state, proceeds to bring an auction mart to rural Nova Scotia and then "civilization" to the stone age tribes of Papua New Guinea, in a modern version of nineteenth-century colonialism. Herriot is more consistent about the negative effects of materialism than about the inequalities of economic class.

Every Living Thing affirms once more a truth that Jim recognized in his first years in Darrowby and subsequently came to know and to appreciate more fully at each stage of his life: A successful and happy life is not one measured in material accomplishment. Instead, it is a life chosen for the personal satisfaction to be found in its daily fabric—complete with challenges, frustrations, and disasters as well as joys—and a life centered on relationships. So Jim recognized when he abandoned his early dream of a Granville Bennett-like practice to stay in Darrowby, where the landscape, the people, his colleagues, and the opportunity to help suffering animals provided a source of constant satisfaction. So he recognized when he married Helen, learning more about relationships in adjusting to marriage and later in adjusting to separation and the alternative relationships of military life. So he recognized when he brought his toddler children on calls, experiencing a close relationship rare among fathers of that time. And so he recognized when he found himself a mentor to younger vets and communing with Ginny. The values at the center of his life are simple and old-fashioned, focused on the bonds of affection and mutual dependence that unite every living thing.

Appendix A
Other Characters in *All Creatures Great and Small*

Individual chapters in Herriot's books usually present independent stories that have their own major characters, plots, and themes. The stories frequently offer parallels to one another and to issues facing James in the framing story of his life, which runs throughout each book. Viewed in relation to each other, the stories in *All Creatures Great and Small* explore competing conceptions of what is important in life. A survey of notable characters from individual chapters shows Herriot's interest in focusing attention on the social dimension of life and on the competing claims of economic success and self-fulfillment.

Mr. Alderson and Candy: Helen's father is a livestock expert and a quiet man who has withdrawn into himself since his wife's death. James recognizes that Mr. Alderson worries about losing Helen to him. He also knows that Mr. Alderson would prefer to unite his farm with his neighbor's farm by marrying Helen to the neighbor's son, Richard Edmondson. In part, their regard for animals brings them together. James succeeds in saving Candy (Mr. Alderson's only Jersey cow, for which he has a special affection) and her calf before announcing his intention to marry Helen. What really makes it right, however, is Mr. Alderson's seeing in Helen and James a parallel to his own marriage: Helen's mother married him for love when no one thought she would have him. (Chapters 48, 65; *ATBB,* Chapter 7)

The Allens—Mr. and Mrs. Allen, Jack and Robbie Allen: A tough, fit, generous farm family, the Allens typify all that James loves about Yorkshire. Their warm response to his marriage seems to give his life choices a seal of approval. (Chapter 67)

The Altons—Tim, his wife, and their oldest daughter Jennie: Tim Alton is a small farmer who is old before his time with the struggle to make a living on poor land. But he is rich in the love of his wife and daughter. James finds the Altons' love amidst poverty more attractive than the Taverners' scorn amidst luxury. The Altons are a positive example of what marriage can bring. (Chapter 61)

The Bellerbys—Mr., Mrs., Ruth, and Bob: Farmers in the high country of the Dales, the Bellerbys seem far from twentieth-century civilization. Their leisurely pace contrasts James's modern living by the clock. (Chapter 10)

Boardman: A wounded veteran of World War I, Boardman does odd jobs at Skeldale House. He used to be a stableman for the old vet before Siegfried and serves as a link to the slower-paced, prewar days of horse and carriage, servants, tended gardens, and veterinary calls in top hat. (Chapters 7, 16, 24; *ATWW*, Chapter 16)

Bob: See *Mr. Dean and Bob*.

Stewie Brannon: One of Siegfried's veterinary school classmates, Stewie has a wife, five children, and a practice that is barely keeping them going. He is cheerful, warm, unambitious, and free of envy. These qualities, in combination with his carefree attitude and affection for his friend, make him an attractive character. He joins the Altons, the Bellerbys, the Coopers, the Rudds, the Watsons, and others who seem to find a happy life outside of worldly success. (Chapters 63, 64; as Brannan in *ATWW*, Chapters 20, 22)

Sam Broadbent: Fat and mentally limited, Sam is a farm worker whose only skill is his ability to imitate the sound of a warble fly. His skill is very useful in herding uncooperative cows, which are scared by the sound. Sam demonstrates that everyone has his or her own niche in life and how important it is to find that niche. (Chapter 41)

Major Bullivant: An artist at running up bills without ever paying anyone, Major Bullivant uses his impressive personality and appearance of inherited wealth to fool everyone for as long as possible before moving on. (Chapter 55)

Phineas Calvert: Calvert is a prosperous farmer whose cheerfulness, messy working clothes, and rough manners are in sharp contrast to the aristocratic Brigadier Julian Cotts-Browne's elegance and snobbishness. It is a mark of James's success when Calvert speaks admiringly of him the way Uncle Dimsdale spoke of Mr. Broomfield in Chapter 1. (Chapter 26)

Mrs. Cooper: A commanding, take-charge woman said to be the boss of her family. But her bossing is motherly in its focus on their health and welfare; she is kind and generous under her tough manner, and her family seems happy. Mrs. Cooper makes an interesting contrast to Miss Harbottle, who is also a commanding, take-charge woman. (Chapter 23)

Frank and George Copfield: In contrast to the dark and thin variety of Dales farmers, the Copfields represent the blonde and heavily muscled variety. James sees their chasing down wild Galloway cattle on foot as the kind of surprising event that makes being a vet in the Dales enjoyable. (Chapter 7)

Isaac Cranford: Cranford is a prosperous farmer who puts making money and keeping it above everything else. He is stingy, selfish, friendless, and intent on winning at any price, including cheating and bullying. Cranford provides a test of James's professional integrity, decisiveness, and determination. (Chapters 28, 29)

Dan: The Alderson's sheep dog, Dan is both a family pet and a working dog. He shows his good nature and his patience when he allows James to examine his dislocated hip without protest. Through his accident, Dan helps to bring Helen and James together for an afternoon as pleasant as their first meeting and paves the way for their second date. (Chapter 60)

Mr. Dean and Bob: Mr. Dean is a widower living in poverty on an old age pension, with his dog Bob as his only companion. When Bob dies of cancer, Mr. Dean insists on giving James a token payment for his services. The situation emphasizes the affectionate relationship between humans and animals, the dignity and honor of the typical Yorkshireman, and the frustrating helplessness of vets to cure some illnesses. (Chapter 11)

Harold Denham: Coming from a wealthy industrial family, Harold Denham is a millionaire who has chosen to spend his life absent-mindedly puttering around his house. His only interest is football pools, although he knows nothing about football (soccer). Harold's idea of what is important in life is clearly different from that of his prominent brother Basil. Like Stewie Brannon and other characters, he chooses happiness over success.

Charlie Dent's pig: A big vicious sow who turns out to be a cowardly bully. The pig is the center of a battle of wills, or wits, between the Farnon brothers. The pig episode is also an example of fear being worse than reality, which is the lesson James learns in the following chapter, in his encounter with Mr. Wilkinson's huge stallion. (Chapter 24)

The Dimsdales—father, son, and uncle: The Dimsdales are silent, patient, and rugged Dales farmers. Uncle Dimsdale compares James unfavorably to his vet, Mr. Broomfield, who can do no wrong. The comparison emphasizes James's inexperience and self-doubt, and shows the difficulty of competing with folk wisdom and dealing with a general distrust of vets. (Chapter 1)

Horace Dumbleby: A butcher, Dumbleby differs from Siegfried's other deadbeat clients. Instead of being charming, he aggravates the vets by demanding immediate service and resenting demands for payment. He also differs in being motivated by greed and stinginess, qualities he has in common with Isaac Cranford. (Chapter 56)

Mrs. Hall: Housekeeper for the Darrowby practice, Mrs. Hall is about sixty and a widow. A typical Yorkshire woman, she is good-hearted beneath her silent, unemotional, rugged exterior. She quietly plays Cupid to James and Helen in Chapter 60. (Briefly throughout; *ATWW*, Chapter 6)

Mr. Handshaw: A believer in folk remedies. James's lack of experience produces what appears to be a defeat for science, a success for a folk remedy, and a long-lasting reminder for the vet of the value of humility. (Chapter 32)

Hodgkin: Hodgkin is Mrs. Pumphrey's gardener, Tricki Woo's ring tosser, and

Nugent's valet. As a stern old Yorkshireman who disapproves of pets, he is sorely irritated by having to play with the dog and pamper the pig. (Chapters 13, 33; *ELT,* Chapter 4)

The Hugills—Walter, Thomas, Fenwick, and William: Married brothers who farm together, the Hugills exemplify a humorously overdeveloped version of typical Dales hospitality and courtesy. (Chapter 42)

Jeff Mallock: As the knacker, Mallock buys dead or unfit farm animals to turn them into animal food or fertilizer. His slaughter yard is a smelly and night-marish place. As a result, his name is associated with death and financial losses for farmers. In contrast to all that, Mallock is a cheerful, cherubic person with a large, beautiful, extremely healthy family. Mallock represents a humorous form of the black magic type of folk wisdom that competes with the vet's scientific knowledge. When farmers ask him an animal's cause of death, he usually names one of four imaginary diseases: stagnation of the lungs, black rot, gastric ulsters, and golf stones. Mallock does this without intending to cause problems for vets, in contrast to people like the Sidlows who are against vets. (Chapter 28; *ATBB,* Chapter 45; *ATWW,* Chapter 32)

Mr. Myatt: A gypsy with a wife and three little girls. All of them seem very foreign to James when he comes to help their sick pony. Countering the popular view of gypsies as dishonest, Myatt pays in advance to show good faith. James notices that the girls love the pony and that Myatt clearly loves his daughters. Later, the girls respond as children anywhere would respond when Siegfried takes seriously their ability to assist the pony's recovery. The Myatts' example seems to show the universal nature of the bond of affection between humans and animals that James has found in Yorkshire. (Chapter 59)

Gobber Newhouse: A representative of the less attractive side of Dales life, New-house is a local drunk and ne'er-do-well. He is one of those who impose on James for a drink in false friendship at Mr. Worley's after-hours bar. He also takes the romance out of James and Helen's movie date by sleeping off his latest bout beside them in the theater. (Chapters 38, 62; *ELT,* Chapter 19)

Dennis Pratt: All of Siegfried's deadbeat clients are so charming that it is hard to stay angry with them or to take legal action—although they do have the money to pay. Dennis Pratt outdoes the rest. Not only is he impossible to shame into paying his bill, but he is also so charming that he talks both Siegfried and James into giving him free medicine. He and Major Bullivant exemplify the homegrown and the imported versions of the master deadbeat, in contrast to the less accom-plished Henry Bransom, Bert Mason, and Old Summers of Low Ness. (Chapter 55)

Major General H. W. St. J. Ransom, Colonel Tremayne, and their wives: Influential in the North West Racing Circuit, General Ransom and Colonel Tremayne con-sider Siegfried for his dream job of supervisory vet for the racetrack in the circuit. The men and their wives emerge as stuffy, humorless snobs even before the unfortunate events at the end of the day. They show the difference between the world of the track and the world of country practice, as well as make clear that the two are not as compatible as Siegfried suggested to James. (Chapters 63, 64)

The Rudds—Dick, Mrs. Rudd, their seven children, and Strawberry: The Rudds exemplify the strengths and values that James admires in the Dales farmers. Dick has the toughness, determination, generosity, and honesty of the typical small farmer. Mrs. Rudd has the ingenuity to stretch their small income to feed and raise seven physically impressive, loving children. Dick's dream is to build a fine dairy herd from Strawberry, his first pedigreed cow. Strawberry's illness demonstrates the uncertainty that threatens both the small farmer's life and the vet's ability to save animals. (Chapters 53, 54)

Mr. Sidlow: A practicer of black magic folk remedies. Since he always calls the vet after his own treatment has almost guaranteed an animal's death, he has many examples of animals dying under veterinary care to show that vets are useless. (Chapter 47; *ELT,* Chapter 4)

John Skipton: A self-made man, Skipton rose from farm laborer to wealthy owner of two prosperous farms. James sees in him evidence that a bond of affection between humans and animals will develop even in the most unlikely places. Skipton still works as hard and lives as simply as a farm laborer, instead of enjoying his wealth. Work is everything to him. Although anything unproductive generally annoys him, he keeps two workhorses from his early days of struggle in luxurious, unproductive retirement. Even Skipton is drawn to see at least some of his animals as more than units of production. Skipton's story, extensively revised and expanded, was reprinted in 1987 in an illustrated version for children, entitled *Bonnie's Big Day.* (Chapter 45)

Mr. Soames: Lord Hulton's farm manager, he is an arrogant bully who is eventually fired for stealing. He provides the first big test of James's judgment and decisiveness. (Chapters 5, 9)

Strawberry the cow: See *The Rudds.*

Miss Stubbs, Prince (a.k.a. ''Mr. Heinze'') Ben, Sally, Arthur, and Susie: Miss Stubbs is bedridden, in pain, and slowly dying, but all of her attention and concern is focused on her three dogs and two cats. She fears death only because she is afraid of being separated from her animals without the possibility of ever being reunited. Her situation emphasizes the bond between humans and animals. In addition, the theological issue that Miss Stubbs raises provides James an opportunity to affirm his growing belief in the strength of that bond. (Chapter 43)

The Taverners—Henry, his wife, and their daughter Julia: Henry Taverner is a very wealthy, warm, friendly man with a wife and daughter who constantly criticize and scorn him. The bleak lovelessness of his household is in sharp contrast to the Alton household. (Chapter 61)

Tip: Peter Trenholm's dog Tip insists on sleeping outside the farmhouse door in all weather, when he could sleep in comfort in the barn with the other dogs. James sees in Tip some of the same qualities of rugged determination that he respects in the Yorkshire farmers, who are, like Tip, determined to thrive in harsh conditions. (Chapter 58)

Colonel Tremayne: See *Major General H. W. St. J. Ransom.*

Terry Watson: A young farm worker with a wife and baby, Terry is small and not very strong. He is barely supporting his family by working and by keeping a few animals of his own. When a nearly incurable form of mastitis threatens to reduce his cow's value, or even to make her a complete loss by killing her, Terry makes a superhuman effort to help her recover. He is an example of the Yorkshire farmers' determination and perseverance in their struggle to survive against difficult odds. (Chapter 36)

Mr. Worley: Mr. Worley is an innkeeper and a pig enthusiast. He keeps an illegal after-hours bar open for a crowd of local scoundrels, who welcome James as a friend and get him to buy a round of drinks. Mr. Worley's devotion to pigs contrasts with James's cautious attitude and Tristan's mixed feelings toward them. The bar crowd also provides an instructive comparison with Mr. Worley's pigs. (Chapter 38)

Appendix B
Other Characters in *All Things Bright and Beautiful*

Viewed in relation to each other, the stories in *All Things Bright and Beautiful* explore responses to social and technological change. They explore especially the status of the individual in mutually dependent social relationships (husband-wife, parent-child, master-pet, etc.). A survey of notable characters from individual chapters shows Herriot's interest in how people meet the challenge of adjusting to new circumstances in their lives.

The Aldersons—Mr. Alderson, Aunt Lucy, Tommy, and Mary: Helen's family. Jim recalls the awkwardness of his courtship in contrast to the comfort of married life. Helen's father is a prosperous, widowed farmer who has little to say to Jim as a suitor to his daughter. Aunt Lucy, his widowed sister, is cheerfully supportive, while Helen's younger brother and sister, Tommy and Mary, are amused by the courtship. (Chapter 7; *ACGS*, Chapters 48, 65)

Alfred the cat, Boris the cat, and the Bonds: Alfred is a wild outdoor cat with a paralyzed eyelid. Boris is a huge, ferocious outdoor cat who beats up other cats, including Alfred. They and many other cats have been adopted by the Bonds, who are London retirees. Large Mrs. Bond is the cat lover, while her small, mild-mannered husband quietly tolerates whatever happens, including Tristan's destructive efforts to capture Boris. The Bonds offer an example of an apparently happy marriage involving accommodation. (Chapter 22)

Walt Barnett: An overbearing scrap merchant turned estate owner and horseman. He has a "downtrodden little wife" (368) and two sullen henchmen, Ginger and Winker. Barnett demonstrates that one's basic personality remains the same despite a change in circumstances. (Chapter 40; *LGMTA*, Chapter 31)

Benjamin the sheep dog: See *Arnold Summergill and Benjamin the sheep dog.*

Bill the bull: Mr. Dacre's bull Bill nearly crushes Jim by trying to scratch himself against the wall, not knowing Jim is between him and the wall. Chance produces both this dangerous situation and Jim's escape. (Chapter 32)

Claude Blenkiron: A popular village policeman, Claude maintains order in his district by personally beating petty violators of the peace and by offering friendly help to all in need of it. This unsettling mixture of questionable means and beneficial ends is reflected in Jim's impression of something threatening beneath his good-natured surface. Claude offers an example of the difficulty of weighing mixtures of negatives and positives or losses and gains, such as those caused by social and technological change. (Chapter 15)

Bonzo the dog: See *The Dimmocks.*

Boris the cat: See *Alfred the cat, Boris the cat, and the Bonds.*

Mr. Brown: A picture of health and an efficient farmer, Mr. Brown is all business—he lacks human warmth even on Christmas Day. He shows one consequence that progress may bring for farming. (Chapter 20)

Ted Buckle's bull: Formidable as he is, Ted Buckle's bull follows his mother quietly back to the barn and allows Jim to finish putting a ring in his nose. The bull offers an example of a bond of affection between animals. (Chapter 43)

Timmy Butterworth: A wirehaired fox terrier, Timmy bears a grudge against Jim for treatment past, just as Magnus does. But Timmy goes beyond the canine equivalent of cursing to seek revenge by nipping Jim's ankles from an ambush. Timmy is an example of memory and individual personality in animals. (Chapter 46)

Cindy the Yorkshire Terrier and Miss Dooley (a.k.a. Mrs. Cook, Mrs. Booby): Miss Dooley demands that Jim misuse science by treating her pregnant Yorkshire Terrier Cindy with drugs to induce labor before the appropriate time. Her mistaken view is mirrored by Jim's mistakes about her name. Miss Dooley invokes the name of Mr. Broomfield to pressure Jim unfairly in much the same way that his name was invoked in Chapter 1 of *All Creatures Great and Small.* (Chapter 33)

Clancy the dog and Joe Mulligan: Clancy has a history of vomiting frequently from eating trash. His story highlights the fact that for Joe Mulligan and the older Dales farmers, life has a casual pace that contrasts sharply with the modern, time-driven pace of the vets' lives. Clancy's case also turns attention to the personalities of the animals treated. Huge and powerful, Clancy threatens violent consequences whenever one of the vets begins to examine him, leading all of them in turn to adjust how they deal with him. (Chapter 4; *ACGS*, Chapter 2)

Mr. Clark: Not a typical farmer, Mr. Clark raises calves in a converted railway car. By indulging Jim's desire to try a new drug to save his dying calves instead of sending them directly to Mallock for slaughter, Mr. Clark benefits from the beginning of the revolution in veterinary medicine. (Chapter 45)

Albert Crump: Mr. Crump's wife and teenage children scorn his enthusiasm for homemade wine, making him "odd man out in his own house" (67). When Jim indulges his enthusiasm out of sympathy, Mr. Crump quickly comes alive. Sharing a glass of wine proves to be pleasant for Jim as well as important for Mr. Crump's self-esteem. The episode highlights the value of supporting other people's enthusiasms, while also showing the danger of overdoing. (Chapter 8)

The Dalbys: When her husband Bill dies suddenly, Mrs. Dalby decides to continue running the farm in order to provide for their sons William, Dennis, and Michael. Inexperience and misfortunes add to the difficulty of her adjustment, but she keeps the farm going through her persistence and her determination to learn what is necessary to succeed. She also demonstrates that making an enormous adjustment does not require a loss of identity. (Chapters 12, 13)

The Dimmocks: The eleven Dimmock children and their parents are poor but happy. Since Mr. Dimmock has never been known to work, they get by on very little. The parents are good-natured people, and the children are courteous, clean, and healthy. They do odd jobs and treat their animals well. Bonzo is the shaggy, mixed-breed dog they share. Nellie, who has a limp from an early illness, gets a boost from being given a dog all of her own. Her dog Toby is a purebred cocker spaniel who is saved by Bennett's surgery. The Dimmocks demonstrate that happiness is independent of economic status and that individual identity can be supported even within so large a family. (Chapters 36, 37)

Dinah the Spaniel and Mrs. Barker: A case for Bennett's surgery, Dinah is an old dog with a severe infection and bad heart. The elderly Mrs. Barker's distress at the possibility of losing her companion is a reminder of the close bond between people and their pets. (Chapter 16)

Mrs. Donovan: See *Roy the dog and Mrs. Donovan.*

Dorothy the nanny goat and the Kirbys: Retired farmers who still keep some animals, the Kirbys restore Jim's good will on Christmas Day by showing that farming is not just a business. Dorothy's attempt to eat Mr. Kirby's summer underwear provides a humorous reminder that animals often have minds of their own. Farming has filled the Kirbys' lives with affection for their animals, each other, and their children and grandchildren. (Chapter 20)

Misses Dunn: Two unmarried ladies, the big and little Misses Dunn get along well despite differences in personality. The run a small farm together on feminine principles, pampering their livestock. The Misses Dunn are more extreme and explicit than their male counterparts in the affection they hold for their animals. (Chapter 42)

Richard Edmundson: Jim sees himself at a disadvantage to the wealthy Richard in courting Helen, despite indications that she is more interested in him than in Richard. (Chapters 7, 11)

John William Enderby: Blinded by competitive spirit, Enderby the grocer has convinced himself that unfair judging cheated him of the best vegetable awards at the fair. Enderby's attitude provides a commentary on the futility of Jim's idealistic effort to judge the best pet contest on merit. It also provides a negative example of competitive contests, in contrast to the positive example offered by Sep Wilkin and the sheep dog trials. (Chapter 11)

Gyp the sheep dog and Sep Wilkin: Gyp is an epileptic sheep dog who has never barked. His owner Sep Wilkin is a hard, practical, highly competitive sheep dog breeder and trainer, but he has an unexpected soft spot in his heart for Gyp. That is why he gave Gyp's more promising brother Sweep to George Crossley earlier. Although he cannot enter Gyp in sheep dog trials and cannot breed from him, Sep adjusts his expectations and keeps Gyp simply because he likes him. When Gyp sees his brother Sweep again much later at a sheep dog trial, Gyp barks his only bark in recognition. Both the hard man and the epileptic dog testify to the powerful pull of affection. In 1985, Gyp's story was published independently as an illustrated children's story entitled *Only One Woof.* (Chapter 34)

Herbert the lamb: Named after Rob Benson's son because they share a fearless determination to plunge into things, Herbert is a week-old lamb abandoned by his mother. Herbert survives by plunging in to take milk from other ewes and his own mother before they can stop him. Later, when he is about two weeks old, undernourished, and still almost as small as a newborn, Herbert's determination wins him acceptance by a sick ewe as a substitute for her dead lambs. Although the substitution can be seen as a form of exploitation, Herbert and the ewe save each other and thrive, offering a positive example of mutual dependence and mutual benefit. (Chapter 3)

Mr. and Mrs. Hodgson: An elderly, kindly, friendly farming couple, the Hodgsons offer a positive example of a married couple. (Chapter 32)

Mr. and Mrs. Horner: The elderly farm couple make literal Jim's belief that married life is fat with benefits by inviting him to share their breakfast of fat bacon, which he loathes. The length to which Jim goes to avoid hurting their feelings puts in another perspective the smaller adjustments that his marriage requires. The Horners' happiness together also offers a positive image of marriage in this humorous chapter. (Chapter 39)

Harold and Mrs. Ingledew: A small, quiet man in his seventies, Harold spends his weekends in wild, drunken singing. When Jim mentions hearing that Mrs. Ingledew "tolerated [his binges] because her husband was entirely submissive at all other times" (3), their relationship becomes the first of many marriage relationships that Jim encounters in the book as he thinks about his own relationship with Helen. Since Mrs. Ingledew never appears and Harold is a pleasant but loud drunk, the nature of their relationship remains ambiguous. On the one hand, it seems to be the stereotypically unhappy combination of domineering wife and henpecked, meek husband who rebels by turning to drink. On the other hand, it seems to be a happy example of mutual accommodation, with Harold indulging his wife's whims during the week and Mrs. Ingledew indulging Harold's on the weekends. Readers are left wondering about their relationship, just as Jim finds himself wondering about his emerging newlywed relationship with Helen. (Chapter 1)

Jock the sheep dog: Robert Corner's dog Jock is a champion car chaser as well as a champion sheep dog. When Corner decides to breed him to sell the puppies, Jock produces seven puppies who quickly become his rivals in car chasing. Jock's story becomes mainly one of a desperate struggle to avoid being overtaken (literally) by the next generation and by change. His story also has a bearing, however, on the issue of relationships in marriage. Before their puppies were born, Jock's mate would join him for the first part of the car chase. But Jim observes that she had no real interest in the sport and seemed to join Jock mainly to indulge his whim. With this observation, Jim turns attention briefly to his own concern about the compromises that marriages involve and what those compromises might mean. (Chapter 2)

Mr. Kendall of Brookside: A hard-to-impress know-it-all, Mr. Kendall is shaken by Siegfried's "magical" removal of his cow's tumor. (Chapter 6)

The Kirbys: See *Dorothy the nanny goat and the Kirbys.*

Mr. Kitson: Mr. Kitson is an old farmer who tries to save money by handling his animals' problems himself until they get so bad that he must call the vet. His refusal to have a dying ewe treated provides the occasion for Jim to discover accidentally the value of heavy sedation as a treatment for infection. Mr. Kitson and Jim provide contrasts in motivation and compassion. (Chapter 30)

Magnus the miniature dachshund: Magnus has a long memory for ill-treatment and a strong animosity toward its source. His owner Danny Beckwith also recognizes Magnus's ability to hold a grudge. Magnus illustrates the ability of animals to remember negative as well as positive emotional relationships, offering a parallel to the examples of Gyp, Ted Buckle's bull, Sam, Roy, Rock, Timmy Butterworth, and Benjamin. (Chapter 46)

Jeff Mallock: As a knacker, Mallock is associated with death and financial losses for farmers. He buys dying and dead animals to turn them into animal food or fertilizer. As a representative of unscientific folk wisdom, he regularly attributes the cause of death in animals to one of four imaginary diseases. He declares the white scour affecting Mr. Clark's calves to be incurable stagnation of the lungs. When Jim's new drug proves him wrong, it marks the coming victory of science over superstition. (Chapter 45; *ACGS*, Chapter 28; *ATWW*, Chapters 32, 34)

Maudie the cat and Colonel Bosworth: A tough old soldier, Colonel Bosworth is shocked and hurt by Maudie's injury. Affection and gentleness coexist with his stern, military manner. (Chapter 23)

Frank Metcalfe: A steel worker from a Dales farming family, Frank tries to return to farming. Although he tries to do it scientifically and does everything right, a series of misfortunes brings failure. Unlike the old farmers who had to struggle through misfortune, Frank chooses to sell out and return to the steel mills. While farming is in his blood, he does not have the rugged determination of the old farmers. A similar sign of change in the Dales comes with the transformation of his farm into a summer home for the wealthy Peters. (Chapter 38)

Joe Mulligan: See *Clancy the dog and Joe Mulligan.*

Roland Partridge: See *Percy the dog and Roland Partridge.*

Penny the toy poodle and the Flaxtons: Penny is dying slowly of an intestinal irritation and of stress and fear concerning it. The young couple who own her, the Flaxtons, are caught in the classic conflict between wanting to save her and not wanting her to suffer. Jim finally saves her by using heavy sedation, which gives nature a chance to heal her. Jim's sedation therapy is a scientifically sound black magic. (Chapter 31)

Percy the dog and Roland Partridge: Percy is Roland Partridge's small, white, shaggy dog. Percy has a knack for self-defense, which he needs when hormone treatments for a testicular tumor attract male dogs from miles around. Roland is a squeamish, refined art lover who has refused to inherit the family farm. Roland wins Jim's admiration for "resolutely doing his own thing" (241) and for his devotion to Percy. (Chapters 25, 26)

Peter the budgie and Mrs. Tompkin: Peter is elderly Mrs. Tompkin's only companion. When Peter dies of fright in his hand, Jim replaces him with another, more talkative budgie without telling Mrs. Tompkin. Although she assumes that Jim improved Peter's personality, the incident shows that the only way to change an animal's personality is to change the animal. (Chapter 32)

Phoebe ("Pheebles") and Victoria: Phoebe, a fat Staffordshire Bull Terrier, and Victoria, a fat Yorkshire Terrier, are the Bennetts' dogs. Jim finds in Granville Bennett's fond pampering of them proof that even a hard-driving specialist can form a close, sentimental relationship with animals as pets. (Chapter 17)

The Pickersgills—Mr. Pickersgill and his daughter Olive: A small dairy farmer with an affection for scientific terms and an unusual ability to mangle them, Mr. Pickersgill has never moved beyond the memory of his two weeks at college while a teen and beyond a reliance on patent medicines. Jim nevertheless convinces him to turn over his milking duties to his daughter Olive. This change simultaneously eliminates Mr. Pickersgill's back problem and his cows' chronic mastitis. (Chapter 5)

Rock the Irish Setter: The opposite of Magnus and Timmy Butterworth, Rock seems to recognize that Jim is trying to help him despite the pain of his treatment. Rock's behavior is an expression of his friendly, good-natured personality and another example that animals have individual personalities. (Chapter 46)

Ewan and Ginny Ross: Ewan is a skillful vet with unusual methods and a preference for working at a comfortably unhurried pace. Ginny is his supportive wife and an excellent cook. The Rosses offer an example of a happily married couple in a country veterinary practice, working under the same conditions and with the same promise of financial success as the Herriots. (Chapter 21)

Roy the dog and Mrs. Donovan: Mrs. Donovan's restoration of the badly abused Roy to health provides an example of mutual dependence and benefit. Lost after the death of her dog Rex, she finds in Roy a new purpose in life. The same trust and good nature that led Roy to endure abuse he now showers on Mrs. Donovan even as she showers loving care on him. Their relationship parallels the relationship between Herbert the lamb and his adoptive mother. It can also be compared to the relationship between individuals in a happy marriage. (Chapter 9)

Sam the dog: Jim's constant companion on his rounds for twelve years, Sam was originally Helen's dog but later adopted Jim. Sam is a tangible form of the positive change produced by Jim's marriage. (Chapters 28, 32; *ATWW,* Chapters 2, 23; *LGMTA,* Chapter 22)

Marmaduke Skelton: A quack veterinarian, Duke is a large unpleasant man given to brawling, to beating his wife and children, and to downgrading Ewan Ross's ability. Unlike Arthur Lumley, who does harm as a quack, however, Duke handles many uncomplicated veterinary procedures competently. Duke meets his match in a prolapsed uterus because his approach is scientifically unsound, whereas Ross succeeds using very unusual methods because he knows the scientific basis for their effectiveness. (Chapter 21)

Arnold Summergill and Benjamin the sheep dog: An extremely friendly Old English Sheep Dog, Benjamin is old Arnold Summergill's only companion on his isolated farm. Arnold has retreated from the modern world, refusing ever to use a telephone or to adjust his stride to walking on populated village streets instead of open hillsides. Jim manages to relocate Benjamin's dislocated elbow almost miraculously, just as he earlier relocated the dislocated shoulder of Helen's dog in *ACGS.* As Jim's last case before leaving for London, his visit to Benjamin and Arnold affirms the value of his chosen profession and the value of dealing with change rather than retreating from it. (Chapter 47)

Harry Sumner and Monty the bull: Young Harry Sumner looks nothing like a typical farmer. He is pale, thin, and sensitive. But he applies himself with energy and determination to the hard work of making a success of the small farm he inherited from his father. A progressive farmer, Harry purchases a prize bull, Monty, to improve his herd and readily accepts the idea of abdominal surgery to save him. Later, Monty grows up true to his kind by changing from a friendly calf to a massive and mean mature bull. Monty serves as a corrective to Jim's tendency to sentimentalize and anthropomorphize animal behavior. (Chapter 18)

Susie the dog and Bert Chapman: Susie is an irresistible shaggy dog dear to big, tough Bert Chapman's heart. Bert and his tiny wife show themselves to be clearly a happy couple as they tease each other playfully about their foibles. (Chapter 35)

Sweep the sheep dog: See *Gyp the sheep dog.*

Toby the dog: See *The Dimmocks.*

Tommy the cart horse: Tommy is prone to colic, dislikes the treatment for it, and is growing smarter about thwarting the treatment. He provides Richard Carmody a lesson in the practical side of veterinary medicine. (Chapter 29)

Cliff Tyreman and Old Badger the horse: Cliff is an old, tough, expert horseman who faces the end of the horse era with the death of the last horse on the Gilling farm, his favorite Old Badger. At almost seventy, Cliff does not try to live in the past. He is enthusiastic about trying new things, like bicycles, tractors, and shepherding. (Chapter 19)

Edward Wiggin and his man Wilf: Wiggin is a frail farmer who fancies himself a cowboy and tries to lasso cows western-style with little success. Wiggin is all show without skill, but his man Wilf is all skill without show. Wilf ropes Yorkshire-style with a halter and succeeds in one try. (Chapter 42)

Sep Wilkin: See *Gyp the sheep dog and Sep Wilkin.*

Appendix C
Other Characters in *All Things Wise and Wonderful*

Viewed in relation to each other and the frame, the stories of the people and animals in *All Things Wise and Wonderful* emphasize the social nature of human beings and animals. A survey of notable characters from individual chapters shows Herriot's interest in focusing attention on the critical importance to happiness—and even to survival—of forming and maintaining supportive relationships.

Eric Abbot and Judy the sheep dog: Eric Abbot's sheep dog Judy seems to act as a nurse to other animals who are sick. She keeps watch with them while they are in discomfort and moves on when they recover or die, going wherever her comforting presence is needed. (Chapter 40)

Ambrose: After skinning his knee in a fall at the Hensfield greyhound track, Ambrose becomes Jim's only paying human patient by giving him sixpence for putting iodine and a bandage on it. (Chapter 22)

Ken Appleton: A big horseman, Ken is one of many large men who faint at the sight of blood in Herriot's books. (Chapter 14)

Mr. Bailey: A poor old-age pensioner with arthritis, Mr. Bailey has a small dog with an age-related chronic cough. Although Siegfried scolds Jim for giving Mr. Bailey free service and medicine, he later matches Jim in generosity and goes beyond by adding some money and a ride home. (Chapter 25)

Terence Bailey, Mrs. Bailey, and Giles: Jim's nightmare concern that he might have spread foot and mouth disease from the Duggleby farm seems to come true when the Baileys report blisters on one of their famous pedigreed cows. Jim's alertness pays off once again when he realizes the blisters are only symptoms of cow pox resulting from the smallpox vaccination that one-year-old Giles received. (Chapter 45).

Flt. Lieut. Barnes: Barnes tries to transform the trainees in Scarborough with unending drills and physical training exercises. (Chapters 10, 12)

Mr. Barge of Cargill & Sons: Mr. Barge is one of the old-fashioned, formally-dressed sales representatives who made ordering veterinary supplies and drugs into a formal social ritual. Mr. Barge's gentlemanly dignity makes it unthinkable to question the value of his firm's exotic and often useless remedies. He is part of veterinary medicine's colorful but less scientific past. (Chapter 29)

Mr. Bartle and Jasper: Jasper, Mr. Bartle's Dalmatian, is one of many dogs to die when a rash of strychnine poisonings hits Darrowby. (Chapter 16)

Mr. and Mrs. Ronald Beresford and Coco: The Beresfords' spaniel Coco howls sharply and steadily when riding in a car. Jim gives Coco Mr. Barge's miracle sedative to quiet the dog on a long car trip before he discovers that it doesn't work. Since the Beresfords are cold and unfriendly people, the torturing howls seem like a form of poetic justice. (Chapter 29)

Ralph Beamish and Almira: Beamish, an arrogant racehorse trainer, places more value on appearances than competence. Because Jim is not part of the horse crowd, Beamish ignores his diagnoses until Jim saves the best horse in the stable, Almira. (Chapter 11)

Mrs. Beck and Georgina: A healthy and probably wealthy woman, Mrs. Beck plays the role of poor widow to take advantage of people. Jim experiences her sharp dealing and miserliness when he spays her repulsive cat Georgina. (Chapter 17)

Benny the collie: To the dismay of four small children and their parents, a swallowed rubber ball has cut off their collie Benny's breathing. When Jim removes the ball and brings Benny back to life, he sees the difference he has made for Benny and the dog's appreciative family as so satisfying that it makes up for the drawbacks of being a vet. (Chapter 7)

Ken Billings: A skilled, careful farmer with two enthusiastic teenage sons, Ken Billings has always had unusually healthy calves until his new ones start dying from apparent poisoning. Ken's well-intentioned use of a new, easier dehorning preparation has produced these deadly results, because the calves are accidentally losing their poison-coated scabs in their food. In the context of Jim's well-intentioned but disappointing service in the RAF, Herriot interweaves the accounts of Ken's situation and of Tristan's similarly disastrous efforts to find easier ways to handle his temporary cooking duties. The unintended poisonings in Chapter 6 also anticipate the malicious poisonings in Chapter 16. (Chapter 6)

Wesley Binks and Duke: A juvenile delinquent who plagues Jim with pranks, Wes turns out to be a neglected and unloved child with the potential to lead a reformed and respectable life. His dog Duke makes the difference. Duke puts Wes into a loving relationship for the first time, and Duke's dependency in his sickness introduces Wes to responsibility. Where all efforts to reform him had failed, Wesley's own desire to help Duke succeeds in making him a model citizen who stays out of trouble and earns money for the medicine and food to restore Duke's health. With Duke's death, however, Wesley's efforts seem to have led only to another rejection. Wes returns to a life of steadily worsening delinquency. In Wesley's brief reform, Jim recognizes how deeply the dependency and love of an animal—if not of another person—can touch and motivate people for the better. More generally, he recognizes how being needed can bring out the best in people. Wesley's example suggests something of Jim's own reasons for entering the RAF, his satisfaction as a vet in restoring dying animals to life, and the pivotal factor in the situations of Paul Cotterell and Andrew Vine. (Chapter 5)

Mr. and Mrs. Birdwhistle, Len Birdwhistle, and Nellie: The Birdwhistles all talk at once, each about his or her own individual interest, producing a very stressful experience for anyone visiting them. Jim has a difficult time with them when he saves their cow Nellie from death by removing her arthritic foot. (Chapter 32)

Mr. Blackburn: Owner of a modern, antiseptic dairy farm, Mr. Blackburn leads a hectic life meeting the inflexible time schedule of the drivers who collect milk for the com.nercial dairies. Jim is reassured to find that, although farming is changing, Mr. Blackburn retains the qualities that Jim has always admired in Yorkshire farmers. (Chapter 36)

Flight Sergeant Blackett: A senior officer at Scarborough with a reputation as a stern disciplinarian, Blackett is revealed as unexpectedly human and kind when he offers Jim hearty congratulations on Jimmy's birth, smiles, and speaks of sadly missing his own three children. (Chapter 13)

Blossom the cow: See *Mr. Dakin and Blossom the cow.*

Boardman, Mrs. Boardman, and Patch: Boardman, a wounded veteran of World War I, is handyman at Skeldale House. He and his wife lose their dog Patch when a rash of strychnine poisonings hits Darrowby. (Chapter 16; *ACGS*, Chapters 7, 16, 24)

Bobby: Mr. Mount's huge shire gelding, Bobby, has a terrible fungus infection in his hoof. The case becomes a test of Jim's pride and good sense when he seeks Siegfried's help instead of trying to do the impossible by handling it alone. (Chapter 30)

Jack Brinham: One of Jim's friends from the Drovers Arms, Jack loses his dog when a rash of strychnine poisonings hits Darrowby. (Chapter 16)

Nurse Brown of Greenside Nursing Home: A registered professional, Nurse Brown is midwife for the birth of Jim and Helen's son Jimmy. (Chapter 13; *LGMTA*, Chapter 17)

The Butcher, Mr. Grover, and Hector McDarroch: The manner and competence of a dentist can greatly reduce or increase a patient's fear of dentists. Jim traces his fear of dentists to feeling overwhelmed by the display of instruments and the huge size and strength of his pleasant but basically insensitive childhood dentist, Hector McDarroch. In contrast, his Darrowby dentist, Mr. Grover, reduces fear by recognizing it, keeping his instruments out of sight, speaking softly, and taking an extremely gentle approach to patients. Jim's first RAF dentist, the Butcher, is his worst nightmare come true. The Butcher is a Hector McDarroch in size and manner, but without the competence. The feeling of powerlessness behind a typical fear of dentists makes Jim's situation with the Butcher a fitting metaphor for his lost independence as a trainee. The picture of the RAF itself remains mixed, however, since Jim notes that every other dentist he met later in the RAF resembled Mr. Grover. (Chapter 3)

Johnny Clifford and Fergus: In his twenties and blind, Johnny is a model of strength when his Alsatian guide dog Fergus is poisoned. To Jim, guide dogs symbolize the "mutually depending, trusting and loving association between man and animal" (138). Only Fergus survives a rash of dog poisonings. (Chapter 16)

Albert Close and Mick: An old, retired shepherd and his old, retired dog, Albert Close and Mick spend their declining years by the pub fire. Mick is in pain and in danger of going blind from a worsening case of inverted eyelids, but Albert is unable to understand or to pay for an operation. Ted Dobson and the rest of the pub crowd come to Albert and Mick's aid by funding the operation. (Chapter 14)

Mr. Coker: Manager of Hensfield's unlicensed greyhound track, Mr. Coker wants Jim to do a rubber-stamp inspection of the dogs in the races. He is angry when Jim insists on doing the job well and disqualifies several dogs. (Chapter 22)

Paul Cotterell and Theo the pub terrier: Paul Cotterell is a quiet young bachelor who seems well-educated, decisive, and self-assured, although he has been struggling with depression. When his dog Theo dies, Paul feels that he no longer has a reason to continue the struggle and commits suicide. (Chapter 37)

Cromarty: Cromarty is a lanky trainee who is too inhibited to join vigorously in the screaming leap planned for the end of a physical training demonstration. His learning not to hold back when he screams leads to his not holding back until the appointed time. His early scream makes chaos of the demonstration. (Chapter 15)

Mr. Daggett: Living an austere life on a remote, primitive farm, Mr. Daggett regularly declares his stockman Ned Finch's efforts to be nearly useless and begrudges Ned's interest in sharing the meager society of a quiet country pub. (Chapter 46)

Mr. Dakin and Blossom the cow: When Mr. Dakin reluctantly sends good-natured Blossom to market as too old to keep, she turns onto the back path and comes home to her stall. Her return touches Mr. Dakin, who has always considered her a favorite and has already regretted sending her away. He is inspired to give her a new role that will justify her staying while also protecting her sagging udder from further injury. Blossom's story was reprinted in 1988 in an illustrated version for children, entitled *Blossom Comes Home*. (Chapter 1)

David: One of the young people who occasionally accompany Jim to see whether they would like to become a vet, fifteen-year-old David sees the quirky side of the profession that has always delighted Jim instead of seeing the demanding and varied picture that Jim intended. (Chapter 39)

Debbie the cat, Buster the kitten, and Mrs. Ainsworth: Debbie is a stray cat who leads a hard life and appreciates comfort, but is too fearful to stay near people for more than ten minutes at a time. Mrs. Ainsworth's kindness and respect for Debbie's timidity cannot change her, but do win Debbie's trust. When she dies, Debbie leaves her kitten with Mrs. Ainsworth. Buster the kitten grows up to delight her by playing fetch, which her basset hounds are too lethargic to do. Reprinted in 1986 in an illustrated version for children entitled *The Christmas Day Kitten*, the episode presents the human-animal relationship as an exchange of gifts freely given. (Chapter 9)

Desmond (a.k.a. Sammy): Jim draws on his knowledge as a vet to reassure his fellow patient Desmond that the surgery for his embarrassing problem will be minor and not, as his teasers suggest, produce greater embarrassment. (Chapter 40)

Mrs. Dewburn and Sidney: Jim's viewing of Sidney, newborn son of Mrs. Dewburn, the local butcher's wife, reassures him that his newborn son's swollen appearance is normal. (Chapter 13)

Ted Dobson: A cowman, Ted talks the rest of his pub crowd into paying for an operation to cure a pub fixture: old Albert Close's dog Mick. (Chapter 14)

Drill Corporal: Jim resentfully thinks him a sadist when the cheerful, cockney drill corporal insists on breaking in new trainees by pushing them to exercise well beyond their comfort level. Later, the value of being as physically fit as possible makes the drill corporal's efforts seem as helpful and well-intentioned as he claimed. (Chapter 1)

Mr. Duggleby: A cricket fanatic, Mr. Duggleby speaks of the sport so enthusiastically that Jim almost misses the symptoms of foot and mouth disease in his piglets—an oversight that would probably have led to an epidemic and the widespread slaughter of farm animals. Jim finds it a reminder of the value of staying alert in spite of distractions and the lulling effect of routine. (Chapter 45)

Mr. and Mrs. Edwards: Young Shropshire farmers, Mr. and Mrs. Edwards share the same qualities that Jim admires in Yorkshire farmers. They are hospitable, hard-working, and good-humored. When Jim is one of several RAF volunteers helping them with the harvest, he is reminded of the generous, supportive side of human nature. He is also reminded that he can help others best through using his knowledge and experience as a vet. (Chapter 26)

Con Fenton: Con Fenton is a retired farm worker and part-time gardener who admires Cedric's (Mrs. Rumney's boxer) friendliness and high spirits. They make a perfect match, because Con leads an active, outdoor life and has lost his sense of smell. (Chapter 4)

Ned Finch: A small, old farm hand, Ned Finch moves vacantly through a hard, abusive life with an air of expectation. His patient endurance is rewarded when he suddenly finds the appreciation of a good woman, marriage, and comfort in Elsie, who is elderly Miss Tremayne's cook-housekeeper. (Chapter 46)

Gertrude the pig: See *William Hollin, Grandad Hollin, and Gertrude the pig.*

Peter and Marjorie Gillard and Kim: The vacationing Gillards bring their injured Golden Labrador Kim to Stewie Brannan's surgery, where Jim is filling in. Jim uses his skill and his ingenuity to save Kim's broken leg. (Chapters 20–22)

Mr. Gilly: A farmer of fifty, Mr. Gilly suffers from an extreme version of Victorian reluctance to swear or to refer to anything related to sex. His restraint is severely tested when a cow kicks him between the legs. (Chapter 19)

Mr. Grover: See *The Butcher, Mr. Grover, and Hector McDarroch.*

Mrs. Hall: Mrs. Hall's absence to care for her sick sister leaves Tristan filling in for her as housekeeper. (Chapter 6; *ACGS*, Chapter 60)

Hamish: See *Miss Westerman and Hamish.*

Len Hampson: A farmer who always speaks in a shout, Len shouts across the marketplace Jim's failure to cure his hopelessly sick pig. His behavior is in contrast to Elijah Wentworth's whispering Jim's success in curing his bull. (Chapter 23)

Miss Harbottle: Secretary to the Darrowby vets, Miss Harbottle does her job here without a hint of the animosity described in *ACGS*. (Chapters 19, 34; *ACGS*, Chapters 14, 17, 20, 23, 52, 55)

Charles Harcourt: A Divisional Inspector at the Agriculture Ministry who must see that bureaucratic regulations are upheld, Charles Harcourt is also a kind and decent man. His wedding gift to the Herriots of a barometer may have an ironic appropriateness, since Jim has raised Harcourt's blood pressure many times and Harcourt has tried to help Jim handle the pressure of dealing with red tape. (Chapter 34)

William Hollin, Grandad Hollin, and Gertrude the pig: When Mr. Barge's miracle sedative proves ineffective on Gertrude, William's sow, Grandad Hollin provides a folk remedy—beer—that calms her enough to allow her newborn piglets to nurse. (Chapter 29)

Mrs. Holroyd: When Jim replaces Stewie Brannan, Mrs. Holroyd serves as his housekeeper. An elderly widow, she is a good cook but untidy and lazy. She gives Jim telephone messages that are amusingly odd, because she writes them without interest in what they mean. (Chapter 21)

Mr. Hopps and Snowball: Mr. Hopps' Victorian inability to speak of anything related to sex brings Jim to his farm unprepared to treat his cow Snowball for infertility. (Chapter 19)

Lord Hulton and Charlie: Lord Hulton has the winning quality of relating to others as equals. Ignoring his superior status as a peer of the realm, he shares in ordinary farm work with his men. He also relies on his farm foreman Charlie for the name of his favorite medicinal cream, and that reliance is a morale booster for Charlie. His unhappy encounter with the slaughterman is a reminder of how class status (and perhaps military rank similarly) is more commonly used to alienate and oppress people. (Chapter 2; *ELT,* Chapters 21, 22)

Lucy and Emmeline: A victim of false pregnancy, Lucy the poodle is inseparable from Emmeline the squeaking rubber doll, treating the doll as her puppy and even beginning to produce milk. (Chapter 39)

Lydia: A barmaid at the Drovers' Arms, Lydia is one of many surprisingly strong women pursued by Tristan. Their date may be his greatest fiasco. (Chapter 41)

Hector McDarroch: See *The Butcher, Mr. Grover, and Hector McDarroch.*

Teddy McQueen: Old schoolmates, Teddy and Jim have a brief reunion while Teddy, now a doctor, anesthetizes Jim for the operation that results in his discharge from the RAF. (Chapter 40)

Jeff Mallock: Mentioning Mallock's name is the equal of a death sentence for a sick animal. A pleasant man, Mallock is in the business of buying dying and dead farm animals to turn them into animal food or fertilizer. (Chapter 32; *ACGS,* Chapter 28; *ATBB,* Chapter 45)

Mr. Mount and Deborah Mount: Mr. Mount is a huge, powerful man who is very protective of his pretty daughter, Deborah. Tristan's jokes backfire by convincing Mr. Mount to forbid her to see Tristan. (Chapter 30)

Mr. Moverley: Unhappy that one of his Ayreshire cows must be slaughtered for having tuberculosis, Mr. Moverley is frantic when Mallock takes his prize pedigreed Ayreshire instead of the infected cow. The Ministry's nit-picking attention to detail and official procedure seems more reasonable when Jim's vague instructions to Mallock lead him to mistake one Ayreshire for another. (Chapter 34)

Jim Oakley, Mr. Bailes, and Rose the cow: Postman Jim Oakley's folk remedy cures Mr. Bailes' cow Rose of a digestive problem after Jim's efforts fail. Later, recognizing a scientific basis for the remedy, Jim uses it himself. (Chapter 12)

Rory O'Hagan: Castrating pigs makes Rory nervous, especially when Jim's scalpel comes close to his fly as he holds the pigs between his legs. While adding to Rory's discomfort by teasing, Jim slices his own finger. This episode anticipates his contrasting easing of Desmond's discomfort over a similar threat and similar teasing in Chapter 40. (Chapter 7)

Oscar: A cat with a taste for people, Oscar goes wherever people gather and stays until the gathering breaks up. He develops a regular pattern of attendance at evening social meetings. Adopted by Helen as a wounded stray, Oscar eventually is returned to his original owners, Sep Gibbons and family. Oscar's story was reprinted in 1990 in an illustrated version for children, entitled *Oscar, Cat-About-Town.* (Chapter 47)

Kitty Pattison: In charge of the office staff at the Ministry of Agriculture, Kitty sympathizes with Jim's inability to master the details of official forms and procedures. Although she tries to help him whenever possible, she frequently must tell him that her boss, Charles Harcourt the Divisional Inspector, wants to discuss his latest error. (Chapter 34)

Police Constable Phelps: When Jim and Siegfried succeed in saving a good-natured but severely injured stray dog, P.C. Phelps saves the dog from being put down as an unwanted animal by taking him home as a pet for his young daughters. In 1989 this story was reprinted in an illustrated version for children, entitled *The Market Square Dog.* (Chapter 33)

Mr. Potts and Nip: The owner of a Clydesdale that Jim foaled as one of his first cases in Darrowby, Mr. Potts has a bad heart condition that has forced him to retire from farming and to live in a bungalow in town, where he misses the country. Jim meets and chats with him daily when Mr. Potts walks his dog Nip in the open country nearby. After his death, Jim walks Nip in memory of him. (Chapter 42)

PT sergeant: Regulations make Cromarty's physical training sergeant virtually powerless to retaliate against him physically or verbally, as the sergeant's absurdly feeble comment demonstrates. (Chapter 15)

Mr. Rogers of East Farm and Bob Sellars: One of Willie Rogers's cows appears to be a case of false pregnancy until Bob Sellars shows everyone where he saw the cow hide her calf, perhaps as a result of a strong maternal urge to keep this calf with her. (Chapter 39)

Mrs. Rumney and Cedric the boxer: Mrs. Rumney and Cedric are outrageously mismatched. Upper-class Mrs. Rumney resembles the beautiful, other-worldly heroine of a Victorian novel and has a Victorian distaste for speaking of bodily functions. Her dog Cedric is friendly but large, clumsy, and afflicted with chronic, very offensive gas. Jim's trying to change Cedric fails, as does Mrs. Rumney's trying to cope. Together, Cedric and Mrs. Rumney call attention to each other's shortcomings, while a change of situation emphasizes their strengths. Cedric finds happiness in a new life with Con Fenton, and Mrs. Rumney finds happiness in a small white poodle. (Chapter 4)

Sam: As Jim's companion on his rounds, Sam the beagle shares and adds to the enjoyment of Jim's impulsive pauses to enjoy the Yorkshire countryside. (Chapters 2, 23; *ATBB,* Chapters 28, 32; *LGMTA,* Chapter 22)

Jack Sanders, Jingo, and Skipper: Jim sees in Jack Sanders's bullterrier Jingo and corgi Skipper an example of a close bond—a comradeship—between animals. When Jingo dies of a fatal disease, Skipper goes into a decline until a new bullterrier puppy fills the void and gives him a new interest in life. (Chapter 31)

Scottish Corporal: This tough and nearly grotesque example of the stereotypical drill corporal reveals the human being behind that role when, after Jim appeals to their shared Scottish background with his accent and talk of Glasgow sports, he sends him on his way to see Helen instead of turning him in. (Chapter 10)

Shep: Part Alsatian, Shep terrorizes visitors to the Bailes' farm by leaping unseen from behind a wall to bark in the visitor's ear and run away. When he confronts and terrorizes Shep in a moment of anger, Jim realizes that the bark is only a game, not an assault, and regrets his action. (Chapter 12)

Simkin: A regular airman who considers himself better than the recruits, Simkin takes pleasure in telling Jim about the Butcher and boasting about using his insider's knowledge to avoid the same fate. The poetic justice of his being switched to the Butcher is both amusing and a negative judgment on being self-serving. (Chapter 3)

Mr. Sowden of Long Pasture: Mr. Sowden is a typical subsistence farmer who must continue working even when he is so sick with a cold that he should be in bed. (Chapter 28)

Mr. Stokill: Although over seventy, Mr. Stokill still single-handedly runs the farm that he worked as a hired hand for thirty years to buy, after leaving school at twelve. His ruggedness makes twenty-four-year-old Jim feel soft. His practical knowledge based on experience succeeds where Jim's theoretical knowledge from books and education fails. (Chapter 8)

Tessa: As a side effect of her false pregnancy, Mr. Rington's dalmatian Tessa suddenly changes from friendly to vicious. (Chapter 39)

Roddy Travers and Jake: A well-liked traveling handyman and hand, Roddy Travers keeps on the move through Yorkshire with his dog Jake. Roddy lives a simple life close to nature. It appears later that Jake is Roddy's only family and that the simple life may be the result of a refusal to put trust in human beings following an unhappy love affair. (Chapter 44)

Miss Tremayne, Elsie, and Wilberforce: An elderly and arthritic but wealthy lady who has moved to Yorkshire and modernized an old manor, Miss Tremayne has many pets (including her aged cat Wilberforce), a generous nature, and a jovial personality which she shares with her cook-housekeeper Elsie. Miss Tremayne is excited about the prospect of Elsie's marrying Ned Finch and their living with her. (Chapter 46)

Trudy: Trudy is a boxer bitch willing to be mated with Mrs. Rumney's Cedric until he exhausts her patience with his incompetence. (Chapter 4)

Andrew Vine and Digger: Andrew Vine is a shy bachelor devoted to his fox terrier Digger. When Digger begins to go blind, Andrew falls into suicidal depression. Appealing to Andrew's devotion to Digger and reminding him of Digger's need for him to serve as his eyes, Jim succeeds in convincing Andrew to make the effort to continue living. (Chapter 38)

Corporal Weekes: Representing the inefficient side of large organizations and the selfish side of human nature, Corporal Weekes is a negative example of the entrenched bureaucrat: fat, lazy, and more interested in perpetuating inefficiency than in serving the soldiers whose laundry and boot repairs he oversees. (Chapter 43)

Elijah Wentworth: A farmer who always speaks in a whisper, Elijah whispers into Jim's ear about the cure of his bull, in contrast to Len Hampson's shouting Jim's failure across the marketplace. (Chapter 23)

Miss Westerman and Hamish: A formidable retired schoolteacher, Miss Wester-man dotes on her Scottish terrier Hamish, who is left in Tristan's care after an operation. Tristan's effort to outsmart Siegfried by combining a date with his babysitting duty produces a series of mishaps, the loss of Hamish, and a rare opportunity for Jim to play a practical joke on Tristan after finding Hamish. (Chapter 41)

Appendix D
Other Characters in *The Lord God Made Them All*

The stories in *The Lord God Made Them All* frequently call attention to the values underlying the characters' actions and lifestyles. A survey of notable characters from individual chapters shows Herriot's interest in human affection, generosity, and nurturing relationships as well as in contrasts between public image and personality.

Amber: A honey-colored, mixed-breed, stray dog who wins Jim's affection as he tries to treat her for a nearly incurable, often fatal skin disease. Amber's case demonstrates both that the vet's professional detachment is an ideal rather than a reality and that human affection and pride can be powerfully irrational forces. In putting down Amber before her suffering increases, Jim must come to terms with losing her and with his failure to save her. (Chapter 15)

Josh Anderson and Venus: A sensitive man who takes pride in his ability as a barber and has a fondness for beer, Josh Anderson is so well-liked that his customers endure his flair for painfully pulling hair out while cutting it. Josh and his wife have adopted Venus, a long-haired dog, to replace their grown children. When, under anesthesia for a minor operation, Venus dies and is revived with the extreme measure of being swung through the air, Jim decides to save Josh the anguish of knowing that detail. But Jim has a scare first when Josh, stroking Venus, speaks of her floating through the air and later when Josh tells Jim, while cutting his hair, that he can sense people's thoughts through their hair. (Chapter 13)

Walt Barnett and Fred the cat: The richest man in Darrowby, Walt Barnett is a hard, unsmiling, ruthless man whose life is ruled by profit. In spite of having a grudge against Siegfried because of an overcharge years earlier, Barnett calls Jim to see a cat that he has adopted, suggesting a touch of human warmth and concern entirely out of character. Someone has tried to attack Barnett by attacking his cat Fred. A year after the second attack, a suspected poisoning attempt turns out to be a fatal virus. When Fred dies, Barnett briefly breaks into tears, lamenting the loss of his only friend, before quickly retreating behind his cold facade. (Chapter 31; *ATBB,* Chapter 40)

Norman Beaumont: A veterinary student seeing practice with Jim, Norman enjoys cultivating the image of a dignified, well-established professional. He is plump, gently humorous, eager to display his knowledge of literary quotations, and determined to master pipe smoking. Norman's pretentions take a dangerous turn when he gives the impression of having expertise in doing cesarean sections only to reveal his limited knowledge while Jim is relying on his guidance to do one. (Chapter 8)

Bella: By miraculously surviving Jim's fumbling first cesarean operation on a cow, Bella turns a scare into a success, living to have eight more calves. (Chapter 8)

Mr. Biggins: A difficult farmer, Mr. Biggins rarely decides to spend money on a vet before his animals are beyond help, and he routinely resists the advised treatment. The vets succeed only once with Mr. Biggins, when Siegfried tricks him into giving his cow the prescribed treatment. (Chapter 19)

Mr. Binns: Mr Binns's wild Galloway cow nearly tramples Jim's three-year-old daughter Rosie, creating first a moment of overwhelming horror for both father and daughter and then intense relief. (Chapter 22)

Captain Birch: The tall, dark captain of the ancient Globemaster plane on Jim's Turkish trip has a commanding presence equal to that of shorter, older Captain Rasmussen on Jim's Russian voyage. (Chapters 29, 32, 35)

Mr. Bogg: Mr. Bogg is so extremely frugal that he even counts pills to see how many less he received than the full thousand he paid for. (Chapter 28)

Bramble the cow: When Jim cures Jack Scott's cow Bramble of a brain disease, she continues to move helplessly in circles from apparent brain damage. Miraculously, Bramble slowly recovers normal movement over the next two years, until only an occasional, slight twitch similar to a silent film star's seductive look remains. The twitch makes such an impression on Brigadier Rowan that he awards her first place in the cattle show. (Chapter 27)

Brandy the Golden Labrador: See *Mrs. Westley and Brandy the Golden Labrador.*

Lionel Brough: A roadman and part-time farmer who keeps an odd assortment of animals in makeshift quarters, Lionel Brough decides to use an inheritance to go into modern, large-scale pig raising. After finding it so much work that he can no longer enjoy the animals and after the stress of nearly losing everything first to swine fever and then to salt poisoning, Lionel turns the pig business over to a younger man and returns to enjoying his old type of farming. Lionel exemplifies the wisdom of choosing happiness over success. (Chapter 37)

Nurse Brown and Cliff Brown: Darrowby's midwife, Nurse Brown has neither forgotten nor forgiven Jim's behavior on the birth of his son, although she treats him kindly on the birth of his daughter and laughs with Helen over his behavior. Her husband Cliff, a big truck driver, is extremely kind and supportive to Jim when Helen goes upstairs at Greenside Nursing Home to deliver. (Chapter 17; *ATWW*, Chapter 13)

Andrew Bruce: An old school friend of Jim's, Andrew Bruce has become a banker in Glasgow, but he feels attracted to the country and asks to accompany Jim on a call. An unusually gory dehorning of huge bullocks at the Dunning farm cures Andrew of any desire to change his job. (Chapter 33)

Mr. Bushel: Mr. Bushel's deafness encourages Jim to ask Norman Beaumont to guide him through a cesarean operation on the farmer's cow. (Chapter 8)

Mr. Casling and his sons, Alan and Harold: The Caslings are nice but rugged, unsmiling men who farm an isolated moor top. Their failure to recognize George Bernard Shaw as a famous playwright and their focus on local matters reminds Jim that fame matters little to people concerned with the challenges of living. (Chapter 23)

Grandma Clarke: In her late eighties, the product of a hard life of farming, Grandma Clarke is now content in her son Matt's farm kitchen. She seems to Jim a vision of goodness, security, faith, and age-old truth. He finds deep truth in her statement that the best time in life is when one's children are young. (Chapter 38)

Humphrey Cobb and Myrtle: Consumed with guilt every time he leaves his beagle Myrtle at home to spend the day drinking and gambling, Humphrey Cobb imagines that she is seriously ill and calls Jim late at night to save her. The situation becomes an example of the complex relationship between human and animal, as well as between vet and client. Jim finds himself responding to Humphrey's need for emotional support, and experiences a feeling of guilt similar to Humphrey's when he treats as another false alarm the only occasion when Myrtle really is sick. (Chapter 2)

John Crooks: Siegfried and Jim's assistant from 1951 to 1954, John Crooks remains a friend after setting up his own practice in Beverley. John talks Jim into taking trips to Russia and Turkey as veterinary attendant to animals being exported from Britain. Jim's promise to speak later about John's assistant days is not fulfilled here but in his last book. (Chapters 4, 29; *ELT*, Chapters 10, 11, 15)

Mrs. Cundall, Ron Cundall, and Herman: Their dachshund Herman provides comfort to invalid Ron Cundall, paralyzed in a mining accident, and his wife. The Cundalls find it very discouraging when Herman develops a back problem and paralysis resembling Ron's, and they finally turn to a harmless quack remedy. Jim refuses to destroy their hope by arguing against its effectiveness, because he is concerned about the well-being both of owners and pets. (Chapter 25)

Ronald Derrick and Mrs. Derrick: Young city people enjoying country life, the Derricks meet a new type of disaster when her goat eats all of Ronald's prized tomatoes, leaving only stalks. (Chapter 28)

Mr. Dunning and his sons, Thomas, James, and William: Mr. Dunning is a small, excitable farmer who regularly speaks in a shout, while his three sons are large, placid men. Mr. Dunning is repaid for his disruptive antics of the afternoon when the last of his bullocks chases him around the farm yard without interference from his sons. (Chapter 33)

Ed and Dave: The copilot and the engineer on Jim's Turkish trip are cheerful Americans in their twenties, who seem to be casual and carefree in their life of travel. (Chapters 29, 32, 35)

Alan and Janet Farnon: Siegfried's young children, Alan and Janet, are very close to their father, accompanying him on calls as Jimmy and Rosie accompany Jim. (Chapter 38)

Fred the cat: See *Walt Barnett and Fred the cat.*

Mr. Garrett: Usually solemn and silent, Mr. Garrett sympathizes from the heart with Jim as one father to another, and agrees that parents need strong nerves. (Chapter 5)

George the bull: Jack Scott's loving treatment has turned George, a bull of dangerous size and power, into a nuzzling, affectionate pet. (Chapter 27)

P.C. Hubert Goole: Despite his reputation for sternly going by the book, Police Constable Goole is drawn into participating in the after-hours party in the cellar of the Black Horse. Goole's affection for his Yorkshire terrier softens him. After several drinks, Goole surprisingly becomes aggressive and noisily resentful of his superiors for passing him over for promotion. (Chapter 17)

Miss Grantley and Tina: Beautiful, unmarried, young Miss Grantley seems to be happy devoting her attention to raising goats, preferring this career to marriage. Although her impression of professional concern and competence determines which vet receives her periodic sample of goat droppings for analysis, the vets (still bachelors at the time) view the droppings as a token of regard in romantic terms. Jim repairs her goat Tina's torn shoulder. (Chapter 11)

Mr. Hammond: Siegfried's test drive of a used car also becomes a test of Mr. Hammond's ability to stay calm under any circumstances. The garage owner, although terrified, manages to maintain his reputation, but decides not to risk it on a second test drive. (Chapter 3)

Peter Hansen: Dark in appearance, the engineer on Jim's voyage to Russia has a ready sense of humor. (Chapter 7, 24)

Wally Hartley: When Wally Hartley wants his new Ayrshire bull's fertility tested, a series of comic misunderstandings and errors follows. (Chapter 26)

Clem and Dick Hudson, Herbert, and George Forsyth: When insurance agent George Forsyth finally succeeds in selling accident insurance to the Hudson brothers and their hired man Herbert, a string of accidents and insurance settlements follow. It seems that the hard-working farmers have discovered that injuries can pay better than farming. (Chapter 20)

Igor: A Mongolian Russian forced to fight for Germany in World War II, Igor is one of many prisoners of war working on Yorkshire farms. Igor's part in a farmer's joke humanizes the POWs as ordinary people rather than threats to anyone. Igor also serves to personalize Jim's later observation that many of the Russian POWs returned home to imprisonment and death. (Chapter 6)

Jumbo: The youngest seaman on Jim's voyage to Russia, seventeen-year-old Jumbo resembles a large Viking. Jim finds that the youngest member of the crew is always called "Jumbo," just as the mess boy is always called "Peter," regardless of their real names. This anonymity gives both characters an abstract quality. (Chapter 18)

Bert Kealey, Tess Kealey, and Polly the pig: Bert Kealey demonstrates how far loving parents will go for their children. To save his eight-year-old daughter Tess from heartbreak over the death of her pig Polly's newborn piglets, the young farmer steels himself to the disagreeable task of regularly stimulating Polly's milk production by internal manipulation until the piglets are old enough to be bottlefed. (Chapter 16)

Albert Kenning: When Siegfried overenthusiastically tests hedge-clippers on the bamboo stakes Albert Kenning, an ironmonger, is holding for him, Kenning fears the loss of his fingers in making the sale. (Chapter 33)

Miss Livingstone and Miss Mullion: Nine-year-old Jimmy's piano teacher, Miss Livingstone, is a pleasant lady in her fifties who exhibits infinite patience with her students. Miss Mullion, who runs Jimmy's school, recognizes Jimmy's performance at the piano recital as typical of him. (Chapter 30)

Luigi: An Italian prisoner of war working on Mr. Harrison's farm, Luigi demonstrates a remarkable ability to subdue a bad-tempered bull mainly by force of his commanding personality. (Chapter 6)

Robert Maxwell: When Jim inadvertently kills Robert Maxwell's cow while curing its foot infection, Maxwell gives Jim a lesson in responding magnanimously to people whose failings have unintentionally caused him harm. (Chapter 10)

Mr. and Mrs. Meynell: The Meynells' reaction to Jim's wearing shorts on a call combines humor with the certainty that expected community standards for dress and behavior must be maintained. (Chapter 28)

Myrtle: See *Humphrey Cobb and Myrtle.*

Noel and Joe: Two Jersey farmers who accompany Jim and their pedigree cattle on the flight to Turkey. Noel, in his thirties, is a pleasant fellow. Joe, in his forties, is tougher at the core and successfully crushes the Turkish vets' refusal to accept one of the cows on a technicality. Joe's quest for a beer lands the three at a Turkish wedding reception. (Chapters 29, 32, 35)

Peter the mess boy: All mess boys, as the captain on Jim's voyage to Russia mentions, are called Peter. This anonymous seventeen-year-old, who is pleasant and subject to seasickness, could be the essence of any youth. (Chapters 7, 12)

Polly the pig: See *Bert Kealey, Tess Kealey, and Polly the pig.*

Hal Preston: Hal Preston has four big, smiling, polite, German prisoners of war helping him on his farm. Their example helps to humanize the POWs, separating the Germans from their negative wartime image as enemy soldiers. (Chapter 6)

Carl Rasmussen: The mate on Jim's voyage to Russia shares the captain's last name, although he is no relation. Carl Rasmussen outdoes everyone in eating. He is plump, reliable, and impressively confident in the captain. (Chapters 7, 18, 21, 24)

Rip the sheep dog: When accidents leave Jack Scott's sheep dog Rip with a paralyzed leg and then a permanently broken leg on the same side, Jack insists on giving him a chance instead of putting him down. Rip somehow manages to run and continue happily bringing the cows in for milking. (Chapter 27)

Mr. Ripley: An extreme procrastination—or laziness—is Mr. Ripley's dominant characteristic. Despite the farmer's promises to change, he has repeatedly presented Jim with the same aggravations. Jim finds reassurance, however, in encountering the familiar aggravations after his time in the RAF. Concerned about feeling at home again in Yorkshire after the war, Jim sees in Mr. Ripley's remaining aggravatingly true to form a reminder of the unchanging essence of Yorkshire, and responds with laughter instead of outrage. (Chapter 1)

Sister Rose: On limited funds, Sister Rose operates a dog shelter behind her house, taking in strays and finding them homes. (Chapter 15; *ELT*, Chapters 47, 49)

Brigadier Rowan: Former soldier, gentleman farmer, drinker, and cattle judge, Brigadier Rowan is so startled to recognize, in Bramble the cow's twitch, the look of someone he once knew that he ultimately awards Bramble first place at the cattle show. (Chapter 27)

Rupe and Will Rowney: Bachelor brothers who do not get along although they run a dairy farm together, the Rowneys even have two different sets of names for their cows. (Chapter 28)

Ruffles and Muffles: The Whithorn's two spoiled and vicious dogs, Ruffles and Muffles, are West Highland Whites, a usually docile breed. Two pleasant puppies of the same breed replace the original Ruffles and Muffles when they die, but the puppies soon become equally vicious, proving that upbringing makes the difference. (Chapter 36)

Sam: Jim's dog Sam continues to accompany him and now Rosie on calls. (Chapter 22; *ATBB*, Chapters 28, 32; *ATWW*, Chapters 2, 23)

Jack Scott: Thin, pale, and gaunt at forty, Jack Scott treats every animal on his farm with affection, which they usually return. He is so full of love that no animal is ever put down just because its condition is unprofitable; Jack gives every animal an opportunity to live. They generally do surprisingly well, as Rip his sheep dog, George the bull, and Bramble the cow among others demonstrate. (Chapter 27)

Alex Taylor: Jim's oldest friend, Alex Taylor, started school with him in Glasgow at four years old. He moves to Darrowby after he too falls in love with Yorkshire during a visit following the war. (Chapter 17; *ATWW*, Chapter 26)

Mr. Thackeray: Four-year-old Jimmy is as impressed with Mr. Thackeray's extraordinary height of 6'7" as he is with the strength of the compact Dales farmers. (Chapter 5)

Tina: See *Miss Grantley and Tina.*

Venus: See *Josh Anderson and Venus.*

Jeff Ward, Mrs. Ward, and Margaret Ward: Jeff Ward and his wife show why parents need nerves of steel, suffering as their daughter Margaret tries repeatedly to correct her mistake and finish her piece at the piano recital. (Chapter 30)

Mrs. Westley and Brandy the Golden Labrador: Mrs. Westley's Golden Labrador is a loving playmate for her four children, diving into the river with them to swim. But Brandy has a taste for finding cans in the trash and getting his tongue stuck in them; he also keeps trying to back onto Mrs. Westley's lap, where he was nursed as a tiny puppy. The Westleys regret complaining about these annoyances when Brandy barely survives pneumonia and is left a weakened, lethargic animal. Then, almost a year later, they rejoice when Brandy suddenly recovers his strength and his interest in cans and laps. (Chapter 34)

Mr. and Mrs. Whithorn: The Whithorns make their dogs insecure and vicious by showering them with an overindulgent love and no firm direction. Jim finds in their negative example food for thought about the proper raising of children as well as animals. (Chapter 36)

Reg Wilkey: Jim and his friends celebrate Rosie's birth in alcoholic, male camaraderie at the Black Horse, where Reg Wilkey, the landlord, agrees to let the party continue illegally in the cellar well beyond closing hours. (Chapter 17)

Appendix E
Other Characters in *Every Living Thing*

The stories in *Every Living Thing* emphasize the importance of penetrating surface appearances and impressions to distinguish underlying truths. A survey of notable characters from individual chapters shows Herriot's interest in calling attention to relationship-centered values as fundamentally important to achieving happiness in life.

Anna and Maggie: Calum Buchanan's menagerie begins to grow when he brings Anna and Maggie, his two Doberman Pinshers, to Skeldale House instead of the one additional dog that Jim persuaded Siegfried to allow. Calum sees Anna and Maggie as gentle, inseparable friends, but Siegfried sees them as threatening and soon finds himself under attack. (Chapters 33, 39)

Mrs. Bartram and Puppy: Huge Mrs. Bartram and her huge dog Puppy look placid but potentially threatening. In fact, Puppy is quite belligerent. He also surprises Jim and Siegfried by taking no interest in beef (unlike most dogs). Fish and chips are his and Mrs. Bartram's exclusive diet. (Chapter 2)

Alan Beech: A farmer friend of Calum Buchanan, Alan Beech tells Jim of Calum's move from Nova Scotia to Papua New Guinea. (Chapter 51)

Mr. Bendelow and Blanco: An expert tailor and procrastinator, Mr. Bendelow may view mending jobs as beneath his ability. He seems to spend his days talking instead of working, and his enormous, white dog Blanco helps him to turn away customers who become threatening over his delays. Blanco sometimes gets pins in his feet, but is good-natured about having them removed. Blanco's mysterious lethargy affects the tailor as badly as Alfred's decline affects Geoffrey Hatfield, until Jim discovers the hidden source of Blanco's condition. (Chapters 5, 6, 19)

Granville Bennett. A small animal specialist, Bennett has taken care of spaying operations and problem cases for Jim until Calum convinces Jim to begin doing them himself. (Chapters 22, 49; *BB,* Chapters 16, 17, 23, 24, 36, 37; *WW,* Chapter 24)

Bill the badger: Calum's third badger, Bill, arrives quietly, to avoid upsetting Siegfried over the rapid expansion of Calum's menagerie. (Chapter 39)

George Birrell, Grandma Marjorie Birrell, and Lucy Birrell: Grandma Birrell and four-year-old Lucy always pamper Jim with new soap and a good towel, in contrast to what he finds at other farms. When Lucy carries on after Grandma's death, Jim sees Rosie and himself in Lucy and her father George. (Chapter 20)

The Birses and Jet: The Birses have lost interest in their family dog, Jet. They are entirely wrapped up in watching television during Jim's visit. Later, they neglect to give Jet the medicinal bath necessary to cure his mange and think about putting him down instead of bothering to bathe him. Their attitude contrasts shaply with that of the Howells and the Farrows. (Chapter 34)

Denny Boynton: Small, strong, and an expert blacksmith, Denny Boynton fearlessly handles the largest and most difficult horses. But all dogs terrify him, even Farmer Hickson's ancient sheep dog Zak. (Chapter 17)

Arnold Braithwaite and Bouncer: A retired builder, Arnold loves his diabetic dog Bouncer and telling stories of knowing major sports figures. His stories seem fictional, but he surprisingly passes a test of their truth. (Chapter 26)

Nat Briggs: After Jim accidentally injects Nat Briggs with abortion vaccine, the big, surly farm worker and newlywed becomes convinced that Jim's mistake will prevent him from having a family. Later, Jim accidentally injects him again. When Nat's wife has twins a year later, his coworkers joke that the second shot was the antidote for the first. (Chapter 41)

Sir Henry Brookly and Lord Darbrough: Influential members of the Milk Committee ruling on Ted Newcombe's T. T. license, Brookly and Darbrough prove that appearances can be persuasive when the quality of Jim's suit and his apparent effort on Ted's behalf win their approval of the license. (Chapter 6)

Mr. Busby and Dandy: Although he originally argues that the monetary value of farm animals makes them more important than pets, Mr. Busby reverses himself when his pet dog Dandy is hurt. His reversal suggests that what Mr. Busby really wants is for his animals to have priority treatment. (Chapter 35)

Mr. Bush: A gloomy farmer, Mr. Bush reacts to the miraculous cure of a litter of dying piglets by complaining about their small size. (Chapter 37)

Mr. Chandler and Don: Old Mr. Chandler's only companion, Don, is an aged dog with a very bad heart. Since Don could go at any time, Jim assumes that Don is dying when Mr. Chandler telephones, but he is surprised to find that his help is wanted with the television instead. (Chapter 28)

Mrs. Coates and Wolfie: Mrs. Coates's dog Wolfie has the contradictory habit of wagging and growling at the same time, catching people off guard. (Chapter 16)

Mr. and Mrs. Colwell and Roopy: The Colwells and their dog Roopy are pleasant and friendly, but their house is extremely dirty and heavily infested with fleas. Jim thought that the gas man's warning was crazy until he found himself covered with fleas after visiting the Colwells. (Chapter 48)

Basil Courtenay: A young father of seven, Basil has a touch of exotic elegance and a gift for conversation that make him seem an unlikely farmer, although he has taken a farming job to feed his family. Basil seems to be handling his job, but Jim discovers that he is not really caring for some sick calves and that he knows farming is not for him. Later Jim learns by chance that Basil has found a job that fits his appearance and conversational skill—as a fancy waiter. (Chapter 29)

Sep Craggs: As rude and aggressive as Major Sykes, Sep Craggs is one of the people whose facade John Crooks is able to get through. (Chapter 10)

Danny, Bert, Hughie, and Joe: Lord Gresham's farm men are unimpressed by Jim's veterinary successes, but they gain great respect for him as a winner of football pools. (Chapter 37)

Mr. Dawson: Everything Jim does becomes miraculously successful in Mr. Dawson's eyes, so much so that Jim wonders if the stories are true. (Chapter 13)

Dinah: Another beagle, Dinah, has succeeded Sam as Jim's companion on calls and on soothing walks in the countryside. Fat and friendly, Dinah makes a hobby of barking at farm dogs from the safety of Jim's car. (Chapters 2, 18, 23, 27, 42)

Mrs. Dryden and Sooty: When Jim treats her cat Sooty, he learns that Mrs. Dryden is selling her house. Bidding for it at auction proves a very negative experience for him, but is very beneficial to Mrs. Dryden. (Chapter 12)

Mr. and Mrs. Farrow: Unlike the Birses, the Farrows and their son welcome Jim warmly and carefully nurse their sick farm animals back to health. (Chapter 34)

Dick Fawcett and Frisk: The cat's mysterious bouts of unconsciousness are explained when Jim realizes that Frisk has been finishing the leftovers from Dick's nightly dose of medicine. (Chapter 14)

Mrs. Fetherstone and Rollo: Jim believes that he has insulted rich, domineering Mrs. Featherstone while under the influence of a brucellosis attack. But, to his surprise, he has unintentionally helped her to see the foolishness of her insisting that her little poodle Rollo be treated for imaginary ailments. (Chapter 9)

Mrs. Gardiner and William: Mrs. Gardiner's terrier William breaks his leg jumping over the garden gate. (Chapter 35)

Jeb and Josh Hardwick: The Hardwick brothers and their wives become convinced that Jim is crazy. In contrast to his experience at Mr. Dawson's farm, everything always seems to go wrong for Jim at the Hardwick farm. (Chapter 27)

Geoffrey Hatfield, Mrs. Hatfield, and Alfred: The confectioner's display of wholehearted devotion to providing exactly the right candy for every customer is the secret of his success, making both his candy and the act of buying it seem special.

His salesmanship is more than an act. It disappears along with his enthusiasm for life when Alfred, his cat and companion in the shop, begins to waste away, and returns when Alfred recovers. (Chapter 3)

William Hawley: Siegfried is as much a miracle worker to old William Hawley as Jim is to Mr. Dawson. William is disappointed when Siegfried, after asking for string, uses it to tie his coat closed instead of to work a miraculous cure. (Chapter 31)

Hodgkin: Mrs. Pumphrey's gloomy, dog-hating, Scottish gardener in charge of exercising Tricki Woo has become too arthritic to continue that activity without complaint. Jim suggests the obvious solution of reducing the exercise to fit the advancing age of both man and dog. (Chapter 4; *ACGS*, Chapters 13, 33)

Miles Horsley: An expert dairyman, Miles Horsley recognizes a fellow perfectionist in Calum Buchanan. (Chapter 15)

Mr. and Mrs. Howell: The Birses' elderly neighbors, the Howells, take over bathing Jet because they like him and know he will be neglected. They convince the Birses to give them Jet by offering to pay his vet bill. (Chapter 34)

Lord Hulton, Marquis of Hulton: Lord Hulton appears briefly when a gale has ruined the gable of Jim's unfinished house. (Chapters 21, 22; *ATWW*, Chapter 2)

Cornelius Ireson: A wealthy industrialist, Cornelius looks physically like his brother Eugene, but, contrary to him, is unsmiling, arrogant, and ruthless. He inherited the family business and wealth. (Chapter 40)

Eugene Ireson and Emily: Oxford-educated and unworldly, Eugene traveled the world before returning to Yorkshire to live simply in a squatter's shack. His brother Cornelius inherited the family fortune, but Eugene is happy living simply with his cat Emily and reading. Tiny Emily produces a huge kitten. (Chapter 40)

Kelly the badger: Calum acquires Kelly as a companion for Marilyn, because he believes that human companionship is not as good a cure for loneliness as another animal of the same species. Later, Jim takes a different view with Ginny. (Chapter 22)

Mr. Kettlewell: Jim and Mr. Kettlewell leap to opposite, equally mistaken conclusions when the farmer's draft horse collapses in a faint after an injection. Jim assumes in horror that the horse is dying and agonizes over how to explain causing the death. The farmer assumes the medicine has unusually powerful side effects. (Chapter 1)

Harry Lumsden: Hugo Mottram's assistant looks very young, but he acts with pluck and loyalty under difficult circumstances. (Chapter 8)

Marilyn the badger: Calum Buchanan's badger travels everywhere with him, giving people qualms until they get to know Calum. (Chapters 15, 18, 22, 39)

Molly Minican and Robbie: Jim's elderly neighbor, Molly, dies shortly after Jim's two years of efforts to cure her dog Robbie of attacks of rigor end in failure. Although Jim is convinced that Molly thought less of him for failing, he discovers that Molly considered him one of her heroes for trying so persistently. (Chapter 47)

Bob and Elizabeth Mollison: Young architects, the Mollisons help the Herriots to design and build a small house that is right for them. (Chapter 21)

Mortimer the monkey: When Diana Thurston's monkey joins Calum's menagerie while she is away, Siegfried accepts it because her father is a big client. (Chapter 39)

Hugo Mottram of Scanton and Match Box: Mottram has difficulty with social relationships, treating neighboring vets as rivals instead of colleagues and being hard on his assistant. But Mottram is a better person at heart than he appears. His love for his horse Match Box brings him closer to Siegfried and Jim. (Chapter 8)

Rupe Nellist and Titch: Rupe Nellist, a prosperous grocer, adopts Titch from Sister Rose's shelter because the neglected but good-natured little dog has a limp like his own limp from childhood polio. Once Titch's leg is repaired, he continues to limp for some time out of habit. (Chapter 49)

Ted Newcombe and Clover: Ted is a hard-working hill farmer and father of two, who has made improving his dairy his main hope for earning enough to live. In order to do that, he needs a live calf from his cow Clover, as well as a Tuberculin Tested (T. T.) license so he can sell his milk at a slightly higher price. Jim succeeds in helping Ted get both calf and license. (Chapter 5)

Gobber Newhouse: Darrowby's bullying drunk meets his match in Blanco. (Chapter 19; *ACGS,* Chapters 38, 62)

Herbert Platt: A local trash collector, Herbert provides Jim and Helen with an account of Ollie and Ginny's wild ancestry. (Chapter 44)

Bert Rawlings: When Jim loses a second house at auction, Bert gives him the surprising news that the house has hidden leaks and rot. (Chapter 21)

Sister Rose: An animal lover and a radiologist, Sister Rose runs an animal shelter at her home. (Chapters 47, 49; *LGMTA,* Chapter 15)

The Sidlows: Prosperous farmers, the Sidlows nevertheless view themselves as struggling and everyone else as out to cheat them. Their actions produce confirmation of their views, as when they call vets only as a last resort, once it is too late to help. Motivated in earlier books by their unshakable belief in the black magic of home remedies, here the Sidlows are motivated more strongly by a miserly desire to save money. (Chapter 4; *ACGS,* Chapter 47)

Bob and Adam Stockdale and Meg: Although the bachelor Stockdale brothers have opposite personalities, they live together in harmony with each other and with Bob's dog Meg. (Chapter 50)

Storm: Large and good-natured, Storm is the first of Calum Buchanan's dogs to arrive in Darrowby. (Chapters 15, 39)

Edgar Stott: A know-it-all, Stott tests Calum by asking him to diagnose a healthy cow as a joke, but Stott finds himself tested when Calum jokes that another cow needs an expensive, messy operation. (Chapter 45)

Tim Suggett: Elderly Tim Suggett enjoys letting young Jimmy discover that milking is harder than it looks and offers to teach him later. When Jimmy goes for a lesson without telling his parents, they worry about his safety. (Chapter 7)

Major Sykes: A small, blustering man, Major Sykes is a bully always on the attack. John Crooks pierces this facade with a friendly response. (Chapter 10)

Bernard Wain and Miss Wain: Middle-aged brother and sister, the Wains are opposites. Miss Wain is older, bossy, and fully in charge. Bernard is meek, repulsed by farmyard smells, and useless in his sister's view. Tristan nicknames Bernard the Cisco Kid because he wears a handkerchief mask to keep out smells. (Chapter 36)

Harriet and Felicity Whiting: Jim embarrasses himself when his efforts to kill a flea at a symphony lead him to paw the prominent Whiting sisters. (Chapter 48)

Bibliography

Herriot's works are identified in references by the initial letters of their titles; for example, *JHDS* stands for *James Herriot's Dog Stories*. Page references in the text are to the paperback editions of his five major works published in the United States (*ACGS, ATBB, ATWW, LGMTA, ELT*) and to the hardcover editions of all other versions of his works, including *James Herriot's Yorkshire* (*JHY*). Although the British versions of his works have been reprinted in paperback editions by Pan Books, Ltd., these editions are not available in the United States and, therefore, not included in this bibliography.

WORKS BY JAMES HERRIOT

All Creatures Great and Small. New York: St. Martin's, 1972; Bantam Books, 1973. (Contains *If Only They Could Talk* and *It Shouldn't Happen to a Vet*.)

All Things Bright and Beautiful. New York: St. Martin's, 1974; Bantam Books, 1975. (Contains *Let Sleeping Vets Lie* and *Vet in Harness*.)

All Things Wise and Wonderful. New York: St. Martin's, 1977; Bantam Books, 1978. (Contains *Vets Might Fly* and *Vet in a Spin*.)

(With others) *Animals Tame and Wild*. Comp. and ed. Gilbert Phelps and John Phelps. New York: Sterling, 1979. Rpt. as *Animal Stories: Tame and Wild*. New York: Sterling, 1985. Rpt. as *Between Man and Beast: True Tales and Observations of the Animal Kingdom*. New York: Bonanza, 1989.

The Best of James Herriot: Favorite Memories of a Country Vet. New York: St. Martin's, 1982; Pleasantville, N.Y.: Reader's Digest Association, 1982.

Blossom Comes Home. Illus. by Ruth Brown. New York: St. Martin's, 1988.

Bonny's Big Day. Illus. by Ruth Brown. New York: St. Martin's, 1987.

The Christmas Day Kitten. Illus. by Ruth Brown. New York: St. Martin's, 1986.

Every Living Thing. New York: St. Martin's, 1992.

If Only They Could Talk. London: M. Joseph, 1970.

It Shouldn't Happen to a Vet. London: M. Joseph, 1972.

James Herriot's Cat Stories. New York: St. Martin's, 1994.

James Herriot's Dog Stories. New York: St. Martin's, 1986.

James Herriot's Treasury for Children. Illus. by Ruth Brown and Peter Barrett. New York: St. Martin's, 1992.

James Herriot's Yorkshire. New York: St. Martin's, 1979; Bantam Books, 1982.

Let Sleeping Vets Lie. London: M. Joseph, 1973.

The Lord God Made Them All. New York: St. Martin's, 1981; Bantam Books, 1982.

The Market Square Dog. Illus. by Ruth Brown. New York: St. Martin's, 1989.

Moses the Kitten. Illus. by Peter Barrett. New York: St. Martin's, 1984.

Only One Woof. Illus. by Peter Barrett. New York: St. Martin's, 1985.

Oscar, Cat-About-Town. Illus. by Ruth Brown. New York: St. Martin's, 1990.

Smudge, the Little Lost Lamb. Illus. by Ruth Brown. New York: St. Martin's, 1991. (Also published as *Smudge's Day Out.* London: M. Joseph, 1991).

Vet in a Spin. London: M. Joseph, 1977.

Vet in Harness. London: M. Joseph, 1974.

Vets Might Fly. London: M. Joseph, 1976.

WORKS ABOUT JAMES HERRIOT

"AMVA Award of Appreciation Given to British Veterinarian-Author." *Journal of the American Veterinary Medical Association,* 167 (1975): 703–704.

"A Bad Ewe-Turn: Author-veterinarian James Herriot Falls Victim to a Surprise Sheep Attack." *People Weekly,* 18 July 1994: 47.

"Best-Selling British Writer James Herriot Dies at 78." *Washington Post,* 24 February 1995: B4.

Brower, Monty. "Long a Success as 'James Herriot,' Yorkshire Vet Jim Wight Says *All Things* Must Come to an End." *People,* 18 March 1985: 91+.

Del Balso, Suzanne. "The Wise, Wonderful World of the Real James Herriot." *Good Housekeeping,* March 1979: 148+.

Dowling, Claudia Glenn. "Life Visits Herriot Country." *Life,* March 1988: 66–69.

Dudar, Helen. "Herriot Finds All Things Brighter—By $3 Million." *Chicago Tribune,* 10 May 1981, sec. 7:2.

"Famed Veterinarian-Author Herriot Visits AMVA." *Journal of the American Veterinary Medical Association,* 166 (1974): 257.

Green, Timothy. "Best-selling Vet Practices As Usual." *Smithsonian,* November 1974: 90+.

Hornsby, Michael. "James Herriot, the World's Most Famous Vet, Dies." *The Times* [London], 24 February 1995: 1–2.

"James Herriot." Obituary. *The Times* [London], 24 February 1995: 21.

Lilliston, Lynn. "Best-Selling Vet Preaches What He Practices." *Los Angeles Times*, 5 December 1973, sec. IV: 1+.

Moorehead, Caroline. "How a Country Vet Turned into a Best Seller." *The Times* [London], 23 July 1976: 12.

"Recovering." *Time*, 18 July 1994: 15.

Roy, Joy N. "Bibliotherapy: An Important Service to Self." *English Journal*, 68 (March 1979): 57–62.

Sternlicht, Sanford. *All Things Herriot: James Herriot and His Peaceable Kingdom.* Syracuse, N.Y.: Syracuse University Press, 1995.

Tabor, Mary B. W. "James Herriot, 78, Writer Dies; Animal Stories Charmed People." *New York Times*, 24 February 1995: A19.

Woods, Audrey. "James Herriot, Veterinarian and Best-selling Author, Dies." *Lawrence Eagle-Tribune*, 24 February 1995: 14.

INTERVIEWS WITH JAMES HERRIOT

Foster, William. "James Herriot Talking to William Foster." *Scotsman*, 16 October 1981.

Gonzalez, Arturo F., Jr. "James Herriot: The Yorkshire Vet Tells All." *Saturday Review*, May–June 1986: 56+.

"Interview with James Herriot." *Maclean's*, 29 May 1978: 4–6.

REVIEWS AND CRITICISM

All Creatures Great and Small

Ames Alfred C. "A 'Miraculous' Talent; It Is Not Too Strong a Word." *Chicago Tribune*, 12 November 1972, sec. 9:1.

Broyard, Anatole. "Of Human and Other Animals." *New York Times*, 14 December 1972: 45.

Bryant, Nelson. "A Place Where the Wind Blows Clean." *New York Times Book Review*, 18 February 1973: 10.

Carlsen, G. Robert, Caren Dybek, and Alleen P. Nilsen. "1972–73 Honor Listing." *English Journal*, 62 (1973): 1298.

Doerner, William R. "How Now, Brown Cow?" *Time*, 19 February 1973: 88.

Evans, R. D. Review of *All Creatures Great and Small*. *Best Sellers*, 1 December 1972: 410.

Felton, Keith S. "Man Who Loves Animals: Bouyant [sic] Memoirs of the Barnyard." *Los Angeles Times*, 4 February 1973, sec. CAL: 50.

Gartner, Janet. Review of *All Creatures Great and Small. Library Journal*, 15 May 1973: 1713.

Gorner, Peter. "A Scot's Tribute to Life's Creatures Big and Small." *Chicago Tribune*, 8 May 1973, sec. 2:3.

Petersen, Clarence. "The Making of a Veterinarian: Better Living Thru Zoology." *Chicago Tribune Book World*, 2 December 1973: 11.

Smith, D. J. Review of *All Creatures Great and Small. Library Journal*, August 1972: 2575.

All Things Bright and Beautiful

Ames Alfred C. "From Dr. Jim, the 2nd Most Satisfying Book of the Decade." *Chicago Tribune*, 22 September 1974, sec. 7:1.

Broyard, Anatole. "Peaceable Kingdom Revisited." *New York Times*, 24 September 1974: 39.

Calloway, E. C. Review of *All Things Bright and Beautiful. Library Journal*, 15 October 1974: 2596.

Lineham, Eugene J. Review of *All Things Bright and Beautiful. Best Sellers*, 1 October 1974: 304–305.

Showers, Paul. "A Country Vet Remembers." *New York Times Book Review*, 3 November 1974: 60+.

Weeks, Edward. Review of *All Things Bright and Beautiful. Atlantic Monthly*, October 1974: 114–15.

All Things Wise and Wonderful

Barnes, Julian. "The Last Detail." *New Statesman*, 20 August 1976: 249.

Cashman, W. J. Review of *All Things Wise and Wonderful. Best Sellers*, November 1977: 243.

Cosgrove, M. S. Review of *All Things Wise and Wonderful. Horn Book*, February 1978: 77.

Hill, M. K. Review of *All Things Wise and Wonderful. Library Journal*, 1 September 1977: 1752.

Lingeman, Richard R. "Animal Doctor." *New York Times Book Review*, 18 September 1977: 13.

Manthorne, Jane. Review of *All Things Wise and Wonderful. School Library Journal*, October 1977: 131.

McNulty, Faith. "The Woof at the Door." *Washington Post*, 11 September 1977: E1+.

Virginia Quarterly Review, 54 (1978): 30.

James Herriot's Yorkshire

Buckmaster, Henrietta. Review of *James Herriot's Yorkshire. Christian Science Monitor*, 3 December 1979: B4.

Fuller, Edmund. "A Sampler of Holiday Gift Books." *Wall Street Journal,* 3 December 1979: 24.

Hill, M. K. Review of *James Herriot's Yorkshire. Library Journal,* 15 November 1979: 2460.

The Lord God Made Them All

Adams, P. L. Review of *The Lord God Made Them All. Atlantic,* July 1981: 90.

Bartolini, Laurie. Review of *The Lord God Made Them All. Library Journal,* 1 June 1981: 1213.

Buckmaster, Henrietta. Review of *The Lord God Made Them All. Christian Science Monitor,* 8 June 1981: 21.

Cosgrove, M. S. Review of *The Lord God Made Them All. Horn Book,* October 1981: 563.

Fuller, Edmund. "Doing Good in Zanzibar, Making Well in Yorkshire." *Wall Street Journal,* 20 July 1981: 16.

Gillebaard, Lola D. Review of *The Lord God Made Them All. Los Angeles Times Book Review,* 7 June 1981: 4.

Gorner, Peter. "Herriot Pens His Fourth Winner." *Chicago Tribune,* 13 May 1981, sec. 2:14.

Johnson, Philip. Review of *The Lord God Made Them All. Saturday Review,* June 1981: 56.

Kanfer, Stefan. "The Marcus Welby of the Barnyard." *Time,* 29 June 1981: 74+.

Smith, N. J. Review of *The Lord God Made Them All. Voice of Youth Advocate,* October 1981: 48.

Sussman. Vic. "Yorkshire's Dr. Doolittle." *Washington Post Book World,* 21 June 1981: 11.

Every Living Thing

Binchy, Maeve. "Make Way for Badgers." *New York Times Book Review,* 6 September 1992: 5+.

Collison, Cathy. Review of *Every Living Thing. Detroit Free Press,* 28 September 1992.

Duree, Barbara. Review of *Every Living Thing. Booklist,* August 1992: 1969.

Gorner, Peter. "Herriot's Back and Yorkshire's Still Got Him." *Chicago Tribune,* 23 September 1992, sec. 5:3.

Hoffman, Preston. Review of *Every Living Thing. Wilson Library Bulletin,* May 1993: 70–71.

Kirkus Reviews, 1 July 1992: 827.

Moore, Claudia. Review of *Every Living Thing. School Library Journal,* December 1992: 151.

Publishers Weekly, 20/21 July 1992: 238.

Publishers Weekly, 2 November 1992: 34.

Schneider, Debra. Review of *Every Living Thing. Library Journal,* 1 October 1992:
    110.

OTHER SECONDARY SOURCES

Buckley, Jerome Hamilton. *The Turning Key: Autobiography and the Subjective Im-
    pulse since 1800.* Cambridge: Harvard University Press, 1984.
Current-Garcia, Eugene, and Walton R. Patrick, eds. *What is the Short Story?* Glen-
    view, Ill.: Scott, Foresman, 1961.
Gunn, Janet Varner. *Autobiography: Towards a Poetics of Experience.* Philadelphia:
    University of Pennsylvania Press, 1982.
Jay, Paul. *Being in the Text: Self-Representation from Wordsworth to Roland Barthes.*
    Ithaca, N.Y.: Cornell University Press, 1984.
Olney, James. "Autobiography and the Cultural Moment: A Thematic, Historical,
    and Bibliographical Introduction." *Autobiography: Essays Theoretical and
    Critical.* Ed. James Olney. Princeton: Princeton University Press, 1980. 3–
    27.
Olney, James. *Metaphors of Self: The Meaning of Autobiography.* Princeton: Princeton
    University Press, 1972.
Olney, James, ed. *Studies in Autobiography.* New York: Oxford University Press,
    1988.
Pascal, Roy. *Design and Truth in Autobiography.* Cambridge: Harvard University
    Press, 1960.
Zinsser, William, ed. *Inventing the Truth: The Art and Craft of Memoir.* Rev. 2nd
    ed. New York: Houghton Mifflin, 1995.

Index

About the Author

MICHAEL J. ROSSI is Associate Professor of English at Merrimack College, where he has been chair of the English Department and Director of the Writing Center. He is the author of *Exploring Literature: A Collaborative Approach* (with Kathleen Shine Cain and Albert C. DeCiccio, 1993). He has published articles and presented conference papers on popular literature, business communication, and writing centers. He is currently teaching a seminar in autobiography.

Other Titles in Critical Companions to Popular Contemporary Writers
Kathleen Gregory Klein, Series Editor

V. C. Andrews: A Critical Companion
E. D. Huntley

Tom Clancy: A Critical Companion
Helen S. Garson

Mary Higgins Clark: A Critical
Companion
Linda C. Pelzer

James Clavell: A Critical Companion
Gina Macdonald

Pat Conroy: A Critical Companion
Landon C. Burns

Robin Cook: A Critical Companion
Lorena Laura Stookey

Michael Crichton: A Critical Companion
Elizabeth A. Trembley

Howard Fast: A Critical Companion
Andrew Macdonald

Ken Follett: A Critical Companion
Richard C. Turner

John Grisham: A Critical Companion
Mary Beth Pringle

Tony Hillerman: A Critical Companion
John M. Reilly

John Jakes: A Critical Companion
Mary Ellen Jones

Stephen King: A Critical Companion
Sharon A. Russell

Dean Koontz: A Critical Companion
Joan G. Kotker

Anne McCaffrey: A Critical Companion
Robin Roberts

Colleen McCullough: A Critical
Companion
Mary Jean DeMarr

James A. Michener: A Critical Companion
Marilyn S. Severson

Anne Rice: A Critical Companion
Jennifer Smith

John Saul: A Critical Companion
Paul Bail

Gore Vidal: A Critical Companion
Susan Baker